D1446801

The Matter of Chance

The Matter of Chance

D. H. MELLOR

CAMBRIDGE

at the University Press 1971

Published by the Syndics of the Cambridge University Press
Bentley House, 200 Euston Road, London NW1 2DB
American Branch: 32 East 57th Street, New York, N.Y.10022

© Cambridge University Press 1971

Library of Congress Catalogue Card Number: 70–152629

ISBN: 0 521 08194 7

Printed in Great Britain
at the University Printing House, Cambridge
(Brooke Crutchley, University Printer)

For my parents.

For the friends I have made while at Pembroke College Cambridge;
who made writing this book compatible with sanity
and sometimes necessary; whom I have ill repaid.

Contents

Preface

I OWE MUCH to many people for what I say in this book. Specific debts
are acknowledged in the text. In discussing other views I use direct
quotation where possible, to avoid attacking straw men or claiming tacit
credit for what is not mine. I have no further interest in academic
patents, and have gone rather to clear expositors than to first authors of
views. But I apologise if I have overlooked a due acknowledgement, and
should be glad to be told of it. References are given in the Harvard
system to a list at the end of the book. This also lists pertinent works I
have read but not referred to. It is not otherwise comprehensive on any
topic I discuss.

Many deeper debts are less traceable. I have discussed all these topics
with many people and gained much from their remarks. Professors
Braithwaite, Kneale and Mackie have taken a particularly careful and
critical interest and made me face problems I should not have seen
unaided. I may not convince them, but I hope they may have helped me
to convince others. I am further indebted to the private comments, as
well as to the published work, of Professors Körner and Giere and
Drs Ian Hacking and John Wilson on topics central to the book. The
first two chapters, written last, owe much to the patient criticism of
Paul Teller.

I have many general philosophical debts. Professors Feigl and
Brodbeck introduced me to the philosophy of science; Gerd Buchdahl
has persistently encouraged me in it; Mary Hesse's and Jonathan
Bennett's astringent interest has been a great curer of complacency; the
stimulus of my colleagues, teachers and students of philosophy in
Cambridge, has left my limitations no excuse. Their stimulus is largely
responsible for what may be of interest in this book. The mistakes are
all mine.

My most practical debts are to Verna Cole, who typed the book,
Charles Jardine, who computed figures 3 and 4, David Papineau, who
checked the references, Harold Frayman, who compiled the index, and
my father, who thought up the title.

I should like to have repaid my debts with a good book, but there it is. Some material, mostly in chapter 6, first appeared in *Philosophy of Science* **32** (1965), 105–22; **33** (1966), 345–59; **34** (1967), 1–9. Some material mostly in chapter 7 first appeared in *The British Journal for the Philosophy of Science* **16** (1965), 209–25; **17** (1967), 323–6; **18** (1967), 235–8; **20** (1969), 366–71. Some material, mostly in chapters 1 to 4, first appeared in 'Chance', published in the *Aristotelian Society's Supplementary Volume* **43** (1969), 11–36, and is reprinted by permission of the Editor. © The Aristotelian Society 1969. I owe thanks to the editors and publishers of these journals for permission to use this material again.

D. H. MELLOR

January 1971

Introduction

> There are certain common privileges of a Writer, the Benefit whereof, I hope, there will be no Reason to doubt; Particularly, that where I am not understood, it shall be concluded, that something very useful and profound is couch't underneath.
>
> Swift. *A Tale of a Tub.* Preface

IT MAY BE THOUGHT rash or superfluous in the Cambridge of Venn, Keynes, Ramsey, Fisher, Jeffreys, Braithwaite and Hacking, to write another philosophical book on probability. The present state of the subject, however, is neither so good as to make it superfluous nor so bad as to make it entirely rash. My project is in any case limited. I am concerned only with statistical probability, which I call 'chance'. The chances of coins landing heads, of people dying and of radioactive atoms decaying concern me; the probabilities inconclusive evidence perhaps lends to hypotheses on these and other matters do not. Inductive probability and the deep problems of confirmation, induction and acceptance that involve it I mention only to show how little chance bears on them. That may serve indirectly to forward the solution of these problems, by limiting them, and I would claim no more than that for this work.

I assume some familiarity with the existing philosophical accounts of chance to which I refer. The ingredients of the present theory are in the literature, but they have hitherto been no more than half baked. The test of the theory is how much sense it makes of what professional usage shows to be thought true of chance. This usage seems to me to embody four important assumptions that other theories cannot make simultaneous sense of: that chance is objective, empirical and not relational, and that it applies to the single case. The chance of a radium atom decaying in the next ten minutes is as objective and empirical a matter as its mass, as little relative to evidence, and as much an attribute of one as of many statistical trials. Frequency theory makes no sense of the single case, personalist theory no sense of chance's objectivity, and classical and logical theory no sense of its empirical and non-relational character.

xi

The present theory takes most if not all chances to display dispositional properties which I call 'propensities'. The idea is not new; the name of the property is taken from Popper (1957). But the details of the theory and its defence against obvious objections are new. My chief concern is to give an acceptable account of the nature of propensity and of its relations to chance and to other dispositional properties.

I start by adopting the positive contribution of the personalist theory of probability. Statements of chance *inter alia* express degrees of partial belief, e.g. in the decay of a radium atom. Arguments are given for the existence and dispositional nature of partial belief and its appropriate relation to full belief. I then present the rationale for one betting measure of partial belief in more than usual detail to support the claim that it is measurable. This is all preliminary to the main claim that chance statements assert some degrees of belief to be made more reasonable than others by objective empirical features of the world. It is contingent that the world has such features; I argue only that nothing in the characterisation and measurement of partial belief excludes further empirical constraints of rationality upon it.

The constraints are then located in propensities, which are such standing dispositional properties of things as the *bias* of coins and dice, the *half-life* of radioelements and the *death risk* of people. The latter examples are given in some detail to support my claims about scientific usage and to show how naturally propensity theory accounts for it. I have deliberately avoided references to quantum theory, for a number of reasons. First the rôle of probability in the foundations of the theory is controversial. But secondly, if the theory provides rational partial beliefs in the happening of macroscopic events, the measure of these will be probabilistic. We may take any such objective chances as displays of macroscopic propensities independently of their microscopic explanation. I do not take the less theoretically "fundamental" nature of my examples to make them less secure cases of scientific knowledge. I have argued elsewhere (Mellor, 1968) against the all-embracing ontological pretensions of physical theories of the very small.

These examples are followed by a discussion of possible objections to propensity as a disposition. I attend in particular to imprecision and inexactness in scientific concepts and show that propensity is not peculiar in these respects. From an account of the sources of inexactness in explanatory dispositions I derive the regulative principle of connectivity, that two physical systems cannot differ in just one such property. When this principle is applied to propensities some plausible classical chance distributions can be derived. I then compare these derivations with related classical and fiducial arguments.

Finally the implications of propensity theory for determinism and the status of natural laws are gone into. 'Determinism' here refers not to the absence of free will but to the thesis that events are governed by non-statistical laws. In this connection and generally throughout the book I address myself only to problems that bear on the relation of chance to other scientific concepts; I am not satisfied that the problems of free will do bear on this relation.

For the same reason I have felt free to adopt controversial positions without argument where the controversy would affect my discussion only in its terminology. For example, objective and realist terminology is used throughout the book. I write as if scientific knowledge is objective and as if such properties as mass, length and temperature exist. The wholesale dissent of subjectivists and nominalists from these presuppositions ought not to bear substantially on the theory here presented of the particular relation chance has to these other concepts.

One or two miscellaneous matters of notation need remarking. I use single quotation marks to form the names of terms and sentences and double quotation marks for other purposes. (In particular I use single quotes where I wish to discuss an author's remarks rather than merely to reiterate them.) Equations and other symbolised statements to which further reference is made are numbered consecutively within each chapter. In representing conditional statements I use ' → ' except where the material conditional is explicitly intended. It should be read 'if... then...', however that is further analysed.

1 The limits of personalism

THE OBJECT OF THIS BOOK is to develop a philosophical theory about statistical probability. I call statistical probability 'chance' for brevity and to mark it off from inductive probability. Statistical probability is what is meant in saying of a coin either

H_1:   The probability of coin a landing heads when tossed is p_1
or
H_2:   The probability of coin a landing heads when tossed is p_2.

Inductive probability is what is meant in saying that on the evidence available of symmetry, results of tosses etc., that

H_1 is more probable than H_2.

My main concern is thus with what Carnap (1962) calls 'probability$_2$' as opposed to what he calls 'probability$_1$'. But I do not share his view (1962, §9; 1955) that these are distinct senses of an ambiguous term 'probability' (cf. Ayers, 1968, pp. 42–50). Nor do I accept his frequency account of 'probability$_2$'.

The theory of this book is that some chance statements such as H_1 and H_2 can be made true by things having a certain dispositional property. Following Popper (1957, 1959a), I call this property 'propensity'. To pursue the example, the *bias* of a coin (or its un-biasedness) is a propensity which makes true some such statement as H_1 of the chance of it landing heads when tossed. Naturally there are many other and more serious instances of propensities. Before discussing them in detail it is desirable to indicate more clearly what this propensity theory of chance asserts and how far it absorbs, denies and supplements other theories of probability.

Propensity theories have been presented before. Such a conception of statistical probability was suggested before Popper by Peirce (1931, volume 2, §664) and has later been developed by Hacking (1965) and adopted by Levi (1967). It will be obvious in the sequel how much the present account owes to their work. But it differs from these earlier accounts in a number of ways. First I attend more to what kind of item a propensity could be and how like it is to other scientific properties.

Hacking is in contrast more concerned with statistical inference itself than with the feature of the world that, as I hold, sometimes makes such inference reasonable. Popper and Levi are likewise sketchy on what propensities are and they do not draw out the detailed consequences of their views. My intention is, by so drawing out consequences, to present at least a clear and detailed view for criticism if not to convert adherents of other views.

Secondly however, I hope also to show that much obvious truth in other views is herein accommodated. The propensity theory is not a comprehensive and exclusive new theory of probability in general but an account of one kind of objective probability statement. It certainly conflicts with such limiting frequency views as those of von Mises (1957) and Reichenbach (1949), although it can be largely reconciled to Braithwaite's (1953) more sophisticated frequentism. On the other hand, propensity theory can observe at least a non-aggression pact with accounts of logical probability statements as in Carnap (1962) and Jeffreys (1961). And it is positively a feature of this version of propensity theory to base itself explicitly on the personalist theories of Ramsey (1926), de Finetti (1937), Savage (1954) and Jeffrey (1965). Personalists have admittedly tended to accompany their theories with a view of probability statements as merely subjective. But that is an incidental defect of personalism which it is my principal aim in this chapter and the next to expose and remove. To this end I generally reserve 'subjective' and 'subjectivism' hereafter for the doctrine I reject, that there can be no objective probabilities. I use 'personalism' to refer to the accounts of chance statements as expressing "partial beliefs", which broadly I accept.

The relation between the propensity and personalist theories is this. According to the latter the making of a probability statement expresses the speaker's "partial belief" in whatever he thereby ascribes probability to, say that a coin a will land heads when tossed. Knowledge of the coin's propensity on the present theory is what in suitable circumstances makes reasonable the having of some particular partial belief in the outcome of the toss. The chance of the coin falling heads when tossed is then the measure of that reasonable partial belief.

It is not usual to base an account of objective probability on a concept of partial belief. It may well be asked why one should do so. Kneale, discussing relational probability rather than chance, puts the question rhetorically (1949, p. 13):

A man who knows that the evidence at his disposal justifies a certain degree of confidence in proposition *A* must know that the evidence probabilifies *A* to a certain degree; for it is only so that the evidence can justify any degree of confidence. But if a man who has a rational opinion knows all this (even although he may not have the terminology in which to state it explicitly), why need we say in addition that he has a degree of confidence in *A* which somehow corresponds with the degree to which the evidence probabilifies *A*? Can we not content ourselves with the assertion that rational opinion is the knowledge that the available evidence probabilifies a proposition to a certain degree?

One might similarly ask of chance: can we not analyse full belief that the chance of heads on a coin toss is $\frac{1}{2}$ without reference to some supposedly corresponding partial belief that the coin will land heads? The reason for denying this is the fact to which Kneale himself draws attention (p. 18) "that knowledge of probability relations is important chiefly for its bearing on action". It follows as Kneale says (p. 20) that "no analysis of the probability relation can be accepted as adequate... unless it enables us to understand why it is rational to take as a basis for action a proposition which stands in that relation to the evidence at our disposal". Similarly with chance. It must follow from our account that the greater the known chance of an event the more reasonable it is to act as if it will occur. What can intelligibly come by degrees, however, turns out not to be reasonableness so much as a tendency to act as if an event would occur. This concept of a quantitative tendency to action is just that of partial belief as it has been developed by personalists. It is thus available to provide in our account of chance that necessary connection with action on which Kneale rightly insists. A great difficulty facing other objective accounts of chance, notably the frequency theories, has been to build such a connection subsequently on to their entirely impersonal foundations (see e.g. Braithwaite, 1966). In proceeding differently we shall of course later need to show that no properly hallowed Humean doctrine is denied.

The other advantage which propensity theory has in basing itself on partial belief is, curiously enough, over subjectivism in being less open to charges of idealisation. We shall see that personalists credit people with partial beliefs whose measure is a probability. Many of their arguments, however, are presented as both normative and limited: e.g. that if a man has certain partial beliefs he can be made to lose money should they not be probabilities. Personalists take their theory to be refuted neither by a person lacking partial beliefs altogether nor by their failing to satisfy such personalist constraints of "coherence".

So de Finetti (1937, p. 111): '[Personalist] probability theory is not an attempt to describe actual behavior; its subject is coherent behavior, and the fact that people are only more or less coherent is inessential.' But de Finetti does not disdain empirical support even on the same page as he disdains empirical refutation: 'The notion of probability which we have described is without doubt the closest to that of "the man in the street"; better yet, it is that which he *applies every day in practical judgments . . .* What more adequate meaning could be discovered for the notion?' (my italics).

But however much or little it matters to personalists that people have suitable partial beliefs, it matters less to propensity theory. Our subject is not partial belief itself but that feature of the impersonal world, namely propensity, knowledge of which can make some partial beliefs more reasonable than others. The actual existence of people with such partial beliefs is as immaterial to propensity theory as that of radio-elements and dice is to games and decision theories. Given that the latter theories provide a suitable concept of partial belief, propensity theory is no further concerned with it in detail than thermodynamics is with subjective feelings of warmth. Subjectivism, on the other hand, offers partial belief as a surrogate for the objective chance that statistical sciences ostensibly refer to. It is very material to one who would dismiss objective chance as a fiction that mathematically suitable partial beliefs exist to take its place.

Nevertheless, even for our purposes more must be said of partial belief if propensity is to be intelligibly characterised in terms of it. It may be as subjective a notion but it is not as plain to the senses as are feelings of warmth. More argument is needed to show that the concept of partial belief will serve our turn; in particular that partial belief is suitably related to full belief, e.g. in a coin landing heads, and to behaviour consequent thereon.

BELIEF AND PARTIAL BELIEF

> Often enough, my cat's behaviour makes it clear to me that he believes he is about to be fed.
>
> Jeffrey, 1965, p. 59

It is a commonplace of personalism that in ascribing a probability one expresses a certain attitude which may reasonably be referred to by such terms as 'doubt', 'expectation', 'degree of conviction' or 'partial belief'. I mostly use 'partial belief' as being the most common and because of the connection to be here discussed with full belief. Similarly, I use 'belief' rather than 'believing', by analogy with 'partial belief'. There would be advantages in keeping 'belief' for what is believed (a proposition) and using 'believing' for the attitude a man has who believes (cf. Russell, 1921, pp. 232–3; Braithwaite, 1932–3, 'The Nature of Believing'; Wittgenstein, 1958, pp. 190–2). But such usage is uncommon enough for it to mislead and I do not wish to add 'partial believing' to an already overloaded vocabulary.

It is usual to take propositions rather than events on the one hand or sentences on the other as the sole objects of belief and partial belief. Cases of belief or partial belief in events or states of affairs can be trivially redescribed. If I believe or partly believe in a coin landing heads I believe or partly believe in the truth of the proposition that it does so. Similarly with belief or partial belief in a state of affairs such as a coin being biased. On the other hand, we do not care what sentence (English, French or whatever) is used to state that the event occurs or state of affairs obtains. It does not, moreover, seem necessary either to belief or to partial belief that the believer have any such sentence of his native language in mind. A believer does not even seem to need a language at all if Jeffrey's cat is a fair example (p. 4 above). It likewise does not seem senseless to ascribe partial belief in his master's front door entry to a dog running excitedly from front door to back as his master approaches the side of the house. Hence for the present I follow Jeffrey (1965, pp. 48–59) in taking propositions rather than sentences as the objects both of belief and of partial belief. In so doing I do not mean or need to insist on the irreducible existence of propositions as bearers of truth. On that large topic I wish to imply no fixed view. But the traditional terminology here conveniently unifies diverse objects of belief and partial belief and begs fewest questions of linguistic competence.

Assuming belief and partial belief to be diverse attitudes towards propositions, what is the relation between them? There clearly is a close relation and we may at least constrain the less by the more familiar notion even if we cannot thereby completely define it.

The ordinary concept of belief is qualitative. One believes a proposition q or not; the matter does not admit of degrees. Similarly with disbelieving q, which I take to be believing $\sim q$. In between it seems clearly possible to have a definite attitude towards a proposition which is yet neither belief nor disbelief but is partial belief. If partial belief is a quantity, it is obviously bounded by belief and disbelief. One extreme of partial belief will be a state of belief, the other a state of disbelief. Certainly less than extreme values will also count as belief. Not all one's beliefs are equally certain and a little doubt may yet fall short of agnosticism. We cannot then take absence of belief as a necessary condition of partial belief. Nor is there any point in asking just where partial belief shades into full belief. It is enough that it must do so somewhere and that our account of both concepts must allow for this necessity.

If absence of belief is not necessary for partial belief, it is even more clearly not sufficient. Lack of belief in q may signify merely a lack of any attitude whatever towards q. Even if one requires also that q be "entertained" (*cf.* Braithwaite, 1932–3, p. 132), it is not clear that a man *must* believe, disbelieve or partially believe every proposition he entertains. To say

'I don't know what to believe'

or

'I don't know whether I believe it or not'

of some topic or proposition is not really to report ignorance of one or other, presumably subconscious, attitude. It is rather to report that the speaker, although conscious of the question, is aware of being unable to come to any of these definite attitudes towards it.

In any case, we shall see later (p. 14) that the notion of entertaining a proposition is both too unclear in itself and too much tied to consciousness to be an acceptable prerequisite of belief. It is no clearer in the case of partial belief for which, for similar reasons, consciousness can hardly be essential if it is not so for belief. Certainly Jeffrey's cat and our own uncertain dog cannot as plausibly be credited with consciously entertaining propositions as they can respectively with believing and with partly believing them. Entertaining q is thus neither an effective nor an intuitively acceptable supplement to the definition one might have hoped for, namely of partial belief in terms of the absence of full belief.

Nor can appeal to the theoretical nature of partial belief make such a definition acceptable. No doubt games or decision theories may often give adequate theoretical grounds for ascribing to a person partial beliefs of which he is quite unaware. But this cannot be assumed to work by definition in every case, even taking partial belief to be a disposition and making every appeal to our unconsciousness of most of our own dispositions. It will be granted by the theory that some pro-positions fail to induce any relevant disposition in a person simply because they have not come, even subliminally, to his notice. (This is not of course to deny that a man may be disposed to believe such a proposition; but that is another matter.) Even some propositions that a man has explicitly thought about, however, may still, as we have just seen, fail to produce in him any awareness of belief or of partial belief. One must not then beg the question by automatically postulating the corresponding unconscious dispositional state. It may still be that the relevant situation would call forth none of the appropriate displays of behaviour on his part. And that in turn must not be ruled out by counting every possible piece of behaviour extracted by compulsion in such a situation as a sign of some such disposition. Measuring partial belief by forcing a man to choose betting odds, for example, presupposes that he has a partial belief which the chosen odds measure. His forced choice does not itself show that he has any such disposition, because he is forced to choose whether he has or not. If he lacks any disposition, he will have to choose odds at random. That a man can always be forced to choose odds in no way shows that he always has even subconscious partial beliefs. An IQ test will analogously show what IQ a child has if it has any. But the mere fact that the test can always be applied is no answer to a sceptic who denies the existence of any such mental capacity as IQ. Like IQs, partial beliefs cannot just be stipulated into existence.

I conclude that partial belief, however highly theoretical a disposition it may be, cannot be defined in terms of full belief, with or without appeal to consciousness. Partial beliefs form a distinct family of attitudes whose existence, nature and relation to the full beliefs that are their bounds must be separately argued for.

THE NATURE OF PARTIAL BELIEF

That there is some such thing as partial belief may reasonably be inferred from common usage. Venn puts the case well (1888, p. 139):

There is a whole vocabulary of common expressions such as, 'I feel almost sure', 'I do not feel quite certain', 'I am less confident of this than of that', and so on. When we make use of any one of these phrases we seldom doubt that we have a distinct meaning to convey by means of it. Nor do we feel much at a loss, under any given circumstances, as to which of these expressions we should employ in preference to the others. If we were asked to arrange in order, according to the intensity of the belief with which we respectively hold them, things broadly marked off from one another, we could do it from our consciousness of belief alone. . .

So far so good, but of what does "our consciousness of [partial] belief" consist? How in particular can so seemingly subjective a feeling of doubt or degrees of confidence or certainty be compared in intensity between one person and another?

At first sight partial beliefs are only subjective in the irrelevant sense that X and Y, with partial beliefs q_X and q_Y of different strengths in some proposition q, do not contradict each other merely by saying so. It is still an objective matter *that* X and Y have these partial beliefs. Y need not share X's partial belief q_X but if he denies that X has it he is objectively wrong.

If partial belief were a feeling, a merely introspectible state perhaps like a sensation of some kind, this appearance of objectivity could be misleading. The comparison is worth pressing in fact, in order to make clear that partial belief is not such a feeling but is rather a publicly detectable disposition. This is indeed widely assumed but it has not been widely argued.

Suppose first that X alone could know, by introspection, what his partial beliefs were. Now try to suppose that on this basis he could accurately report the strength of his partial beliefs. These assumptions still seem to provide no public method of correlating X's reports with the similarly couched reports of other people. To suppose that Y could be wrong, or even right, about X's partial beliefs now lacks clear sense. He could predict that X would use the expression 'q_X' to report his partial belief and could certainly be right or wrong about that. But he would seem unable to know either what X applied 'q_X' to or whether he, Y, would apply the same term to a similarly strong partial belief. As for the terms Y uses to report the strength of his own partial beliefs, he would have no way of telling if they were rightly applied to X. He would effectively be unable either to assert or to deny the accuracy of X's reports. The rest of us, not being X either, would be similarly impotent. In short, second and third person ascription of partial belief would be pointless and its apparent objectivity spurious.

Arguments like this are now widely recognised to be ineffective in showing sensations to be incommunicable; but the standard reply to them is not available in the case of partial belief. The point is that even if a sensation is private, the terms in which it is reported are not. They can for instance also be applied on the basis of standard causes of the sensation being present, which is an entirely objective matter. My confidence that my present visual sensation of sunlit grass is rightly reported as being like yesterday's similarly caused sensation relies heavily on my knowledge that it *is* similarly caused. Through such appeal to standard causes we can even give objective sense to such remarks as

' *X* sees yellow more green than *Y* does'

by getting *X* and *Y* to match a standard yellow light against various standard mixtures of red and green light (Gregory, 1966, p. 127). The tests of matching are of course objective behavioural tests of ability to discriminate such as are used to test and measure colour blindness. We can then afford to concede the obscure claim that *X* and *Y* cannot compare absolutely the sensations they respectively receive from the same standard sources of coloured light. It is enough that they can match other colours objectively against such public standards and so describe and compare their visual sensations in these public terms.

Could we not similarly assess *X*'s introspectible feeling of partial belief by getting him to match it with that induced by some standard source of it? It may, that is, be as senseless (or at least as immaterial) as it is with visual sensations to remark that we cannot compare absolutely the states of mind of *X* and *Y* induced by some standard cause of doubt. So long as doubt can be matched against what some standard causes induce we may have all that is needed for objective comparison of felt partial belief, as we do with seen colour.

Up to a point, indeed, the analogy holds, and has been used to characterise degrees of partial belief. Suppose *X* to be in doubt about the truth of a proposition *q* which will be settled by some agreed future observation. Let it be one of the usual propositions about the result of throwing a die or that a man dies or that some atom decays in the next year or day. Then *X* is offered the following choice of bets: a fixed prize either if *q* turns out true or, alternatively, if a standard coin that everyone agrees to be unbiased lands heads on a given toss. If *X*'s partial belief in *q* makes him indifferent for all prizes which of these prospects of gain he will take, one may surely conclude that whatever it feels like to him it matches in the relevant respect his partial belief in the standard coin landing heads. The coin is moreover a very plausible inducer of a standard doubt. For *X* to believe it unbiased is by the same test for him to have equal partial belief in it landing heads and tails; he would presumably feel indifferent between getting the prize on the one and getting it on the other.

This test is in fact appealed to by Ramsey (1926, p. 177) to show *inter alia* that partial belief is objectively measurable. Where it differs from the colour matching test is that the latter presupposes the existence of objectively coloured objects. Reference to the light sources having standard colours cannot be replaced by reference to them *looking* red, green, etc. The whole point is that there are no behavioural tests of whether a given standard really "looks the same" colour to different observers. Hence the objective colour of the standard source is needed precisely to give sense to second and third person application of the concept of something looking of that colour. Now if partial belief were similarly accessible only to introspection, lacking behavioural tests of its strength, Ramsey would equally have to rely on the standard coin actually being unbiased. It would not do for it merely to induce similar feelings of partial belief in it landing heads in different people. The whole point of the coin would be to give sense to such statements of similarity in feelings of partial belief. Ramsey's test would have to presuppose the existence of objectively equal chances of the coin landing heads and tails. Of this one would have to be convinced in any particular case by checks of symmetry, frequency, etc., just as one checks the specification of a standard source of red light. In each case one could be shown to be wrong, but only by reference to a further standard whose objective chance or colour was not in question.

This is of course a fantasy. Partial belief cannot possibly presuppose objective chance in the way coloured sensations may presuppose coloured objects. Perceiving objective colours is obviously a vastly more direct process than perceiving chances. I do not insist that the colour of sensations *is* thus definable in terms of their standard causes. But even if it were, that would give no reason to assume the same of partial belief. It is quite clear that our concept of partial belief could be applied just as well in a deterministic world devoid of chance. A subjectivist like de Finetti (1937) must indeed suppose this to be our situation. His view may be false but it is certainly not a contradiction in terms. On the other hand, Ramsey's is a patently reasonable device for comparing partial beliefs. Partial belief therefore cannot be a merely introspectible feeling. There must be independent public criteria for its presence and strength.

Partial belief may of course often be attended by related feelings; as

Braithwaite remarks (1932–3, p. 142) in the extreme case of full belief, "in a great number of cases I have a feeling of conviction when I believe: indeed I think that this feeling of conviction may reasonably be used as evidence for the existence of the belief". The evidence of course is inductive, based on correlation of the feeling with independently attested belief. This correlated feeling no doubt explains why one generally knows more than others do about one's own beliefs.

We may readily concede similar correlations of partial belief with feelings of "partial conviction" by which a man may become peculiarly well informed of his own doubts, as yet publicly undisplayed. That does not make feelings part either of belief or of partial belief, nor need feelings by any means always accompany them. Thus Braithwaite observes (1932–3, p. 142) that "I believe quite thoroughly that the sun will rise tomorrow, but experience no particular feeling attached to the proposition believed." Kneale similarly notes (1949, p. 15) that "when we realise that $2 + 2 = 4$, we do not sweat with any feeling of supreme intensity".

Whether or not partial beliefs are correlated with introspectible feelings of doubt and certainty, the latter are not our concern. Kneale's mistake in denying more than marginal relevance to partial belief follows directly from his taking it to be such a kind of feeling (1949, pp. 14–17). He observes of himself that he "can discover no such feeling" (p. 14); complains of it that it could not be adequately measurable (p. 15); and remarks in the above quotation the absurdity of supposing full belief to be an extreme of it.

Oddly enough, one of Venn's objections to partial belief as a foundation for chance is precisely that it is *not* an introspectible feeling; and so not, Venn thinks, accessible except by reference to the frequency with which the corresponding full belief is displayed. In this he contrasts it (1888, p. 158) with surprise, "to which we are thus able to assign something like a fractional value" and which "has what may be termed an independent existence; it is intelligible by itself...Hence...it is as applicable, and as capable of any kind of justification, in relation to the *single event*, as to a series of events. In this respect...it offers a complete contrast to our state of belief about any one contingent event". Venn is quite right in thinking that whatever is needed to characterise chance is not measurable by introspection, and right also in pointing to the crucial difficulty of justifying partial belief in a single event. He is wrong only in supposing that states of belief must be measurable by introspection if at all, and in supposing the problem of justification to be soluble by dismissing partial beliefs in favour of frequencies.

We find that partial belief is no more definable as a feeling, measurable by introspection or by reference to its standard causes, than it is definable by absence of full belief. We are left with the alternative account of partial belief as a disposition to indulge in publicly describable behaviour, e.g. specifically behaviour in betting situations. The detailed justifying of this specification will concern us later. Here I note merely, before giving a suitably related account of belief, that this view is implicit in all the main personalist theories. Ramsey in particular, proposing his measure for partial belief, takes it to be dispositional. While explicitly avoiding any commitment to subjectivism, Ramsey as carefully avoids any appeal in characterising partial belief to the existence of chances. The standard coin does not have to be unbiased, only to be thought so, i.e. to induce equal partial beliefs in it landing heads and tails. Equality of partial belief itself is characterised dispositionally by "belief of degree $\frac{1}{2}$ as such a belief as leads to indifference between betting one way and betting the other for the same stakes". (Ramsey, 1926, p. 178.)

THE NATURE OF BELIEF

The view of belief as dispositional is naturally congenial to one who takes partial belief to be so. It is surprising only that the two have so rarely been related. Personalists on the one side have given scant and superficial attention to philosophical accounts of belief; on the other, Price (1969) for example treats Locke and Cardinal Newman as the leading writers on whether belief admits of degrees. No doubt much that needs saying about belief is not germane to our enquiry. We need satisfy ourselves only that our view of belief is consistent with the extreme cases of our view of partial belief. For example, as partial beliefs of increasing strength shade into full belief, we shall not want to transform a steadily changing disposition abruptly into an essentially introspectible mental act of assent. It will also be as well before developing a behavioural measure for partial belief, to check that the two extremes of such behaviour are plausible manifestations respectively of belief and of disbelief.

It is now widely agreed that belief at least contains a dispositional component. The dispositional account of belief is well given by

Braithwaite (1932–3), and has largely been conceded by Price (1969). It is not just that one has certain dispositions to believe propositions one is not actively considering. A sleeping man, for instance, will obviously be credited with this amount of dispositional belief however his state of conscious active assent to a proposition is further analysed. The important claim of the dispositional account is that active assent, whatever it may feel like, cannot rightly be ascribed to a man who would not exhibit appropriate behaviour in relevant circumstances. The relevant behaviour moreover is substantially non-verbal. The crucial test of belief is normally how a man acts, not whether he says 'yes' when asked. We may wish to discourage lying and self-deceit, but can hardly hope to make them logically impossible.

Price (1969, pp. 256–9) is wrong, however, to distinguish as sharply as he does on these grounds between speech and other action. It is just as feasible to simulate action that characterises a belief as it is to lie. One can even deceive oneself in some non-verbal display of belief. An actor may wordlessly portray belief in some tragic event, and an audience may be unselfconsciously moved thereby to tears. Or a jealous husband may carefully set out to convince even himself by his displays of trust in his wife. Verbal behaviour is only less conclusive in that it is usually the easiest and cheapest method of deceit, and consequently often the least reliable evidence of belief.

Linguistic evidence of belief may be permissible, but Jeffrey's cat (p. 4) strongly suggests that it is not necessary. I have indeed taken propositions as the objects of belief (p. 5) precisely to avoid making linguistic competence a prerequisite of it. That it makes sense of ascribing beliefs to speechless creatures need not of course be a merit peculiar to the dispositional theory. It might make sense to credit cats and dogs with characteristic feelings of both full and partial belief. But only if belief is also evidenced in their necessarily non-linguistic behaviour could we ever have grounds for doing so. Such ascription of belief would be quite inexplicable unless belief is essentially dispositional.

It is a further merit of the dispositional account of belief that it makes clear sense of unconscious beliefs, as Price characterises them (1969, pp. 300–1): ' '*A* believes that *p*' can still be true, even though *A* does not assent to the proposition *p* when he entertains it and attends to it.' This covers the cases both of self-deceit and where *A* is simply unaware that he has any belief on the matter at all. This possibility and that of animals having beliefs cast doubt, however, on the force of requiring dispositional belief sometimes to be "entertained" as well. The idea is that the state of active assent, at least, must include entertaining the proposition believed (Braithwaite, 1932–3, p. 132), or have done so on some past occasions (Price, 1969, p. 251). Now there is only force in this requirement if 'entertaining' here refers to some conscious awareness of *p*. But then it seems to rule out belief in animals, who cannot with clear sense be said to entertain consciously what they admittedly could not formulate. And if "entertaining" may be credited to a believer just because he exhibits the behaviour to which the belief disposes him, the requirement is empty. If given greater content, moreover, it would rule out also unconscious beliefs of which a person has never been aware. Yet surely one can discover that one had always unconsciously assumed, without ever thinking about it explicitly, that the quickest way from London to Tokyo was over the North Pole.

A dispositional as opposed to an "occurrence" account of belief need not in fact proceed in two stages. It need not tack on to the undeniable disposition to active assent that a sleeping or inattentive man must be credited with, a separate dispositional account of active assent. It need only credit the believer with a single disposition, namely to indulge in the relevant behaviour. No doubt behavioural displays of belief in people will normally be accompanied by conscious awareness of the belief displayed. That has been noted already in the discussion (pp. 10–11) of partial belief, as has the main point that such awareness or feeling of conviction is not essential.

The dispositional theory has apparent difficulty in explaining how someone can seemingly be directly aware of beliefs that he is not outwardly displaying. This objection has, I think, been adequately met by Braithwaite (1932–3, pp. 139–43). His appeal to correlated feelings of conviction affording evidence for one's own beliefs has already been referred to (p. 11). He notes in addition that we can have "(1) A direct induction from my knowledge of my behaviour in the past to knowledge of my behaviour in the future. (2) By means of *Gedankenexperimente*: I may consider how I shall act in the future in a given situation, and infer that I shall act in the way I think I shall act."

Braithwaite similarly (pp. 137–9) meets objections that a dispositional account is implausible of beliefs which have only remote implications for action, for example beliefs about the past. I find his rejoinders convincing; but in any case such difficulties would not impair the theory's adequacy for our present purposes. I am concerned with partial belief and therefore with belief itself only in future physical happenings that can have chances, such as the fall of dice and men, the decay of atoms, the spread of disease. The relevance to possible action of belief in such future events is not doubtful, as it might be thought to be with events in the remote past. No doubt chancy events occurred then too but it is the partial belief of someone to whom they would then have been future that is our concern.

In the case of partial belief, moreover, it is a great merit of personalist theory that it is able to prescribe a single kind of action to display dispositional belief in events of every kind, e.g. choosing odds for a bet on its occurrence. The homogeneity that can thus be imposed on the most diverse partial beliefs indeed justifies treating them as a single family of attitudes. It is easier with partial belief than with belief itself to specify what can count as a display of the alleged disposition and the dispositional account of partial belief is accordingly the less contested.

There must, however, be a connection between the actions that respectively display belief and partial belief if the former is to be taken as an extreme case of the latter. The connection is indeed reasonably evident. Suppose that with given desires and other beliefs a belief in q would be displayed by action A in situation S. Suppose that partial belief in q steadily increases as measured by acceptable odds on its truth. Now try to suppose that a partial belief, so measured and so increasing, never turned into full belief. This is surely incoherent: to be disposed to risk an indefinitely great loss (for a given stake) should q prove false, but not otherwise disposed to display belief in q by doing A in S. In other words, if S is an appropriate betting situation, being prepared to offer sufficiently short odds on q – varying no doubt with q and the believer – just is one way of displaying belief in q. Belief, as Price (1969, p. 294) says, "is a multiform disposition, which is manifested or actualized in many different ways". What our account needs, and what seems to be true, is that this betting behaviour is always one way of manifesting belief at least in the events to which chance might be ascribed.

Naturally much else is true of belief which needs showing to be possible of a disposition. The main points have been made in the literature and need not be laboured here. Price (1969, pp. 246–7) notes that a disposition need not persist any great length of time, and Braithwaite (1932–3, p. 139) that it can intelligibly change without ever being displayed. Thus the facts adduced by Venn (1888, chapter 6, §§ 7–8) and others about the fluctuating nature of belief and the influence on it of other emotions count not at all against it being a disposition. Analogous instances come readily to mind. My weight is undeniably nothing but a multiform disposition, *inter alia* to depress excessively the bathroom scales. Yet it fluctuates incessantly without my being weighed, some-times indeed because I worry, being made too directly conscious of it by correlated feelings of grossness.

I find, then, no objection to construing the propositional attitudes called 'partial beliefs' as a family of dispositions which shade appro-priately into the dispositional attitudes of belief and disbelief. These attitudes are what personalists rightly claim to be expressed in the making of probability statements. But is it true, as subjectivists allege, that probability statements can do nothing else? To that question we now turn.

SUBJECTIVISM

> I met a timid old lady [once in a railway train] who was in much fear of accidents. I endeavoured to soothe her on the usual statistical ground of the extreme rarity of such events. She listened patiently, and then replied: "Yes, Sir, that is all very well; but I don't see how the real danger will be a bit the less because I don't believe in it."
>
> Venn, 1888, p. 157

The propensity theory is an *a priori* theory about what, if anything, makes some chance statements true. It does not itself assert that any chance statements *are* true, that is it does not deny that the world may be entirely deterministic. I suppose some chance statements to be true since I believe as a matter of fact that some things have propensities. Anyone who accepts this account of chance will suppose so too if he believes with natural piety the sayings of statistical science. But there is, for example, no logical necessity either in a coin being biased or in it being unbiased. There is no question of trying to prove a coin's bias or lack of it by this or any other *a priori* theory. Naturally, there might neither be nor have been thought to be chances, and scientists might never have proposed and seriously tested statistical laws. The theory would then have been of as little interest as a theory of the conceptual ramifications of witchcraft now is to most of us, but it would be none-theless capable of truth. It is no part of the propensity theory itself that there are any propensities. It is a part of it, however, that there can be propensities and that it is the province of statistical science to settle whether there are or not.

While, therefore, I need not argue for the existence of chances, I do need to meet *a priori* arguments against them. Such arguments may lead to a stronger or a weaker conclusion. The stronger conclusion would be that the concept of chance is incoherent. Statistical statements then, ostensibly about chances, would have to be given some more plausible alternative reference in order to be capable of truth. The weaker conclusion would be that true statistical statements always could be given such alternative reference even if they did not have to be. We would have, and statistical science would give us, no reason to assert the existence of chances except as logical constructions out of such other things as frequencies or personal betting rates. Objective chance would be at least redundant and at worst conceptually impossible, if such arguments were sound.

Arguments tending to these conclusions are associated with those who have developed the personalist theory of probability although notably not with Ramsey (1926) himself. Thus de Finetti (1937, p. 141) comments on such an assumption as that a coin has a fixed but unknown bias, so that tosses of it could be "independent events with constant but unknown probability p": 'one would be obliged to suppose that beyond the [subjective] probability distribution corresponding to our judgment, there must be another, unknown, corresponding to something real...From our point of view these statements are completely devoid of sense.' Since a statement "completely devoid of sense" must, one supposes, necessarily fail to be true, we have here an expression of the stronger subjectivist conclusion. Jeffrey (1965, p. 190) tentatively proposes the weaker conclusion: 'in the interest of conceptual economy one might wish somehow to reduce the objectivistic concept [of probability] to the subjectivistic one. I shall now propose a reduction of a sort.'

Many personalists admit that subjective doctrines are really incidental to personalism, and profess only sceptical agnosticism about objective probability. This agnosticism, however, relates less to chance than to the possible success of Carnapian attempts to argue *a priori* the existence of *inductive* probability. Thus Savage (1954, pp. 6–7) supposes that "until the contrary be demonstrated, we must be prepared to find reasoning inadequate to bring about complete agreement [in subjective probability]". Savage does not seriously suppose that empirical chance, as opposed to the reasoning of inductive logicians, might justify such agreement. That is because he assumes that if chance exists it must have a frequency analysis which disclaims any relevant relation to subjective probability. But a personalist who accepted a propensity theory could let some of his agnosticism be resolved by the results of a statistical science. Whether the rest of it could also be resolved by an *a priori* inductive logic is not for propensity theory to say.

THE OBJECTIVISM OF USAGE

In challenging the need for personalism to be subjectivist, some seemingly trite things need to be said and argued for. First of all that chance statements are rarely, if ever, meant just to convey subjective attitudes of partial belief. Chance statements certainly do express such attitudes, and their doing so indeed gives an essential point to making them. What is at issue is whether expressing partial belief can be all a chance statement does.

When two people express different partial beliefs about a proposition, they clearly do not thereby contradict each other. That is true however similar their situations, knowledge or preferences may be. So if all probability ascription ever did was to express such an attitude, it would never assert the existence of any objective probability and *a fortiori* never of any chance. Chances might still exist, but the supposition that they did would be pretty pointless since no statistical utterance could bear on it. For suppose ascriptions by two people of different chances to the same event (or set of events) expressed only diverse beliefs about the corresponding proposition (that the event or events occur). Since they would necessarily fail to contradict each other, no sense would be given to one rather than the other being objectively correct. If there can be chances, then the ascription of one (e.g. 0.5 to heads on a coin toss) must be able to contradict the ascription by someone else of a different one (e.g. 0.3) to the same event. To admit even the possibility of chances, we must take chance statements not only to express a partial belief but also or instead to assert that it is in some way objectively more justified than is the expression of some other partial beliefs, regardless of whose they are.

It may of course be, if there are objective probabilities, that what justifies some partial belief is not a property of an event but some relation the proposition partly believed bears to other propositions. The other propositions may even be characterised in an apparently subjective way as those known or reasonably accessible to the believer. This is done for instance in Carnap's requirement (1963, p. 972) that a rational man should assess the probability of a proposition by its relation to his "total evidence" for and against it. But that probabilities may be relational, even in such a way, does not show at all that they are subjective. A man can be objectively wrong both about what is known or reasonably accessible to him and about its relation to a proposition he partly believes. A Carnapian probability statement which asserts the utterer to be right on these matters does more than a subjective expression of an attitude could. Even Keynes' clear insistence (1921, p. 4) on this elementary point, however, has not prevented repeated confusion of relational with subjectivist views and consequent misappropriation of the former to the latter category (e.g. by von Mises, 1957, pp. 75–6).

Thus probability ascriptions merely expressing attitudes make no more sense of objective probability as a relation between propositions than they do of it as a property of events. Two people may address themselves to precisely the same relation between precisely the same propositions and still they will not contradict each other in expressing different attitudes or in reporting that in relevantly identical situations they do or would have different partial beliefs. Even one man only contradicts himself straightforwardly if he both asserts and denies of a proposition that he has a given attitude to it at one time. Subjectivism thus entails that ascriptions of different probabilities are sufficiently reconciled by numerical diversity in the ascribers. Given such diversity, a subjectivist must hold that the truth of one ascription can never entail the falsity of the other. This is just what any objective theory of probability, relational or not, logical or propensity, must deny. A personalist who wishes also to deny it must therefore deny that all a probability statement does is express partial belief.

So the first thing to show is that probability ascriptions are in fact normally taken to do more than express partial belief. To show this some preliminary sampling of common usage suggests itself.

In English a wide variety of words may be used in making a sentence make what everyone would agree to be a probability statement. Take some mildly forensic examples:

(1) 'We don't really know, but *most probably* the robbery occurred yesterday.'

(2) 'The way the lock was forced makes it *most improbable* that it was an inside job.'

(3) 'They were *much more likely* to have used a chisel than a pen knife.'

(4) 'I *expect* they took their time over it.'

(5) 'We were *pretty sure* some attempt would be made.'

(6) 'The *probability* is, being amateurs, they didn't realise that it is virtually unsaleable.'

(7) 'The *chances* are enormously against them pulling another job here so soon.'

Of these sentences, only (4) and (5) would naturally be used merely to convey attitudes, and it is significant that neither contains any of the terms 'probable', 'improbable', 'probably', 'probability', 'probabilities'. Not that invented instances prove anything, but it is in fact very difficult to construct naturally subjective English sentences explicitly in terms of probability.

Moreover, closer inspection shows incidental reasons for (4) and (5) appearing to be subjective. Suppose their hearers, as good subjectivists, reply with sentences so negated as to give as little appearance of contradicting (4) and (5) as possible:

($\sim$ 4) 'I do *not* expect they took their time over it',
(i.e. not ' I expect they did *not* take their time over it');

($\sim$ 5) 'We were *not* pretty sure some attempt would be made',
(i.e. not: 'We were pretty sure some attempt would *not* be made').

First, ($\sim$ 4) and ($\sim$ 5) might be used to convey a lack of any attitude at all (see pp. 6–7). If so, clearly no question arises of their use being intended to deny objective justification to the attitudes conveyed by (4) and (5). And even if ($\sim$ 4) and ($\sim$ 5) are used to convey positive attitudes, they might secondly be used to remark a difference in the objective situation or knowledge of the hearer which would account objectively for his different attitude being equally appropriate. Thus he might supplement ($\sim$ 4) with

'I've seen these chaps before, which you haven't, and they don't hang about on jobs like this';
or ($\sim$ 5) with

'We hadn't been told, as you had, that they knew the stuff was here'.
Thirdly, the past tense of (5) and ($\sim$ 5) makes them irrelevantly subjective where the present tense statements might well not be so. Compare:

(i) 'I said that q'

reporting a past assertion which in no way reasserts that q with

(ii) 'I say that q'

expressing a present assertion that q. The reply

'I deny that q'

may clearly be used to contradict (ii) even though the reply

'I denied that q'

obviously in no way contradicts (i). Similarly, the relevant subjectiveness of the present tense version of (5),

(5') 'We *are* pretty sure some attempt will be made',

must not be inferred from the obvious failure of ($\sim$ 5) to conflict as a reply with (5) itself.

Making every allowance to us on these grounds, a subjectivist might still insist that such present tense sentences as (4) and (5') can naturally be used subjectively. Granting that, it remains doubtful, as I have hinted, that their merely subjective sense survives translation into explicit terms of *probability*. Let us admit that

'I expect that q'

merely expresses partial belief in q; it is less clear that

'I think that q is probable'

or even that the less stridently objective

'I think q probable'

does so. The reply

'I do not think that q is probable'

would normally be understood as relevantly opposed, neither remark being taken merely to report what the speaker's private opinion was. The speakers would, I suggest, be taken as asserting their conflicting opinions (*a*) that q is (objectively) probable and (*b*) that q is (objectively) improbable. The prefix 'I think that' in 'I think that r' indeed generally signifies tentativeness in the speaker's opinion that r or his awareness of lacking conclusive evidence that r. Nevertheless, I think that an utterance of 'I think that r' is, in general, an assertion, however tentative, that r. If this is so, special reasons must be adduced for us to make an exception just when r happens to be explicitly a probability statement.

But whether or not sentences of the forms 'I think q probable', 'I think q improbable', etc. are normally used to make merely subjective statements, the sentences (1), (2), (3), (6) and (7) above, which lack any such qualifying expression as 'I think that' are clearly never so used. On this point personalists have sometimes been disingenuous in their choice of examples. Thus Savage: 'If, for example, a statistician were to say, "I do not know the p of this coin, but I am sure it is at most one half," that would mean in personalistic terms, "I regard the sequence of tosses of this coin as a symmetric sequence, the measure M of which assigns unit measure to the interval $[0, \frac{1}{2}]$".' (1954, p. 53.) That is too easy: the statistician's remark is subjective to start with. The question is what plausible alternative the personalist has to a statistician's utterance, however tentative, of

'The p of this coin is at most one half'
and whether *that* would be as convincingly subjective as Savage's sentence beginning 'I regard'.

SUBJECTIVE SURROGATES FOR CHANCE

> ...proceed to consider what a wise man would think and call that the degree of probability.
>
> Ramsey, 1926, p. 163

That we mostly mean our probability statements to be objective disposes of no positive subjectivist argument. What it does is put on subjectivists the onus of accounting for what they must take to be a popular illusion of objectivity. Subjectivism must first account for the wide intersubjective agreement on some probability statements which gives their objective truth such *prima facie* plausibility. These are just the standard cases of chance with which we shall be concerned: the chances of radioactive decay and of other physico-chemical transitions, of the outcomes of gambling trials and genetic experiments, of death, disease and accidents in various clinical and social settings. Of these the subjectivist must tell a causal story showing how perception of entirely non-probabilistic features of the world leads diverse people to similar partial beliefs in the truth of the propositions in question. This causal story is the subjective surrogate for the objectivist account of agreement as resulting from a shared perception of objective chances. To this subjective surrogate, which personalists have tried to provide in the precepts of Bayesian inference (see e.g. de Finetti 1937, p. 152), we shall return in chapter 2 (pp. 45–9).

Subjectivism must not only account for agreement on chances, it must also give a subjective point to the widespread activities of asserting, disputing and modifying chance statements. Since he must hold all these statements to fail in their intended reference to objective probabilities, a subjectivist must suppose them to fail uniformly of truth. This failure may be put in terms of the statements lacking truth value or of not being made at all by the use of statistical sentences (Strawson, 1950, 1952). De Finetti's description of sentences referring to unknown chances as "devoid of sense" (see p. 17) seems best taken this way. With Russell (1905, 1919), I prefer to construe sentences that fail to refer as making false statements; in this context the difference is only terminological. If in these terms all chance statements are supposed equally false, the point of debating them cannot be that of picking out the class of true ones. There must be a subjective surrogate for truth, if the objectivist presuppositions of usage are to be explained away.

There is nothing terrible in the discovery that a presupposition of common usage is mistaken. The fact that, as Kneale (1949, p. 7) puts it, "we think it possible to argue about probabilities and maintain that some men's judgements are better than those of others" does not of itself dispose of subjectivism. Statistical talk may presuppose objective probability, but that does not make its existence part of the meaning of 'probability'; and if it did, that still wouldn't prove that objective probabilities exist. One might as well conclude that a subjective account of Christian discourse and objective atheism must both be wrong because Christian discourse presupposes God's existence. Or that England must have existed for centuries because historians all write as if it had. These are not conclusive answers to scepticism either about chances, God, or the past.

But a subjectivist, to meet the facts of usage, must give alternative sense to the utterance, and acceptance by others, of one chance statement rather than another. The required sense can be provided by a notion of *sincerity* which is available to personalists. We are agreed that an essential role of a chance statement is to express partial belief, and whoever makes it may or may not have the partial belief it expresses. If he has, let us call the statement 'sincere'; if not, 'insincere'. Then the subjectivist surrogate for truth in his reconstruction of objectivist usage will be sincerity. The "right" (if trivially false) chance statement to make will be one that truly expresses the speaker's partial belief. A "wrong" chance statement will be one that expresses some partial belief the speaker doesn't have. What is wrong about it will be not that it is false – a trivial defect for the subjectivist, shared by all chance statements – but that it is insincere.

Some objections and complications to this notion of sincerity need brief remark. In its normal sense 'sincerity' requires more than is granted here. In particular it normally requires belief in the truth of the statement made. In this sense a subjectivist cannot be sincere in making a chance statement. But to complain of that would be trivial; if we are to trade on the virtues of sincerity, we must settle for a weaker notion to which having the appropriate partial belief is sufficient as well as necessary.

The complications arise from the dispositional account we have given of partial belief which makes it possible to be unaware of one's partial beliefs. So a man may deceive himself and sincerely (in its normal sense) express in his chance statement a partial belief which, when it comes to the behavioural test, he does not display. Whether this ever or often happens is not of much consequence: we may either say of such cases that the man 'thought himself sincere' or add self-knowledge to sincerity in the subjectivist criterion for propriety of statistical utterance. The essential point is that making a chance statement is at least a standard way of expressing a partial belief, namely the one the speaker would have if sincere and not self-deceived.

We may also admit what one might call 'group sincerity', where a probability statement is approved as expressing the shared beliefs of some group of people. The prestige of some scientific group may even make statements of their shared beliefs of such weight and interest to the public at large that they provide a standard by which deviant beliefs can be dismissed as erroneous. There is thus even a subjective surrogate for objectivity itself, endowing the consensus of professional physicists, say, with infallibility at least in matters of chance. This may be less than congenial to those outside the nuclear or genetic temples, but it obviously carries a shrewd appeal to the high priests within. Thus Borel (1924, p. 50) affirms:

There are cases where it is legitimate to speak of the probability of an event; these are the cases where one refers to the probability which is common to the judgements of all the best informed persons. . . One could, in order to abridge our language, while at the same time not attaching an absolute sense to this expression, call these probabilities objective probabilities.

Now it is doubtless desirable to defer from time to time to the informed opinion of physicists in talking of "the probability that an atom of radium will explode tomorrow" (Borel's example), but that is hardly what it *means* to talk so. An objectivist would find it a bizarre conclusion that the properties of radium have respectfully altered down the years to match the changing but ever-infallible consensus of "the best informed persons" at the Cavendish laboratory and elsewhere. (The subjectivist, of course, would retort that his claim is precisely that there is no such probabilistic property of radium.)

Here, however, we must distinguish general from specifically probabilistic subjectivism. Borel takes this supposed probabilistic property of radium to be "a constant of the same kind as the density of copper or the atomic weight of gold...always at the mercy of the progress of physical–chemical theory". But the truism that even well informed opinions may change on objective matters affords no argument for general subjectivism. Anyway, as Hacking (1965, p. 211) has observed in this context: "if all flesh is grass, kings and cardinals are surely grass, but so is everyone else and we have not learned much about kings as opposed to peasants". I need not dispute a general subjectivism whose acceptance would affect only in terminology a discussion of the relation of chance to other supposedly objective concepts. I take the subjectivist then, unlike Borel, to deny the existence only of chance properties in radium, leaving it possible for even "the best informed persons" to be objectively wrong about such matters as its density and its atomic weight.

Bizarre as the subjectivist rewriting of our supposed knowledge of radioactivity may seem, we could be forced to accept it by sufficiently compelling independent arguments for subjectivism. The objectivist assumptions of usage could then be explained away in the fashion I have outlined. But compelling independent argument is needed for so strained a reconstruction of physical theory; otherwise the general presumption must remain that people can sometimes be right in what they mean to say about chance as about other matters.

I have emphasised that an objectivist need not assume physicists' talk to be infallible in the way subjectivists must assume their shared partial beliefs to be so. All the probabilities I am concerned with are empirical. Apart from logical and mathematical errors, the most well informed physicist may just be wrong in taking the half-life of radium (the length of time in which the chance of a radium atom decaying is $\frac{1}{2}$) to be t_1. It might in fact be t_2 ($\neq t_1$) or, *pace* current theory, there might be no half-life at all. It is logically possible that what is chemically identified as radium simply is not, despite appearances, a radioelement as currently understood. Many current assumptions about chances might be false and they could conceivably all be rejected in the light of future science.

But that, as Borel admits, is nothing peculiar to chance. If subjectivism is to be as impervious as it must claim to be to the apparently objective successes of the statistical sciences, it must be content to rest equally unsupported by their hypothetical future failures.

In developing propensity theory it will be necessary to deal with other arguments against the possible existence of chances. Some of these stem from metaphysical determinism, some from supposed consequences of a Humean view of laws of nature or of induction. None are compelling enough to warrant taking subjectivist substitutes for the intendedly objective chance statements that we need to suppose true. It may be conceded to Savage (1954, p. 53) and company that "the *meaningfulness* of such [objective] propositions does not constitute an inadequacy of the personalistic view of probability" (my italics). What does constitute the incompleteness of personalism as an account of chance and the falseness of subjectivism is the intended meaning of such propositions and with it their possible truth.

2 Measuring partial belief

It is not enough to measure probability; in order to apportion correctly our belief to the probability we must also be able to measure our belief.

Ramsey, 1926, p. 166

SINCERITY for an objectivist, like patriotism for Edith Cavell, is not enough. Also like patriotism, perhaps, it is not even necessary. A chance statement is not made true by sincerely expressing the speaker's partial belief. What makes it true is a correspondence between the partial belief it expresses, sincerely or not, and some objective feature of the world. We take the feature to be quantitative, as in the continuously variable bias of a die. For an appropriate correspondence to be possible we want a similarly quantitative measure of partial belief. Consider a person aware of the changing bias of a die: we wish to be able to urge him to change by some corresponding extent his partial belief in it landing six when thrown.

It is not immediately evident that our wishes can be fully gratified. Partial beliefs might be comparable only in terms of greater or less. We should then be able to say only that a partial belief grows or lessens and our statements of correspondence would be limited accordingly. When the chance of throwing six with a die rises by 0.2, we could only ask the corresponding partial belief to become greater than that corresponding to any smaller rise in the chance. There would be no further sense in asking how much change occurs in a partial belief or how much greater one partial belief is than another. Kneale (1949, p. 15), mistaking partial belief to be a feeling, claims that "it is absurd to say of one feeling that it is just twice as intense as another of the same kind, because feelings of great intensity do not have parts which are themselves feelings of less intensity". We have already seen (pp. 8–12) that partial belief is not a feeling, but even so one might wish or be obliged to confine oneself to comparative statements about it. Koopman's development of personal probability has a comparative basis with the primitive relation

'a on the presumption h is no more probable than b on the presumption k' where a, b, h, k are all such "experimental propositions" as that a coin lands heads in such-and-such a time and place, and the relation is what "a given individual at a given moment may be regarded as assenting to" (Koopman, 1940, pp. 162–3).

Personalist theory has however given sense to stronger than comparative measures of partial belief. The technical part of this achievement is well known; in what follows I attend more to its rationale. I concentrate in particular on one underrated personalist argument that uses betting behaviour to measure partial belief. Its conclusion is that there is a quantitative measure of partial belief that is a probability (in the sense of having at least the main properties mathematicians ascribe to probabilities). The present importance of the argument is in showing partial belief to have a quantitative measure. Once that is shown there are a number of independent arguments for the measure being probabilistic (see Hacking, 1968, p. 53; Lucas, 1970, chapter 3).

It is by no means an unmixed blessing that the measure of partial belief is a probability. It certainly justifies personalists in calling partial belief so measured 'subjective probability' and in making free with many theorems of the probability calculus. It justifies them also in claiming to have given at least a very plausible interpretation of that calculus. But it has also caused a good deal of philosophical confusion. Whether any objective probability statements are true is quite unsettled either way by the same calculus happening also to provide a measure for partial belief. That fact does not begin to show that no objective empirical quantity is also a probability. Had the calculus not applied to partial belief, that would equally not have shown that there had to be objective probabilities to make sense of applications of the calculus. Nor would it have shown that objective probabilities could not correspond to partial beliefs. It is neither logically necessary that empirical applications of the calculus should be successful; nor that correspondence with chance requires partial belief to have the same measure as chance.

The question of what statisticians apply the probability calculus to would naturally arise if it measured neither partial belief nor any objective quantity suitably linked thereto. The question has a frequentist answer, namely that the calculus applies to certain objective frequencies (or limits of them) which can easily be shown to satisfy it. In that sense a frequentist supposes there to be objective probabilities. What a frequentist denies existence to is any probabilistic feature of the world that is irreducible to frequency and peculiarly related to partial belief.

The propensity theory asserts that there can be chances which are not reducible to frequencies. I also suppose with the personalists that partial belief in fact has a probabilistic measure. This makes feasible a conveniently concise statement of the objectivist thesis: some personal probabilities can be made more reasonable than others in a person suitably situated by his being aware of a corresponding objective probability. Normally the two probabilities will be of the same numerical value although there are some special cases in which they differ (see e.g. pp. 60–1).

It is a pleasant coincidence that chance and partial belief can have the same measure. It is naturally not coincidental, given this fact, that the same measure is actually chosen to apply to both. Betting quotients are preferred to betting odds as measures of partial belief just because they can be constrained to be probabilities. The propensity view, it is worth remarking, gives this preference a point lacking in both frequency and subjective accounts. For the frequentist the probability axioms are, at least with finite classes, "arithmetical truisms" (Ramsey, 1926, p. 158) about proportions, e.g. of coin tosses that land heads. If chance is now defined in terms of such proportions, then arithmetical truisms its axioms remain. It is gratuitous for a frequentist to impose these also on the seemingly irrelevant subject matter of partial belief.

Similarly, subjectivist arguments for adopting the standard probability axioms must rest entirely on plausible premises about the nature of partial belief. Personalists have indeed established the major axioms in this way, but an axiom not so supported that is put to fruitful use in statistics shows only inadequacy in a subjectivist account of chance. A problem of this kind has bothered personalists who have tended wrongly to feel that they should adopt subjectivism: no evident feature of partial belief warrants the assumption that personal probabilities are countably additive. Now statistics assumes countable additivity extensively of chance especially in treating of continuous distributions. It is thus not clear whether an important class of theorems which require this assumption are generally true of partial belief. To adopt them when needed, on the grounds that statistics applies them successfully and has partial belief as its subject matter, is to beg the question (see Savage, 1954, p. 43).

There is no problem here for propensity theory, because it does not take partial belief to be the subject matter of applied statistics. Assuming countable additivity to be true of chance requires on this view no peculiarly esoteric justification. It is enough that the assumption is mathematically convenient and theoretically fruitful in applied statistics itself. The justification is the same as for making comparable assumptions about any other objective quantity. For example, no direct measurement of length could conceivably be so precise as to require the use of real rather than merely rational numbers in stating its result. Yet nobody objects on these grounds to the universal assumption that there are irrational lengths. It is very convenient and fruitful to assume certain relations between continuous lengths, areas, volumes, distances, times and other quantities, for instance in the mundane application of Euclidean geometry. But these assumptions entail that some lengths being rational requires others to be irrational. Whenever the side of an Euclidean square is of a rational length its diagonal must be irrational and *vice versa*. The fact that this particular consequence of our physics is not amenable to direct experimental test is not taken to count against the otherwise well confirmed system from which it follows. It would be unreasonable of an objectivist to accept such merely indirectly testable assumptions about other commonplace quantities and yet without special reason to rebel against them in the case of chance.

The same assumptions, made about partial belief, may of course be similarly fruitful in the theories of games and decisions based on it. If so, that will as much show them to be true of partial belief as applied statistics has shown them to be true of chance. Such justification is a *sine qua non* of an adequate subjectivist account of chance. But it is a matter of only mild interest to propensity theory. There would be a certain aesthetic appeal in a demonstration of complete identity of measure between partial belief and chance, but no more than that. The arguments against subjectivism rest on stronger ground than the unprovenness of such an identity. Meanwhile, since our theory in no way requires it, we may assume for expository convenience what a subjectivist should show. After outlining a rationale for one personalist derivation of the main axioms, I shall refer thereafter without further qualification to mathematical probability as being alike the measure of chance and partial belief.

BETTING AND BELIEF

I follow many personalists in taking betting behaviour to provide one measure of the partial beliefs that may be displayed in it. This course has many advantages and some drawbacks. The great advantage has been remarked above (p. 15) that the same measure then applies to partial belief on all subjects, however diverse, that can be bet on. Different measures are not needed for partial belief on different topics, and partial beliefs on the most disparate matters are thereby made quantitatively comparable in strength.

The drawback is that some topics cannot be bet on. A bet must be settleable either way to the satisfaction of the parties to it and in some currency or benefit whose value can be assessed before the bet. These may seem modest requirements but they may not always be satisfied. Consider for example a bet on an afterlife as that is normally conceived. If the belief in an afterlife is false, at least one party to the bet will be unable to collect his winnings. If the belief is true, the subsequent value is still obscure of any stake that might be supposed also to survive the settling of the bet (see Mellor 1969*a*, p. 229 for further discussion of this case). Similarly with a case of tentative belief in a general but vaguely characterised theory of evolution. There are almost endless and unspecified possibilities for modifying the theory either to accommodate new data or to fall foul of them. It is not clear what the parties to a bet on its truth will be able to agree on as settling the bet either way. It cannot be assumed in such cases as these that a betting measure applies at all, nor consequently that sense is given by it to talk of quantitative partial belief.

Before a betting measure of partial belief can be applied to any topic it needs showing that the topic can be bet on. Otherwise the reference to betting is an idle metaphor. In the wide class of cases that might involve propensities, however, the possibility of betting is not seriously disputed. Trials with dice, coins and scintillation counters are easily conducted and their outcomes easily observed; as are the deaths and diseases of men, the yields of crops and the sex and other genetic characters of the offspring of biological species. No doubt there will always be hard cases but nothing to warrant labouring their epistemology here.

Some trivial idealising of the betting situation is obviously in order. We cannot for instance conduct and settle bets as fast as some radio-elements decay (with half-lives of 10^{-6} seconds) or as slowly as others

(10^7 years). But the time taken over the mechanics of a bet is so little of its essence as to make this fact immaterial. We could if need be bet instead on some more convenient record of such happenings. In the same way, many partial beliefs are measured only indirectly through some further partial beliefs related to them by a statistical theory accepted by the believer. The partial belief of a modestly mathematical gambler that heads will result on three successive coin tosses may reasonably be inferred from his measured partial belief in heads on one such toss. Again, the bearing of unaided observation may be remote on the settling of a bet about some obscure quantum transition. But provided the parties to the supposed bet can agree on what will settle it, and in due course that it has been so settled, it is immaterial how "theory-laden" their joint assumptions are.

These assumptions, needed to show the feasibility of betting in typical statistical situations, are indeed trivial. The assumption which chapter 1 (pp. 6–7) showed not to be trivial is that such betting displays a dispositional partial belief. In particular, even when a man has some such partial belief, extracting quantitative behaviour from him in a bet does not show the partial belief to be correspondingly quantitative. A man may be in a state of partial belief that is in quantitative terms very imprecise. He may think something probable without having any feeling of it being very probable rather than fairly probable or *vice versa*. If made to bet, he will have to behave, e.g. in his choice of odds, more precisely than his disposition dictates. We must not then read back into his partial belief the precision we have imposed on its display. We might analogously make a colour-blind man pick out one patch on a colour chart; we must not infer from his enforced choice between the red and the green patches that he can see a difference in colour between them. The temptation of spuriously investing a measured quantity with too great a precision, because the method of measurement yields it, is not peculiar to partial belief. Accountants notoriously suppose million pound transactions to be capable of valuation to the last penny; engineers feed computers data good to two significant figures and solemnly process the fifth and sixth figures of the resulting output.

Although the temptation of specious precision is general and has been generally discerned (see chapter 6, pp. 101–9), it is worth noting the means available to resist it in the betting measure of partial belief. Otherwise the measure could be wrongly convicted of irrelevance or falsity in ascribing to partial beliefs a precision they do not possess.

Instead of referring to the odds a person will choose when forced, we could as well refer to the range of odds he will *not* choose. The man who merely thinks something probable need only be taken to be disposed by his partial belief *inter alia* to avoid odds corresponding to probabilities not greater than $\frac{1}{2}$. The exposition that follows of how partial belief can be measured could have been rewritten in these terms, but the consequent complication seemed to me needless. It should be enough for those rightly sceptical of personalism's power to precisify our doubt that the rewriting can evidently always be done. The admitted diffuseness of much partial belief need be no ground for rejecting the personalist measures of it.

Before betting behaviour can be taken to provide a measure of partial belief, two things must be done. First some suitably quantitative feature of the behaviour must be isolated that is a function *inter alia* of the gambler's partial belief. Secondly the influence on this feature of all other factors must be discounted or eliminated. The strength of this personalist argument lies in the plausibility of its claims to have done these two things.

The two obviously quantitative features of betting behaviour that are affected by partial belief are (i) how much a man stakes and (ii) the odds he bets at. The more a man inclines to believe a proposition q, the more he will stake on its truth at fixed odds and the shorter the odds he will offer on it at a fixed stake. Personalists have used (ii) to measure partial belief; but it is illuminating to see why (i) will not do, especially as it has recently been proposed (Watling, 1969, p. 37).

The arbitrariness of monetary units unsuit them as measures of partial belief. Nobody would wish to base such a measure on a particular currency or on a temporarily fixed set of exchange rates or on gold. None of these has any theoretically plausible connection with human attitudes, useful though any of them might be as indicators on a particular occasion. A particular thermocouple or mercury thermometer might analogously be in widespread use to measure temperature and yet would not provide an acceptable definition of that measure. Even in a fixed currency the value of a given stake is undesirably related to the gambler's wealth. £1 is worth less to a millionaire than to an impoverished student. Willingness to risk £1 on a proposition may therefore indicate a greater faith in its truth, other things being equal, on the part of the student.

One might reasonably allow for a gambler's wealth by supposing him supplied with an amount of money that was fixed and large enough to swamp the influence of his private resources. In itself this is no more artificial than the betting situations actually proposed by personalists. It becomes so, however, when we try to allow for the effect of the odds on the proffered stake. It has been suggested that the odds could be ignored, but that would be absurd. If I were offered ten million to one on snow tomorrow (in a fine cold English May) I might well put £1 on it; while at evens I should risk no more than 25p on rain. Nobody would conclude, I hope, from this modestly rational behaviour that I had a stronger partial belief in snow tomorrow than I had in rain. There can be no doubt that the odds are among the other factors, affecting how much a man will risk losing, whose influence must be allowed for or removed before we can accept the proffered stake as measuring his partial belief.

The main objection to this proposed measure stems in fact from the strong influence of the odds on it. No plausible way of allowing for the effect of the odds leaves any quantitative measure of partial belief at all. Suppose we try stipulating that all bets are to be at even odds. A vast number of prospects will now attract equally negligible stakes even though the gambler's doubts about them are plainly unequal. Compare for instance the prospect that a date picked blindfold off a calendar will be a Sunday with the prospect that a flipped coin will land on edge. Nobody in his right mind would put money on either prospect at even odds. Yet my partial belief in the former, weak as it is, is clearly stronger than my partial belief in the latter. Different odds would discriminate partial beliefs of these two strengths: at eight to one the Sunday bet would attract money which the other would not. But there would still be other unequal partial beliefs which stakes at these or at any other fixed odds would not discriminate.

The plain moral is that the shortest odds at which a person will bet at all is a much more plausible general measure of partial belief than is the stake he will put up at any fixed odds. The reason is simply that the influence of what money is available on the shortest acceptable odds is vastly less than is the effect of odds on the size of stake. If odds are the basic measure, vagaries of the money supply can be countered without making the situation so artificial as to invalidate appeal to our knowledge of behaviour in real betting situations. The alternative of taking stake size as the basic measure after allowing for the odds is like taking the speed of a wind in preference to its temperature as the basic measure of its coldness. It is true that higher speed makes a cold wind colder, but for no fixed temperature will wind speed measure all detectably different coldnesses, which the temperature of still air readily does.

We start then by taking the shortest odds at which a person will bet at all as one provisional measure of his partial belief. We must next take account of the other factors besides partial belief that may also affect such odds. If need be we may restrict the supposed betting situation in some reasonably natural way so as to render their effects either calculable or negligibly small. A man with very little money, for example, may be reluctant to bet even the smallest amount possible in a given currency except at longer odds than would attract an equally doubtful but richer man. To minimise this effect we might suppose the gambler to be supplied with enough money to bet at whatever stakes are required. We should then assume the shortest acceptable odds to be impervious to wide variations in the (relatively small) proportion of his wealth committed to the bet.

The above is a natural assumption and is doubtless satisfied in many bets. It would still be preferable to be able to dispense with it by placing some suitable constraint on the betting situation. Even with a fixed and adequate supply of cash a man's gambling tendencies may well be affected by considerations of scale. Some might disdain bets for small amounts except at very long odds and others of a more prudent or nervous disposition might be similarly averse to wagering fortunes. Either way it will be hard to assess and allow for the effect of the stake proposed on the shortest acceptable odds. We therefore restrict the situation to one into which such considerations cannot enter. The gambler is allowed neither to choose the stake nor to know what it will be before he decides what odds are acceptable. We achieve this by making his opponent choose the stake after the gambler has specified the odds, provided always that the stake is reasonably within what the gambler has been supplied with.

This raises yet a further problem, the solution to which however also enables us to deal with another irrelevant factor. The problem is that our gambler may well refuse to bet at all under the conditions we have imposed. If stake size affects the shortest acceptable odds – and if it didn't these precautions would be needless – the gambler may be unable to specify them without knowing what the stake is. Observe that we cannot as things stand compel him to bet in order to extract the required choice of odds. We want to know the shortest odds that are acceptable to him, i.e. such that he would refuse to bet at any shorter odds. If we are going to make him bet whatever he says, there are no odds at which he can refuse to bet. No odds can be unacceptable to a man who is compelled to bet in any case. The concept of choosing the shortest acceptable odds has no application in that situation. And if we make him bet but give him a free choice of odds, the gambler will clearly choose the longest odds the rules allow regardless of his partial belief.

We seem then to face the alternative of abandoning shortest acceptable odds as our measure of partial belief or of reverting to the inelegant idealisation that they are unaffected by stake size. The right choice is made plainer by considering how another irrelevant effect on the odds can be disposed of. A gambler's choice of odds on q may well be affected by whether he wants q to be true or thinks it should be true. A Conservative might feel that he should not put money on Labour winning a general election. It would therefore take longer odds to tempt him to bet on such a dreadful prospect rather than against it. It being again almost impossible to assess and hence allow for such irrelevant effects on what odds are acceptable, the betting situation must be so restricted as to eliminate them. This can fortunately be done in an obvious way which simultaneously resolves our other dilemma.

The solution is to let the gambler's opponent not only set the stake after the odds are fixed but also choose then which way round the bet goes. For example, his opponent decides whether our Tory gambler is to bet on Labour or on the Conservatives winning. It will no longer be within the gambler's power to choose which side he backs. He will have to bet one way or the other and will not know which until after he has fixed the odds. His choice can thus not be affected by his knowledge of which way the bet is to be. In this situation it is unnecessary to assume as Ramsey does (1926, p. 178) the doubtful existence of an "ethically neutral proposition, believed to degree $\frac{1}{2}$".

Better still, now that his opponent settles the direction of the bet the gambler need not be confined to the shortest odds acceptable to him. For odds that are longer one way are shorter the other. Our Tory cannot aim to profit by setting odds on Labour much longer than he would in fact accept in an unforced bet. If he did, his opponent could turn his expected profit into an expected loss by making him back the Conservatives at the correspondingly shorter odds. Being thus able to abandon reference to the odds being the shortest that are not unacceptable, it now makes sense to compel the gambler to bet.

A gambler's choice of odds might of course be affected if he believed he knew what stake and bet direction would be imposed on him. He must obviously not only be in a position of ignorance but realise that he is so. In specifying the betting situation we prescribe that the gambler be brought to or left in this psychological state. The condition is not implausible. I have remarked (pp. 6–7 above) the possibility of lacking both belief and partial belief on a topic. Where the topic is other people's intentions I find that their incomprehensible behaviour frequently actualises this possibility in me.

One plausible measure of a man's partial belief is thus the odds he will determine if compelled to bet where his greedy but otherwise mysterious opponent subsequently decides both the stake size and the direction of the bet. From this situation the irrelevant effects are absent of a man's other beliefs, of his itch or distaste for gambling, of his preference for high or for low stakes, of his desires that some things should be true and others not and of the variable utility of money. The claim is that the only remaining factor disposing a man to settle on some odds in preference to others just is the strength of his partial belief, of which the odds are therefore a fair measure.

It seems to me that all one can or need do in support of such a claim is to account as I have outlined for the other known influences on the odds, since it will hardly be denied that partial belief is one such influence. Then it will not do to reject the claim merely on the grounds that there might be other influences unaccounted for, we know not what, which distort the proposed measure. It would be as reasonable to refuse credence to the readings of a thermometer shielded against all known sources of possible error on the grounds that it might after all be affected by some field or cosmic exhalation as yet unthought of.

Even so, more needs saying in defence of this betting measure of partial belief. The objection to be met is not like a querying of the accuracy, on a thermodynamically justified scale, of readings given by some practical thermometer. It is more like denying the claim of such a scale to be a measure of comparative warmth, where we hold the latter concept to have been available long before the advent of modern thermometry. Such objections have been repeatedly raised to projects of the kind that Carnap (1962, 1963) has called 'explication' and taken to be common both to science and to philosophy. Objectors such as

Strawson (1963) have taken explication to be common to science and to what Carnap does, e.g. in his construction of confirmation theory, and to be in either case irrelevant to philosophical analysis of everyday concepts. I have no wish to enter here upon the general dispute; if I did I should start by denying the shared assumption that "explication" in science is like what Carnap does. It is pertinent, however, to ask in the present case how a supposed disposition to rather abstruse, elaborate, artificial betting behaviour is related to doubt and uncertainty as we commonly understand them. A man can surely doubt and be certain who has never heard of betting, who even lives in a primitive community that uses no money, exchange or barter of any kind. Betting behaviour, it might therefore be urged, can be no part of what is meant when one is said to be in doubt or in this or that state of partial belief.

Consider an analogy. The Newtonian concept of mass is widely agreed to provide a quantitative measure of roughly "how much there is of" everyday things including people. The measure relies on elaborate concepts of acceleration, of exotic behaviour in artificial situations; or so it may seem from the viewpoint of some everyday lives. Yet men were surely said to be 'massive' (not only 'heavy' but literally 'hard to push around') before any of this Newtonian conceptual apparatus was constructed. And surely men can still be massive in just this sense, with which Newton can consequently have nothing essentially to do?

The proper reply to such remarks would be that the everyday use of 'massive' and related terms has come to be extended and refined. In particular comparative and quantitative judgments of massiveness have been added. For this extension Newtonian mechanics has provided sense and the successful sciences that deal in Newtonian forces have provided application. The sense of 'mass' is tied to no one sort of Newtonian force – contact, pressure, friction, viscous, electrical, magnetic, electromagnetic, gravitational – by which Newtonian masses can be affected. But the existence and mechanically interchangeable nature of these diverse forces is what gives sense to ascribing to objects finely graded dispositions to resist them. The objects of course include people, and that they may be unaware of having such dispositions is obviously neither here nor there. Most everyday remarks, although they intend no such elaborate implications, can be construed equally well as suitably imprecise statements about Newtonian mass. Of course it needs showing in each case that the everyday forces which we credit people with some ability to resist are quantitatively Newtonian. Where they are not, as when one refers to a man's "massive" stubbornness (his ability to be unmoved by forceful arguments), one's use of the terms becomes metaphorical.

The relation here, whatever it is, seems to me similar to that between everyday doubt and its explication as a disposition to indulge *inter alia* in suitably quantitative betting behaviour. The uses of such quantitative talk are comparably sophisticated, given point by theories of games and decisions relating them to similarly extended uses of terms referring to preference and utility. For such talk to be truly applied to a person, he has no more to have heard of money or of betting than Goliath had to have heard of Newton in order to be quantitatively massive. What is needed, as with mass, is that the everyday doubt thus elaborated is in something which the related quantitative concepts can be applied to. We have seen (p. 31) that because it cannot be bet on, the prospect of an afterlife can only be shown by the present account to attract quantitative partial belief in the metaphorical way a man can be massively stubborn.

If most or even many of our everyday doubts had to be thus ruled out as metaphorical, we should rightly reject the proposed betting measure as inadequate if not completely irrelevant to them. But not every, and perhaps not any single, use of everyday terms can be counted analytic and many uses in new situations are not specified at all. So new rules of use can well be added and existing ones to some extent revised during the scientific development of an everyday term without any need to suppose that a new concept has been introduced. This seems to me to be as much the case with partial belief as it is with mass. A person can bet as we have prescribed on the truth of most propositions that he can in everyday terms be said to doubt. We have a criterion then for saying of a man who doubts such a proposition that he is in what Johnson (1921, chapter 11) calls a 'determinable' dispositional state of partial belief, namely one of which "determinate" values can be distinguished by the various odds he could choose in the specified betting situation. It may of course be false that he is in any such state and it may be as we have noted (p. 32) that his partial belief is not precise and would be equally well displayed by any choice of odds in some interval. These count no more as objections to a betting measure of partial belief than a rainbow's lack of mass, or imprecision in mass of vaguely bounded objects like mountains, count against the explicatory value of Newtonian mechanics.

COHERENCE

I have argued the case for taking betting odds rather than stake size as the betting measure of partial belief. It is usual in fact to take not the odds themselves but a simple function of them, namely the betting quotient. The reason is that betting odds are not probabilities. This title is not withheld because odds lack such mathematical refinements as countable additivity (p. 29) but because they violate the most basic axioms of the probability calculus. Betting odds are ordered pairs of real numbers (usually integers, for convenient staking in the units of a discrete currency) each of which may take on any positive value. Probabilities are in contrast single real numbers (or at least rationals– see Braithwaite, 1953, pp. 130–1; Kyburg, 1961, pp. 64–5) confined to the interval [0,1] (Kolmogorov, 1933, p. 2). In this, probabilities resemble betting quotients, which can be defined in terms of betting odds as follows: if the odds on a proposition q are $n:m$, the betting quotient on q is $n/(n+m)$.

What the expressions 'odds on q', 'quotient on q' are intended to imply about the direction of the bet is best shown by an example. Suppose I say that I agree to odds of 1000:17 on q. Then if I am betting on q, I put up 1000 units for every 17 my opponent puts up. Whoever wins collects the total stake of 1017 units. If q turns out to be true, I win; if false, my opponent wins. The betting quotient on q is thus the fraction of the total stake put up by whoever will win it if q is true.

Although betting quotients must be like probabilities in lying between 0 and 1, they could for all we have yet shown fail to satisfy other basic axioms of the calculus. The probabilities of the members of a set of mutually exclusive and jointly exhaustive propositions must add up to 1 (Kolmogorov, 1933, p. 2). Betting quotients that do satisfy this constraint are called 'coherent' or 'fair'. (The former is the better term because Carnap (1962, p. 166) has also applied 'fair' more restrictedly to just those coherent betting quotients that are also warranted by an objective probability relation.) But it is not yet clear why a person's betting quotients should be assumed to be coherent. To take the simplest example, a person disposed to adopt quotient p on q in one bet is not *prima facie* thereby disposed to adopt $1-p$ on $\sim q$ in a simultaneous bet. If we are to credit betting quotients in general with the coherence they need to be probabilities, a general argument is needed to rule out alternative incoherent quotients. The standard argument for this is the

"Dutch book" argument that incoherence in his quotients makes a man liable to lose money whatever happens, i.e. whether q turns out true or false. The mathematics of the argument is simple and well known (see e.g. de Finetti, 1937, pp. 103–4) and it will be enough here to illustrate it. What is more important is to show that (and how) the argument applies to the betting situation we have specified above.

The Dutch book argument works by making a person with incoherent quotients take on a number of bets, on each possible outcome of which his total losses exceed his total gains. It is taken to be irrational to expose oneself to certain net loss in this way and the betting quotients of rational beings are consequently assumed to be coherent. (A stronger argument which we need not here consider deems it irrational to combine bets with at least one possibility of net loss and none of net gain, see Kemeny, 1963, pp. 719–20). Now a gambler could normally avoid a Dutch book in a number of ways without making his quotients coherent. He could refuse one or more of the fatal combination of bets, or veto the stake sizes or bet directions, or alter his quotients, after these other factors were safely fixed, to some suitable but still incoherent values. While these alternatives remain open the desirability of avoiding a Dutch book affords no strong argument for coherence. But in order to establish betting odds (and hence the betting quotient) as a suitable measure of partial belief, we have already ruled out these alternatives on independent grounds. Our gambler has to bet at quotients which he fixes first, after which his opponent freely determines the stake size and bet direction. In this situation the gambler's only method of stopping a Dutch book against him is to make his betting quotients coherent.

A Dutch book may be illustrated by the example above, with incoherent betting quotients of 0.7 on q and 0.2 on $\sim q$. Our gambler's opponent chooses to stake £7 on q in a bet (i) at the 0.7 quotient and £2 on $\sim q$ in another bet (ii) at the 0.2 quotient. It is easily seen that on this combination of bets our gambler will make a net loss of £1 whether q is true or false.

	q TRUE	q FALSE
Bet (i)	−3	+7
Bet (ii)	+2	−8
Net	−1	−1

GAMBLER'S PROFIT in £s

The question remains, however, why the betting quotients that measure a person's partial beliefs should be assumed to be coherent.

We have of course the independent arguments for a probabilistic measure of partial belief referred to on p. 28, but the betting situation we are using to measure partial belief should furnish its own rationale. Some trivial objections to the Dutch book argument are easily met. A philanthropist with a taste for gambling might no doubt purposely submit to a Dutch book as a congenial method of giving money away. His betting quotients will be incoherent; equally, they reflect other factors than his partial beliefs. Indeed, such a use of a betting situation is freakish enough to call its sense in question. Certainly what is staked in a bet need not be actual cash, whether pounds or roubles, and a betting mechanism could incidentally be used to give cash away. But a bet needs some suitably transferable quantitative object of desire that can be possessed and so staked and won or lost. The term 'goods' is conveniently used here to refer indifferently to any such desired stuff. Then what makes a betting situation is that each party has the object of winning by means of it whatever goods the other is by the same means prepared to lose. If our philanthropist really is betting, as well as dispensing cash in a pointlessly complex way, there must be some goods he desires to win but might lose. They might be the quantity of happiness in others that could be produced by the difference between his greatest and least possible loss of cash. Whatever his goods are, in terms of them our philanthropist will wish to avoid a Dutch book however he behaves in cash terms. To accept betting behaviour at all as a measure of partial belief is surely to accept as legitimate a constraint such as coherence that is needed to give a minimal betting sense to it.

Nevertheless, the usual way of justifying coherence in terms of 'rationality' can be misleading. It makes it seem a merely normative constraint too much like the further constraints an inductive logic would impose (Savage, 1954, pp. 6–7). But inductive logic is in no sense subjective; it is quite immaterial that actual partial beliefs do not satisfy its constraints. Personalism on the other hand purports to deal in real partial beliefs (Jeffrey, 1968, p. 169). We shall see that it even purports to provide in Bayesian precepts a causal account of how scientists' partial beliefs converge on agreed values (pp. 45–9). I have remarked that personalists hedge their bets on this point (p. 4), but a stronger case can be made for what they ought to say. The case may not in the end be strong enough for subjectivism but it will be strong enough for us.

What observations of incoherence mostly show is that everyday betting behaviour is rarely an accurate measure of partial belief. In the same way, many casual tape-measure operations do not constitute accurate measurements of length. The kinds of situation in which lengths and partial beliefs can be given accurate direct measurement are both highly artificial. In the case of partial belief, we have seen that it must be so if irrelevant influences on the betting quotient are to be excluded. The same is true of the precautions needed in making accurate length measurement. Specifying the precautions seems no more normative in the one case than in the other. It is plausible to assume that people in, and fully seized of, the carefully constrained betting situation we have specified would in fact be coherent if the consequences of incoherence were made explicit. And it is as dispositions to produce different betting quotients in precisely this situation that partial beliefs are here discriminated as being of different strengths.

The application of the Dutch book argument is not restricted by the fact that partial belief is often measured otherwise than by betting behaviour. It does not matter even that some partial beliefs (un-conscious ones and those of animals) cannot be measured by betting at all. There is analogously no way of laying a metre rule alongside a light wave to measure its length. In neither case should we infer that the concept is not subject to the same measure. In each case other connota-tions give the concept application and impose on it what would be true of the results of this method of measurement. A measurement of any quantity may be corrected by one of a different kind, as when a mercury thermometer reading of a temperature is corrected by that of a thermocouple. For this to be possible, clearly the measure must be the same by whatever method it is applied. And so it is with partial belief, whose strength may be inferred equally from choice among uncertain options and independent measures of their utility. Any idealisation in all this, in applying the correlations on which alternative measures of a quantity rely, is scientific and theoretical rather than normative in the manner of an inductive logic.

The degree of idealisation is certainly greater with partial belief than it is with length and it is neither necessary nor plausible to impose coherence over the whole range of a person's partial beliefs. People may as well have incoherent partial beliefs as they may have logically inconsistent full beliefs. The idealisations to consistency in full belief and coherence in partial belief still have a descriptive point and their limitations can be similarly accounted for. Both belief and partial belief have been taken to be dispositions to action, being given content and application in explanatory theories thereof. Now consider full belief: the paradigms of action are deliberate, and certainly beliefs that are consciously seen to be inconsistent cannot be held simultaneously. Plausible explanation of deliberate action will therefore ascribe consistency at least to those conscious beliefs motivating it. One is therefore generally reluctant to ascribe inconsistent dispositions because they would not deliberately be displayed together in one action. One or other would be changed and to that extent a believer will deliberately act as if he had never held simultaneously inconsistent beliefs.

Still we may observe inconsistency amongst beliefs indirectly and account for its possibility in terms of unawareness and lack of joint display in deliberate action. Since beliefs may moreover be changed by coming to consciousness, past inconsistency may be inferred even where none is presently displayed. In the example of p. 14, my becoming aware of my belief about the quickest way from London to Tokyo might lead me to change it because I now see it to be inconsistent with other, previously unrelated, beliefs about geography and airline routes and speeds. I may likewise be separately conscious on different occasions of beliefs which I should see to be inconsistent and hence modify if I considered them together.

Similarly, the use and limitations of assuming coherence amongst partial beliefs can largely be accounted for descriptively. I have suggested (p. 42) that it is as conceptually impracticable in our specified betting situation to display incoherent partial beliefs as it is to display together consciously inconsistent full beliefs. Now the deliberate actions under uncertainty that partial belief is invoked to explain (e.g. marketing and other business decisions) are assumed to be treated by the agents as displaying what such betting would alternatively measure. In so far as the successful application of the theory to these actions justifies this assumption we may conclude that bringing partial beliefs to consciousness, preparatory to deliberate action, tends to make them coherent. This is the justification for idealising partial beliefs into coherence at least in the explanation of much deliberately risky action.

This justification is anyway quite adequate for our present limited purposes. A person who wishes to distribute correctly his partial beliefs in sundry prospects according to his knowledge of their chances must first make his partial beliefs coherent. That, however, is his problem, not ours. As we have already remarked (p. 30), it is of no consequence for propensity theory if indirect tests or associated feelings of doubt suggest from time to time that some of a person's unconscious, uncompared or unacted on partial beliefs are incoherent.

BAYESIANS AND THE LIMITS OF COHERENCE

Let us then, instead of that idle and not very innocent Employment of forming imaginary Models of a World...turn our Thoughts to what we experience to be the Conduct of Nature with respect to intelligent Creatures.

Butler, 1736, p. viij.

We can now revert to a topic left over from chapter 1 (p. 22), namely the subjectivist surrogate for the perception of chances. In terms of coherent betting quotients (CBQs), physicists for example share remarkably similar partial beliefs in the occurrence, within fixed intervals of time, of certain well known nuclear transitions. Plain men account for this as the natural result of their shared perception of an objective chance. Subjectivists must be more subtle: they must explain causally how the shared perception of quite non-chance features of the world leads men of diverse initial opinions into the ultimate concordance of partial belief that we observe. As de Finetti (1937, p. 152) puts it, if

it is a question of showing that there is no need to admit, as it is currently held, that *the probability of a phenomenon has a determinate value* and that it suffices to get to know it,

then it will be necessary

to show that [1] *there are rather profound psychological reasons which make the exact or approximate agreement that is observed between the opinions of different individuals very natural, but that* [2] *there are no reasons, rational, positive, or metaphysical, that can give this fact any meaning beyond that of a simple agreement in subjective opinions.*

(de Finetti's italics; my underlining).

Chapter 1 produced reasons of usage against part [2] of de Finetti's project. I now enquire into the success of part [1], what the "rather profound psychological reasons" might be that lead physicists to agree on objectively non-existent half-lives for radioelements. Part [1] of the project of course has no force on its own as an argument for subjectivism, however successful it may be. The existence of chances does not preclude a causal account of how physicists come to agree on them. On the contrary, for any objective quantity that we can come to know there is presumably a discoverable causal process of perception by which we come to know it. If scientists can investigate and agree on temperatures, for example, they can investigate the causal conditions under which such agreement comes about. The process is not normally esoteric nor are its conditions obscure: clear-sighted men look straight at a well-calibrated, suitably placed thermometer, reasonably close and in a good light. In these conditions, as de Finetti (1937, p. 99) says of probability,

one can get a clear idea of the reasons, themselves subjective, for which in a host of problems the subjective judgements of diverse normal individuals not only do not differ essentially from each other but even coincide exactly.

One would not take this mundane truth as a ground for "refusing to admit the existence of an objective meaning and value" (de Finetti, 1937, p. 99) for temperature, mass, electric current and the like; nor is it a ground for such refusal in the case of chance. In general, the truth of a scientific theory of perception, about how scientists come to agree in the opinion that they have objective knowledge of some kind, does not entail or even suggest that their agreed opinion is false. And if it did, chance would be no worse off than any other major scientific concept.

Subjectivists nevertheless need their surrogate for the perceptual process and have thought to provide it in the following way. Among the theorems of the probability calculus true of partial belief (measured e.g. by CBQs) is Bayes' theorem (e.g. Feller, 1957, p. 114). Subjectivists would interpret Bayes' theorem as relating a person's CBQ on a proposition q to a hypothetical CBQ on q conditional upon the truth of another proposition r. A Bayesian in these terms is one who on learning of the truth of r adjusts his actual CBQ on q to equal this previously hypothetical CBQ. In doing this he is said to 'conditionalise' his subjective probability assignments on the acquired evidence that r is true. Then as Savage (1954, p. 68) puts it:

In certain contexts, any two [Bayesian] opinions, provided that neither is extreme in a technical sense, are almost sure to be brought very close to one another by a sufficiently large body of evidence.

This is the fact cited by subjectivists as their causal explanation of how scientists, initially allowed to have widely divergent CBQs, are brought by the piling up of shared evidence into the close agreement that is observed in their chance assignments.

Not only does this account of Bayesian consensus fail to show that there is nothing to agree on, but the CBQ measure of partial belief fails in two ways even to entail Bayesian consensus. First, personalists have not in other respects presented arguments for coherence as a scientific theory about real betting quotients. They have presented the conclusion of the Dutch book argument as a canon of rationality restricting betting quotients proffered simultaneously by one person to those of which *inter alia* Bayes' theorem is true. When a person's simultaneously proffered quotients are found to violate this restriction, personalists do not take their account to be refuted; his behaviour is rather to be condemned as incoherent (see chapter 1, p. 4). So construed, the account could neither be confirmed nor be infirmed by evidence of actual behaviour. By the same token it could not entail or explain actual behaviour as would a real psychological theory of how scientists come to agree on assignments of probability.

I did my best in the last section to construe the Dutch book argument more descriptively. But no evidence has been produced that its premises are true of the processes leading to the scientific agreement on chances which is to be explained. No one supposes the committees who settle and revise values of radioactive constants to proceed by conditionalising CBQs. Nor is it really pertinent that Bayesian committees would be able to agree just as real ones do. The fact that a flat earth would share many features with the real one does not make the flat earth hypothesis an acceptable explanation of those features. (It could of course be said that a flat earth at least provides a model for them. What Bishop Butler called 'that idle and not very innocent Employment of forming imaginary Models of a World' (see p. 45) is always in fashion with mathematicians as being both easier and more elegant than finding out the empirical truth of the matter.)

However the Dutch book and other arguments for coherence in partial belief are construed and applied, the really serious objection is that behaviour can perfectly well be coherent without being Bayesian. Coherence applies only to a person's actual simultaneously proffered betting quotients, not to hypothetical or conditional quotients. The Dutch book argument for example does not work with conditional bets. If a gambler can be taken up on old conditional bets whose antecedents have been realised, he can be made to lose money whether he conditionalises or not. To see this it is necessary to make more distinctions than are usually made in the literature (except by Ramsey, 1926, p. 180).

There is first the concept of *conditional probability* defined in the calculus (e.g. Feller, 1957, p. 105). Taking propositions for the moment as the bearers of probability, the definition may be put thus:

$$p(q,r) =_{\mathrm{df}} \frac{p(q\&r)}{p(r)}.$$

When the unconditional probabilities $p(r)$ and $p(q\&r)$ are interpreted as CBQs on the truth of r and $q\&r$, my conditional probability $p(q,r)$ is simply the corresponding function of my CBQs.

Secondly there is the concept of a *conditional bet* made at a *conditional betting quotient*. I may not only be disposed to bet on q at an unconditional quotient $p(q)$, but also to undertake a bet on q subject to the condition that r be true. If r is true, a bet on q takes place at my conditional quotient; if r is false, no bet takes place. My quotient for this conditional bet may well be different from $p(q)$ if I believe the truth of r to bear on that of q. It does not follow that it will be the same as the conditional probability $p(q,r)$.

Thirdly, there is the new unconditional quotient on q I adopt after learning of the truth of r.

Suppose the Dutch book argument applied to conditional betting quotients. Surely when I learn r I should equate my new unconditional quotient on q with my previous quotient on q conditional on r? For otherwise a Dutch book could be made against me by combining bets at my present unconditional and my past conditional quotients. There is however a fatal flaw in any such argument for Bayesianism. The argument will not entail conditionalising unconditional betting quotients unless we further identify conditional betting quotients with conditional probabilities. But once that is done a Dutch book can be made against me in any case. Bayesian behaviour will not preserve me and so is not picked out by the argument as particularly rational.

We have seen that the Dutch book argument to be effective requires that the gambler is compelled to bet at the quotients he specifies. If it is applied to his conditional probabilities on q interpreted as conditional betting quotients, he can subsequently be taken up on any such quotient whose condition is realised. Let two such mutually compatible conditions be r and s, where the gambler's partial beliefs before learning of their truth were such that $p(q,r) \neq p(q,s)$. He thus committed himself to betting on q at two different quotients should both r and s turn out true. Now that they have done so his opponent has only to enforce a suitable combination of these two bets in order to make a

Dutch book. It is immaterial how the gambler has subsequently changed his unconditional quotients.

This absurd consequence can be avoided by not applying the Dutch book argument to conditional probabilities. This is indeed essential to the argument's use above in establishing coherence in unconditional betting quotients. There is in any case no plausible need to appeal to conditional bets. A measure of my partial belief at any time in every proposition I could bet on is provided by the unconditional quotient I would produce at that time. The most that my conditional quotients could be supposed to measure is my prediction of what my partial beliefs would be in possible future situations. I cannot see great import-ance in measuring predictions of partial belief, certainly not at the cost of destroying an argument for coherence in the measure of partial belief itself.

It should be clear anyway that coherence in my partial beliefs at one time can no more determine what they should be at another than logical consistency can in the case of full beliefs. The constraints of coherence cannot compel a person to change his partial beliefs from time to time in a Bayesian or in any other way. Just as, on a subjective view, two people may have the same or widely different CBQs on the same event, so one person may from time to time preserve or alter his CBQs on that event in any way to which he is disposed. That this is so is well illustrated by a personalist's assertion that

there are cases in which a change in the probability assignment is clearly called for, but where the device of conditionalisation cannot be applied because the change is not occasioned simply by learning of the truth of some proposition. In particular the change might be occasioned by an observation. (Jeffrey, 1965, p. 154.)

Equally of course any change called for by conditionalisation can be cancelled or modified to any extent by such effects of inconclusive ob-servation. Whatever the other merits of this assertion (see Levi, 1967*a*, 1969; Harper and Kyburg, 1968) it shows at least the compatibility of coherence and non-Bayesian behaviour (see also Hacking, 1967).

Recent unpublished work by Paul Teller has persuaded me that there are arguments at least for the generalised form of conditionalisation advanced by Jeffrey (1965, chapter 11). I am not convinced that they establish in it the causal explanation of agreement on chances that subjectivists need. Certainly what I have yet seen publicly advanced does not do so. And we have seen that it will not be matter for more than sympathetic concern to propensity theory if and when this lacuna in subjectivism is filled.

3   Frequencies and trials

FREQUENCY ANALYSES have become accepted as the standard accounts of chance, and their inadequacy has been the most potent subjectivist argument against its existence. Philosophers have felt forced into subjectivism by elimination, just as they feel scientists have been forced into frequentism. As Savage puts it (1961, p. 576), "rejecting both necessary and personalistic views of probability left statisticians no choice but to work as best they could with frequentist views". With statisticians frequency views have predominated among objective accounts of chance. A symposiast introducing a Royal Statistical Society discussion can quite naturally say: 'The term *frequentist* applies to any analysis or analyst of the "objectivist" school, where...there is a tendency to interpret probability solely in terms of relative frequencies in large scale replication' (Aitchison, 1964, p. 161). For Savage (1954, p. 3) also "objectivist views hold that...evidence...for the magnitude of the probability...is to be obtained by observations of some repetitions of the event, and from no other source whatever".

Having thus identified objective with frequency views, the subjectivist of course concludes that "the difficulty...in any objectivistic view [is that] probabilities can apply fruitfully only to repetitive events... it is either meaningless to talk about the probability that a given proposition is true, or this probability can be only 1 or 0" (Savage, 1954, p. 4). This is indeed the chief defect in any view that is properly called 'frequentist' but, as Giere (1969, p. 382) has noted, it is not as endemic to objectivism as personalists have supposed. Propensity theory at least is free of it and can satisfy, as his own theory does not (see chapter 7 below, pp. 136–46), Kneale's demand for a tenable "objectivist analysis of an A-thing's being B which is yet not a frequency theory" (Körner, 1957, p. 80).

The disease from which frequency accounts of chance suffer is too much operationalism; not, as de Finetti (1937, pp. 148–9) believed, too little. It relates the concept of chance too closely to one particular method, namely measuring frequencies, by which chances are ascertained. That chance is a property of which "observed frequencies are to be thought of as measurements" (Loéve, 1955, p. 5) is of course a commonplace among statisticians. It does not follow that frequencies provide an acceptable definition of chance any more than metre rule operations provide an acceptable definition of length. The frequentist error, as Kneale (1949, pp. 193-4) observes, is "that of confounding evidence with that for which it is evidence...My evidence for stating that another man is in pain may be that he winces and says he is in pain, but this is not what I mean by my statement." It is superfluous today to spend time razing the largely abandoned ruins of operationalism, but erstwhile tenants who continue to squat in frequentist outhouses ought perhaps to be evicted...

The attractive starting point for frequency analyses of chance is the relative frequency or proportion of G (i.e. things having the property G) in some finite population of F. Thus Braithwaite (1953, p. 122): 'On the assumption that the class β is neither the null class nor is an infinite class,...the probability of a β-specimen being an α-specimen can be identified with the proportion among the members of β of those which are members of α.' (See also Russell, 1948, p. 371.)

The frequency theories of von Mises (1957) and Reichenbach (1949) ostensibly define probability only for certain infinite classes which von Mises calls 'collectives'; but this is not to be taken literally, as von Mises in effect admits (p. 11): 'In order to apply the theory of probability we must have a *practically* unlimited sequence of uniform observations.' (My italics.) Few if any empirical classes, however, are known to be infinite and those which are open are most plausibly supposed finite. Thus Kyburg (1961, p. 143): 'I have already supposed that all rational classes are finite, and even that the number of their members must be less than two to the googolplex $[10^{10^{100}}]$.' A frequency theory must certainly apply to the finite case if it is to have even *prima facie* plausibility, since frequency is undefined in infinite classes. It is only the sequence of frequencies in finite classes from which von Mises constructs limits for his collectives, that gives his theory any frequency sense. If these finite frequencies are denied to be chances it is hard to see why von Mises' pseudo-mathematical limits of them should be admitted to be so. Determinism in general cannot seriously be supposed a consequence of the Universe having only a finite number of individuals, nor in a particular class of β-specimens of that class being finite.

I therefore follow Russell (1948, p. 382) in assuming, "in order to make Reichenbach's theory as adequate as possible, that, where finite classes are concerned, the definition of [p. 371] is to be retained, and that the new definition is only intended as an extension enabling us to apply probability to infinite classes. Thus his $H_n(O,P)$ will be a probability, but one applying only to the first n terms of the series." The extension to infinite classes is not trivial. Von Mises had difficulty reconciling the condition that G occur randomly in a collective of F with the condition that there is a limit to the frequency of G in increasing classes of F (see Kneale, 1949, §§32–3; Popper, 1959, §§50–65; von Mises, 1957, pp. 87–93). Such difficulties need not concern us. Our objections are rooted equally in the finite cases from which frequency theories ultimately derive their sense.

It is tempting to identify chance with frequency because frequency, in the finite case at least, is an objective property, in principle easily measurable, which trivially satisfies the probability calculus. "When probabilities can be identified with class-ratios whose denominators are finite numbers which are not zero, no further problem arises about them. All these probabilities are rational numbers lying between o and 1 inclusive, and all the logically necessary laws connecting related probabilities appear as arithmetical propositions connecting related fractions" (Braithwaite, 1953, p. 122). The trouble is that the frequency of G in a class of F is a property that cannot intelligibly attach to the individual members of the class. Hence the frequentists' inability to make sense of a named individual a which is F having a chance of being G as well as having the property G or the property $\sim G$ (von Mises, 1957, pp. 11, 17–18; Reichenbach, 1949, §72). This is precisely the inability, put as that of assigning an objective probability to the proposition that a is G, which Savage attributes to objectivists in general (p. 50 above).

The difficulty may be more plainly seen as follows. Suppose a has the properties $F_1, F_2, \ldots, F_i, \ldots$, where the corresponding classes (of things that are F_1, F_2, etc.) are all finite. On a frequency view the chance that F_1 is G is the frequency of G in F_1, the chance that F_2 is G is the frequency of G in F_2 and similarly for any other property F_i. These frequencies in general differ and so therefore do the chances defined by them. Which, if any, of these alleged chances is to be ascribed to the individual a? If none, how are they to fulfil chance's intended rôle of constraining the CBQ it is appropriate to offer on a being G? If no one frequency can be picked out to fill this rôle the definition, whatever it is of, is not of chance.

Kneale (Körner, 1957, p. 19) and Ayer (1963, p. 200) have pointed out (*pace* Salmon, 1967, p. 96) that this is the frequency analogue of a difficulty for the view that probability statements express logical relations between two propositions, e.g. a hypothesis and inconclusive evidence for it. The difficulty is to decide how much evidence should be invoked to yield a non-relational probability that could constrain a CBQ on the hypothesis. One may say that all, or all available, evidence should be invoked (Carnap, 1963, p. 972). The frequency analogue of such a "total evidence" requirement is that the chance that a is G should be identified with the frequency of G in the most closely defined class of which a is a member, namely the class of things that are F_1 *and* F_2 *and*...F_i *and*...; but unless some limit is set to the increasingly detailed specification of this "reference class", a will be its sole member. The frequency of G in the reference class will be 1 or 0 as 'Ga' is true or false. This is the fact analogous to the total evidence – the set of all true propositions – containing either the hypothesis that a is G or its negation, so that the logical probability of 'Ga' on the total evidence is either 1 or 0 (Ayer, 1957, p. 16).

Frequency and logical relation theorists have never overcome this obstacle to their accounting for plainly non-relational objective probability statements (Hempel, 1968; Kyburg, 1970a). Their attempts founder on the problem of setting a non-arbitrary limit to the amount of evidence, or closeness of specification of the reference class, to be invoked in making the probability assignment. The problem might be overcome, for example by an adequate explication of the notion of "available" evidence (Ayers, 1968, pp. 21–2). But the resulting definition of probability would then rest on other considerations than frequency or the logical relation holding between two propositions. Frequentists faced with this problem have generally adopted the Procrustean solution of denying that there is a chance that a is G. Thus von Mises asserts (1957, pp. 17–18):

We can say nothing about the probability of death of an individual.... It is utter nonsense to say, for instance, that Mr X, now aged forty, has the probability 0.011 of dying in the course of the next year. [Mr X] is...a member of a great number of other collectives...for which the calculation of the probability of death may give as many different values. One might suggest that a correct value...may be obtained by restricting the collective to which he belongs...by taking into consideration more and more of his individual characteristics. There is, however, no end to this process...we shall be left finally with this individual alone...the collective will cease to exist.

This view makes it quite inexplicable how statistical data can be given individual application. Reichenbach (1949, §71) rightly insists that "it is the *predictional value* that makes probability statements indispensable" but is reduced to the following account of how this indispensable rôle can be fulfilled (§72):

> An individual thing or event may be incorporated in many reference classes, from which different probabilities will result. . . . We then proceed by considering *the narrowest class for which reliable statistics can be compiled*. . . . We do not affirm that this method is perfectly unambiguous. . .we are dealing here with a method of technical statistics.

Of course we are dealing with nothing of the sort: we are dealing with a crucial test of the adequacy of any proposed definition of chance. The same goes for Salmon's (1967, p. 91) alternative appeal to the "*broadest homogeneous reference class*" in providing for the application of statistical data to the single case. It will not do to relegate this "extremely practical affair" (Salmon, 1967, p. 92) of obtaining "weights that can be used in practical decisions" (p. 95) to "rules [that] are part of methodology, not of probability theory" (pp. 93–4). The process of picking particular reference classes is no doubt extremely practical; but if the process is what makes probability statements indispensable probability theory should at least make sense of it. The issue cannot be disposed of just by calling single case chances 'weights' and the problems of determining their values 'methodological'. Single case application is so central to the use of probability statements (cf. Ayers, 1968, p. 23) that no account of their meaning can be acceptable which rules it out.

Nor is it sufficient to refer as von Mises (1957, p. 16) does to the profits of casinos, lotteries and insurance companies in order to show that chance statements are used predictively. No one seriously doubts our knowledge of their predictive usefulness, just as "one would appear ridiculous, who would say, that 'tis only probable the sun will rise tomorrow" (Hume, 1739, book 1, part 3, section 11). What we want in each case is an account of how such knowledge is possible. It is just this that frequentists, as a consequence of their definition, cannot provide. "When frequency theorists claim that they can provide a justification for the practice of insurance companies. . .they delude themselves by abandoning their own definition of probability at a crucial point in the argument." (Kneale, 1949, p. 167.)

If frequentists deny that their definition applies to the single case, what does it apply to? What sense can be made of 'the chance that *an F* is *G*' which denies all sense to 'the chance that *this F* is *G*'? It seems to me that two common kinds of situation have lent frequency analyses their *prima facie* plausibility. One is where an *F* is selected, with each *F* having an equal chance of selection. It then trivially follows that the chance of the selected item being *G* is equal to the frequency in the class of *F*. This is what gamblers take the situation to be in drawing cards "at random" from a deck. The description of the situation clearly affords no frequency definition of chance, since chance has to be independently invoked in giving the description. But the situation is one in which, *given* the concept of chance, it is plain why frequency should be a measure of it, i.e. should warrant a partial belief on the possible outcome that the selected *F* is *G*. The fact that the selected *F* may also be F_1, F_2, etc. is irrelevant; it is given that the selection device ignores these characteristics. If *a* is *F*, it has a chance of being selected that is independent of its other properties; if *a* is $\sim F$, it has no chance of being selected whatever its other properties.

The other kind of situation in which the frequency analysis appears most plausible is where a population is generated by some device, as the human population is. Some humans (*F*) are male (*G*) and others not. The frequency of *G* in the population of *F* may be explained in terms of the chance of the event that the creation of an *F* will also be a creation of a *G*. If this chance, *p*, is the same for each such event, then it follows from the strong law of large numbers (e.g. Feller, 1957, p. 190) that there is a very high chance that the frequency, *f*, of *G* in a large population so generated will not differ by more than a specified small amount from the chance *p*. (I assume for simplicity that *G*s and $\sim$ *G*s that are *F* do not differ in their chances of death; where this is false, *f* will also be a function of such chances.) Here again it is easy to see how the concept of chance as warranted partial belief can be applied: one can bet on the outcome (male or female) of a single process of conception and delivery; on the outcome of many such processes one can bet that the frequency of men in the resulting population lies in the specified limits. Given this concept of chance, it is easy to see also that the observed frequency might be used as a measure of the chance that a single birth is male. The temptation to regard this commonplace though important fact about chance as giving scope for a frequency definition is well illustrated in Cramér (1945, p. 149):

Whenever we say that the probability of an event E with respect to an experiment . . . is equal to P, *the concrete meaning of this assertion* will thus simply be the following: In a long series of repetitions of [the experiment], it is practically certain that the frequency of E will be approximately equal to P. [My italics.]

But all the law of large numbers really tells us, as Kyburg (1961, p. 20) notes, is that "given a probability statement, we can...roughly anticipate the result of a long experiment; given the result of an experiment we may decide what probability statement to accept on the basis of a decision technique". It is, of course, essential that probability statements be testable in this way but that does not make them thereby definable.

In situations of both these kinds, where frequency in a population is closely and plainly connected with chance, some other item than the population is involved and there is some possible event on the occurrence of which a person could bet. In the one case the extra item is a sampling device and the event is that the F sampled is G; in the other case the extra item is the generating device and the event is that the F generated is G. It is an irrelevant though possibly misleading fact that in some cases the sampling or generating device may itself be F, as when it is people who sample from or breed a population of persons. The fact is irrelevant because no assumption is used about the extra item being F or $\sim F$; it could be misleading if it suggested that nothing but populations of F and G need be invoked in describing the situation as being one of chance.

Where no such extra items are present and no possible event is contemplated on whose occurrence a bet could be made, there is no obvious use for the concept of probability. What use is there in saying that the chance of a card in a deck being an ace is $1/13$ except in some context of manufacturing decks or of selecting cards from them? It is true that in other contexts the frequency definition makes 'probability' a synonym for 'frequency', but it is precisely this feature that generates the frequentists' problems. Because there is a frequency of G in every finite population of F, F_1, F_2, etc. the frequentist is obliged to suppose a corresponding probability. But no accepted inference from frequency to chance or from chance to frequency would be invalidated if this identification were abandoned. The laws of large numbers, as theorems of the probability calculus, in no way presuppose a frequency account of probability. Nor do the statistical decision techniques by which they are applied to finite data and through which they adequately explicate the everyday conception that what is probable is what happens more often than not. To define chance in terms of frequency adds nothing to this explication; it merely makes needless nonsense of inferences to the single case.

Braithwaite's (1953, chapters 5–7) theory is perhaps unfairly called 'frequentist' (by its author amongst others). It essentially treats chance as an implicitly defined theoretical concept in a hypothetico-deductive system. This is an eminently reasonable approach and, as Kyburg and Smokler observed in 1964 (p. 4), "most statisticians today hold views which, while not so formal and explicit as Braithwaite's, are not essentially different from his". Feller (1957, p. 5) for example observes, congenially to the present thesis, that "we shall be concerned with theoretical models in which probabilities enter as free parameters in much the same way as masses in mechanics". On to this theory Braithwaite has however grafted a number of gratuitously frequentist features. He gives a frequency definition of chance in the finite case (quoted on p. 51 above) that his theory does not use and which it could easily abandon. He then adds a dispensable Campbellian analogy (see Campbell, 1920, chapter 6; Mellor, 1968) with his "Briareus model" (pp. 129–33), in which finite frequency statements correspond to probability statements in the theoretical calculus. The Campbellian rôle of the Briareus model is to make the calculus acceptably intelligible by giving it an alternative interpretation in terms of frequencies. That does not make probabilities frequencies, as Braithwaite shows in remarking on "the fact that the model [requiring] a restriction of probabilities to rational numbers makes probabilities *more analogous to* class-ratios [i.e. finite frequencies] than they would otherwise be" (p. 131, my italics). But his Briareus model does make Braithwaite's theory look more like a frequency theory than it needs to do.

The crucial part of Braithwaite's theory is his account of how chance statements are tested against observed frequencies. It has been criticised on points of detail (Hacking, 1965, pp. 114–17; Kyburg, 1958) but its chief defect is taking "the meaning of a probability statement [to be] given by its rejectability by appropriate statistical [i.e. frequency] evidence" (p. 191). Now Braithwaite admits on the same page that "reasonable belief in probability statements may be based on quite other data than those concerned with frequencies which correspond to the probabilities". He declines only to admit that these other data could be as analytically related to chance as frequencies are. Consequently he is left with the problem: 'Why is it reasonable to base a betting rate upon an estimate of chance?' which he considers in a paper of that title

(Braithwaite, 1966). All we need to reconcile Braithwaite's account with propensity theory is to strip it of the operationalist bias that ties chance needlessly tight to a frequency measure of it. Braithwaite's problem then becomes: 'Why is it reasonable to use frequency as an estimate of chance?'

Abandoning frequency views of course still leaves the positive task of analysing the relation chance has to other concepts including, where relevant, that of frequency. But the latter is not the hard part of the task. As a result of the work of Braithwaite and others, and as the simple examples above partly show, the relation of chance to frequency is quite well understood except that it is not one of definition. What really need looking into are its relations with other scientific concepts.

CHANCES AND TRIALS

I propose to account for chance in terms of a feature of the world, ascertainable by the methods of science, that warrants adopting some partial beliefs rather than others. For frequentists, the sort of item of which chance is a feature is a class of things of some kind. The feature is the frequency, in that class, of things of some other kind. Of what kind of thing is it a feature, on the propensity view, that the chance that F is G is p, and how is this feature related to others?

It should be clear from the discussion so far that one kind of situation to which propensity theory could apply the concept of chance is one in which something can be bet on. Typically the situation is one in which the occurrence in the near future of an event of some observable kind is possible but not certain. Among such situations are the examples above in which a population is being generated or sampled from. Other obvious examples are those in which it is noted whether a person dies, falls ill or recovers, or some such transition as the decay of a radioactive atom occurs, in a given period of time. In all such situations there are two or more possible events, one or other of which is bound to occur. To apply the concept of chance to the situation is, on the present view, to say that and how the situation warrants certain partial beliefs on the occurrence of these possible events.

This usage is conveniently consonant with the more ascetic usage of mathematical probability, where 'event' is used of anything to which a probability can be assigned. The calculus is stated in terms of a set of "sample points" called a 'sample space', of which events are subsets.

Numbers are assigned to sample points, and thence to events containing them, so as to satisfy the probability axioms (see Cramér, 1946; Feller, 1957; Kolmogorov, 1933). In the present interpretation of the calculus I largely adopt Hacking's (1965, pp. 13–14) terminology. A situation to which the concept of chance can be applied is a *"trial*...each trial must have a unique *result* [sample point] which is a member of a *class of possible results* [sample space]...the possible results for any trial are mutually exclusive. A set of possible results on any trial will be called an *outcome* [event]. A trial will be said to have outcome E when the result is a member of E." A chance is normally assigned to an outcome but may for brevity also be assigned to a result, meaning by that the outcome whose sole member is the result.

The term 'trial' too much suggests a contrived situation or experiment as opposed to one that occurs naturally. The concept of chance may be applied to either, as the examples of death and radioactive decay show. However, while not ideal, 'trial' is an accepted term and I adopt it as such rather than add yet another to the literature.

Given this terminology, I return to the question: to what should the feature I call 'chance' be ascribed? It is trivially true that an outcome "has" a chance; to ascribe a chance to an outcome of a trial is no more than to restate that there is an objective constraint on the partial belief reasonably held on its occurrence. But the chance of it happening is not a property that can be ascribed to an event without taking it to be the outcome of a trial. It must indeed be the trial itself of which it is a feature that the chance of an event is p. For typically an event that occurs as the outcome of a chance trial contains more than one possible result. The event that a throw of a die yields an odd number for example contains the possible results one, three and five. Its chance p is therefore determined in part by the chances of results that have not occurred and are consequently hardly available to be their ultimate bearers. Hence the pertinent feature of the trial cannot just be the chance of the result that actually occurs but the chance distribution over all possible results, which yields in turn the chance of every possible outcome.

There is of course normally no objection to saying that it is a property of a throw of a die that the outcome {five} has a chance say of 0.3. On the contrary, this will be entailed by the chance distribution over all the results just as that a rod has a length > 20 cm is entailed by it having a length of 30 cm. The point is that this usage must not be taken to license the inference that the chances of {five} and of {six} are distinct properties susceptible of independent explanation, perhaps by reference to each other. In the same way the length of a rod being < 40 cm is not an extension of it independent of it being > 20 cm and susceptible of independent explanation. Both are entailed by the length of the rod being 30 cm, and this is the single extension of it that laws connect with other properties and relations of the rod.

These remarks should not be misconstrued, as they have been by Watling (1969, p. 41), as an admission that chance is relational. It is not a matter of choice either that an event is an outcome of a chance trial or of what trial it is an outcome. A coin may land heads on being tossed when biased, on being tossed when unbiased and on being carefully lowered to the ground heads up. In the first two cases the chances of it landing heads differ; in the third no chance is involved at all because the event is not an outcome of a chance trial. In general, an event may be identified under a description whose satisfaction could be bet on, and many events distinguished by their spatio-temporal locations may satisfy such a description. Some will be outcomes of chance trials and some will not. Those that are outcomes of trials have chances and the others do not. Any given event either is as a matter of fact such an outcome and so has a definite chance or is not and has no such chance. Watling's own examples (pp. 41–2) show that here is nothing relational. Of course the chance of a radium atom decaying in N years depends on whether it is bombarded during that period. Any given atom either is bombarded and its decay has one chance or it is not bombarded and its decay has another. (See chapter 5 below, pp. 91, 97–100 for details of this example.) No one decay of a radium atom need have two chances; there is no conflict of properties to be resolved by recourse to relations.

Similarly with Watling's horse racing example (p. 48). If horse races really are chance trials (which I doubt) then the chance of horse A winning may well depend on whether it rains or not. Suppose the chance is 0.6 if it rains and 0.2 otherwise. If we do not know the state of the weather we do not know A's chance of winning, although we may know it to be in the interval [0.2, 0.6.] A probabilistic confirmation theory covering this situation could conceivably be to hand, with rules for detaching probabilities on specified amounts of evidence. Suppose that relative to such evidence the theory confers inductive probability 0.5 on the hypothesis that it will rain. In this (perhaps barely) conceivable position of quantifiable ignorance we might be entitled to adopt and recommend a partial belief of strength 0.4 on *A* winning. All the example really shows is that if there can be chances we may be as ignorant of them as of anything else objective.

This situation must be sharply distinguished from that in which one and the same event really could be said to have two or more chances. That happens when the occurrence of one chance trial is itself a possible outcome of another chance trial. This could be the case here: whether it rains or not could be a chance matter. Then if rain is the outcome a further trial occurs, namely a race in which *A*'s chance of winning is 0.6. If the outcome were fine weather the further trial would be of a different kind, namely a race on which *A*'s chance of winning would be 0.2. Suppose the chance of rain is 0.5 and that in fact it does rain. Then the event of *A*'s winning seems to have two chances: 0.6 as the outcome of the rainy race and 0.4 as the outcome of the composite trial. Another example is Laplace's case of a coin the direction of whose bias is unknown. Heads seems to have a probability of $\frac{1}{2}$ on the first toss as well as the chance that displays the bias. See chapter 7 below, pp. 131–6.

Is this an inconsistency or a complication? It certainly provides another reason, if one were needed, for taking chances to be features primarily of trials rather than of events. Talking of an event having a unique chance is normally natural because the event is an outcome of a trial whose occurrence is not in turn the outcome of another trial. We are able to classify such simple situations into kinds of trial with characteristic chance distributions. According to the propensity theory this ability is parasitic on our ability to classify certain physical things into kinds, with characteristic propensities. The dispositional nature of propensities in fact affords natural scope for making one trial result from another. (See p. 72 below). But in any case our classification of simple trials enables us to account for more complex situations, as an outcome of which an event can plausibly be said to have more than one chance.

I need also to emphasise that in contrast to Hacking (1965, pp. 18–20) I ascribe chance distributions primarily to trials rather than to *kinds* of trials. We might of course distinguish two trials as being of different kinds just because they had different chance distributions over their possible results. We might e.g. wish for that reason to distinguish waiting a day from waiting a year to see if a person dies as being trials of different kinds. This is not in fact done (see chapter 5, p. 98) but we may for the moment and the sake of argument suppose that a given chance distribution over given kinds of results characterises a kind of trial. There is however a danger in using the noun 'kind' in this way. For while ascribing the chance distribution to the *kind* of trial is a convenient symptom of this usage, it may then tempt one to deny the propriety of ascribing chance distributions to trials themselves. The temptation is particularly strong for a frequentist. Something that is at least like a frequency of one kind of result can readily be ascribed to a kind of trial, namely the frequency (or its limit) of such results in some class of actual or hypothetical trials of that kind. But such frequencies cannot, as we have seen, be ascribed with sense to any single trial of that kind. Now this is only a fact about frequencies that in itself makes the frequency account of chance unacceptable. While that account is in question it cannot be claimed to be a fact about chances in support of the frequency view – at least, not without using what Flew (1966, p. 73) calls the 'My-best-friend-is-a-Jew-but' gambit (in which all the evidence counts against the conclusion drawn from it).

On the present analysis, ascribing chances to single trials expresses the fact that their function is to warrant certain partial beliefs on the possible outcomes of such a trial. One cannot bet on a kind of trial because a kind of trial is not itself a trial. One could warrant as strong belief on all trials of a certain kind were trials so classified (which they are not) that this followed from its being warranted on any one trial of that kind. That is all that talk of ascribing chance distributions to kinds of trial could signify. It could not in the least follow from it that distributions should not also be ascribed to individual trials.

I conclude provisionally that the "feature of the world ascertainable by the methods of science' (p. 58 above) with which we are concerned is expressed in a chance distribution over the possible results of a trial. This feature is to be regarded as primarily a property of the trial and only derivatively of the events that are its actual outcomes or of a kind of trials characterised by possession of the feature. But this kind of entity, the trial, and the feature expressed in the chance distribution over its possible results, still bear an obscure relation to the other entities and features of science with which it is clear they are connected. In the following chapter the dispositional concept of propensity is introduced to clarify the relation. Although it may in due course displace chance distribution as the primitive objective concept, the two are not at all the same. We shall find reason to distinguish them more carefully than has hitherto been usual.

4 Propensity

Chance distributions display dispositions called 'propensities'. To assess this claim we have first to discuss dispositions. The psychological dispositions of belief and partial belief have been considered; now a more general discussion is needed of what a disposition is. Dispositions are ascribed not to trials but to more permanent entities which are reidentified through apparent change as unchanging bearers of changing properties. The paradigms of such entities are the common physical things with which science begins its enquiries. The paradigms of such properties are the dispositions we ascribe to people.

Such a sentence as

'*a* is of a generous disposition'

is used of a person *a* to explain a regularity in his behaviour. It is not an unconditional regularity like the sun rising every day. *a* is being accused neither of continuous generosity nor of periodic fits of it. *a* is rather said to be such that situations of a certain kind regularly evoke a more generous response from *a* than they do from most people. The situations are of a kind where alternative actions differ in the extent to which they are generous. Dispositions in people thus explain what might be called 'conditional regularities'.

The characteristically generous action that a situation evokes may be called a 'display' of the agent's generous disposition. The point of the disposition is that it is ascribed to the person at a time whether he is then in the situation or not. The situation calls forth a display of the disposition, i.e. a piece of behaviour which in that situation is explained by the fact that the person is generous.

Some features of psychological dispositions do not carry over to other cases. People may choose to display their dispositions by bringing about appropriate situations. *a* may contrive occasions for his generosity as well as responding generously in uncontrived situations. (A person's action in contriving a situation in which to display a disposition might of course itself count as a display of it.) The essential feature which does carry over is that whenever the bearer of the disposition is in

[63]

a suitable situation that situation has a characteristic feature. The feature normally is that the situation has a certain result, e.g. the result of the generous act. The feature need not however be a result even in the human case. An orchestral conductor may for example have the dispositional ability to give exciting performances of Berlioz. But this quality of the performance, which displays his ability, is not in any normal sense a result of it. The present importance of a disposition's display not needing to be a result of the display situation is that in the case of propensity it never is (see below pp. 68–70).

To say then of a person or thing a that

    a has disposition F at time t

is at least to say that

    if a were involved in a situation of kind K at time t,

    the situation would have property P.

A statement ascribing a disposition thus entails what is best called a 'subjunctive' conditional. 'Subjunctive' is better than 'counterfactual' even though in English it also normally implies falsity in the antecedent, because that implication has to be shed here. The conclusion would be ridiculous that a person's generous disposition had to lapse whenever he was in process of displaying it.

Physical dispositions are like psychological ones in that they do not have to display themselves continuously, periodically or even at all. The solubility of a substance is always available to account for a property of situations in which it is mixed with water, namely that a certain amount of it dissolves; but a sample of the substance is no less soluble for never being mixed with water.

Nor must the use of the word 'always' in the last sentence be misconstrued. It is true as a matter of natural law that chemical substances may be characterised *inter alia* by their solubility. Soluble objects cannot in general become insoluble without changing in chemical composition. An object identified under a chemical description therefore cannot change in this respect from time to time. A piece of salt that is soluble at one time is soluble at all times. But this is an empirical consequence of the laws relating solubility to chemical constitution, not a logical consequence of solubility being a disposition. What makes an object soluble when it is not dissolving is not that it *will* dissolve in the future but that it *would* dissolve *now*. What is invariable is not that objects will always be soluble if they are ever so, but that they will always dissolve if mixed with water while they are soluble. It is in the latter sense that dispositions are invariable, not the former. Conversely the fact that a usually soluble object may sometimes not be soluble gives no licence to the view that soluble objects might sometimes not dissolve in water. An object that fails to dissolve when suitably mixed with water is thereby shown to be insoluble at that time, however soluble it might be at other times. It is the same with quantitative dispositions. An object that accelerates differently at different times under the same force has different inertial masses at those times.

Human dispositions are arguably not always so invariable. One might conceivably truly call a man 'generous' even while he acted meanly, if mean acts were sufficiently unusual with him. I should prefer to say that his usual generosity had temporarily deserted him, but the point of usage is not important. What is important is the invariable character of the physical dispositions to which chance is to be related. Hereafter I intend 'disposition' to imply invariability in this sense, and use 'tendency' for what can admit unexplained exceptions to the regularities of behaviour it purports to explain.

Physical dispositions of objects then are invariable in their display but changeable in their presence. The events that are their changes must be sharply distinguished from the events that are their displays (Ayers, 1968, p. 83). Dissolving an object is not the same as making it soluble, taking its temperature is not the same as heating it, and declining to weigh oneself will not of itself keep one's weight down. But if dispositions are changeable, what serious test can there be of their presence in an object while it is not displaying them? Is it not trivially and thus pointlessly easy to make a changeable disposition "always available" to account for every fluctuating conditional regularity that we choose to read into an object's behaviour? It would indeed be too easy to explain a regularity in terms of a disposition solely constrained to account for it. Hence the notorious and exaggerated inadequacy of a drug's dispositional "dormitive virtue" to explain the sending to sleep of those who take it. We require therefore of at least the explanatory and explainable dispositions introduced by the sciences that they be linked to other properties and relations of the entity (see chapter 6). Thus they are properly ascribable on the basis of other regularities than the ones they serve to explain. We have seen for example that solubility is ascribable on the basis of chemical constitution, and inertial mass is ascribable on the basis of weighing. A drug's dormitive virtue that was detectable also by smell or chemical analysis would be a perfectly respectable disposition. The links between dispositional properties that make them nontrivially usable in explanation are the laws into which they enter, however loosely these may be formulated. What laws a disposition enters into is of course contingent. It is no part of the meaning of 'soluble' that solubility is connected specifically to chemical composition. But the fact that no other property is necessarily connected to solubility does not refute the rule that some other property must be contingently connected to it. Being a rule governing the explanatory scientific use of all disposition terms, it tends not to be cited as part of the particular meaning of any one of them. It tends to be overlooked by those who have not familiarised themselves with scientific usage.

PROPENSITY

> The die has a certain "would-be"...a property quite analogous to any *habit* that a man might have.
>
> Peirce, 1931, volume 2, §664

The commonplace remarks of the last section leave many problems about dispositions, some of which will have to be attended to in this and later chapters. But they may serve initially to show the concept of a disposition to be sufficiently familiar and plainly independent of probability to warrant its use in our account of chance. Even if Popper is wrong (1957, p. 70) in supposing all physical properties to be dispositional, certainly most are. We have already had solubility, mass, weight and temperature as examples. We could as readily have had length, volume, pressure, electric charge, current, fields of every kind, with the capacities of things to react to and affect them, without exhausting even the macroscopic domain. Whatever problems remain in further analysing dispositions, a successful dispositional account of chance can fairly claim to have dealt with those which the peculiar nature of chance has posed in statistical science.

I have already remarked that a dispositional view of chance is not new. It occurs in the quotation above from Peirce, is referred to by Braithwaite (1953, p. 187) and has recently been strongly revived by Popper (1957, 1959a) and Hacking (1965) and adopted by Levi (1967). But these authors' accounts of what such a view entails seems to me either incomplete or defective enough to justify another attempt.

The view is that the feature I have taken to be expressed in a chance distribution ascribed to trials of some kind should be regarded as the display of a dispositional property ascribed to more permanent entities. I follow Hacking (1965, p. 13) in calling the entity a 'chance set-up' and Popper (1957, p. 67) in calling the property 'propensity':

The probabilities...may be looked upon as *properties of this arrangement. They characterise the disposition, or the propensity,* of the experimental arrangement to give rise to certain characteristic frequencies *when the experiment is often repeated.*

Despite his emphasis on frequencies and repetition, Popper is clear (p. 68) that

we now take as fundamental *the probability of the result of a single experiment,* with respect to its *conditions,* rather than the frequency of results in a sequence of experiments. . . . A statement about propensities may be compared with a statement about the strength of an electric field...[which] speaks about certain dispositional properties of the field. And just as we can consider the field as physically real, so we can consider the propensities as physically real.

Hacking (1965, p. 13) characterises a chance set-up as "a device or part of the world on which might be conducted one or more *trials,* experiments or observations" and identifies propensity (which he calls 'chance') with what the chance distribution would be, would have been or will be on such a kind of trial. Hacking differs from the present account in taking chance to be a property of a kind of trial rather than of a trial (see p. 61 above). For this reason he needs a so-called 'frequency principle' to relate his chance to what may be expected of the single case: 'If all we know is that the chance of E on trials of kind K is p, then our knowledge supports to degree p the proposition that E will occur on some designated trial of kind K' (Hacking, 1965, p. 135). The symbolising of this principle has led to problems and controversy that are of more mathematical than philosophical interest (Miller, 1966 and 1966a, 1968; Popper, 1966, 1966a; Mackie, 1966; Bub and Radner, 1967; Rozeboom, 1969). It is of the essence of chance that some such principle is true, and I do not doubt that it can be consistently framed. Providing a frequentist rationale for it is essentially the task undertaken in Braithwaite's (1966) paper referred to on p. 57 above. But it takes a frequentist to need a rationale for such a plainly analytic truth. The present account, taking propensity to be displayed in single trials, avoids the need for such complications; nor is it thereby cut off from truths about long runs.

In asserting the dispositional nature of propensity Hacking (1965, p. 10) draws an explicit analogy with such a property as the fragility of a glass: 'If a wine glass would break, or would have broken, or will break when dropped, we say the glass is fragile. There is a word for the active event, and another for the passive dispositional property.' But this analogy needs more careful statement on the present view. The *fragility* is the dispositional property of the glass that it has whether or not it is being or ever has been or will be dropped. The *breaking* is the characteristic property of the "trial", namely of the dropping of the glass, which the glass's fragility explains and which it therefore shares with *all* trials of the same kind, namely all droppings of fragile glasses. It is not immediately obvious what are analogous respectively to fragility and breaking in the case of single trials on a chance set up. On Hacking's account (1965, pp. 10–11) the "active event" is the "long run frequency" on many trials of the same kind. Elusive as this item notoriously is, it is certainly not to be found in our single case.

PROPENSITY: DISPOSITION OR TENDENCY?

The breaking of a fragile glass would normally and rightly be called the 'result' of dropping it. It is tempting then to take the result (or some outcome containing the result – see p. 59 above) of a chance trial as the corresponding "active event" that displays a chance set-up's propensity. But we cannot both yield to this temptation and construe propensity as a disposition. If the breaking of a glass displays a fragile disposition it must be the *invariable* result of suitably dropping fragile glasses. A glass that does not break when so dropped is at that time not fragile. A glass that sometimes breaks when dropped and sometimes not (supposing it reconstituted from its fragments – it is incidental that the display of this disposition destroys the object) is not "disposed to be fragile"; sometimes it is fragile and sometimes it is not.

The result of a chance trial however must not be invariable. A coin that never lands heads when tossed is not in that respect a chance set-up at all. (I exclude for the present the degenerate chances of 1 or 0.) It is essential to the concept of a chance set-up that repeated trials should sometimes lead to one result and sometimes to another. A coin with a moderate bias towards tails must be expected to land heads sometimes. A coin that does not land tails on a suitable toss is not thereby shown to lack its normal bias at that time. (This is not like the occasional lapse we might allow in the display of a human disposition (p. 65 above). A person might possibly act meanly while retaining his generous disposition, but no one supposes that he has to.)

We face the following dilemma. Either propensity is not a disposition or results and outcomes of chance trials do not display it. Let us test the first horn of the dilemma. The result of a chance trial could be taken to display what I have called a 'tendency' (p. 65 above). To say for example that

    a tends to act generously

is plausibly to say that in situations where generous action is possible but not certain

    a acts generously more often than not.

The tendency does not require, as a disposition would, that when *a* fails to act generously he lacks the generous tendency. All a generous tendency needs is a preponderance of occasions on which generous action is forthcoming. Analogously, to say that

    tails is probable

where tails is a possible result of tossing a coin *a*, would be taken to say that

    a tends to land tails

meaning merely that in suitable tossing situations

    a lands tails more often than not.

We might refine this concept of a tendency to cope with comparative and quantitative chance statements.

    'Tails has a higher chance than heads'

said of the coin *a* would come out as

    '*a* has a stronger tendency to land tails than it has to land heads'.

We would suppose a numerical scale of "tendency-strength", with weak tendencies to land tails corresponding to chances of tails $< \frac{1}{2}$ and strong tendencies to chances $> \frac{1}{2}$. It is certainly true that tendency admits of degrees of strength in a way that dispositions do not. Although we can say

    '*a* is of a more generous disposition than *b*'

that means something else. It means either that *a* acts more generously than *b* in situations of the same kind or that he acts generously in kinds of situations in which *b* does not. But to be more generous in this sense is to have a different disposition, just as to be longer or heavier is. There is not the difference of degree exemplified in saying that

    a has a stronger tendency to be generous than *b*

where *a* more often acts generously than *b* does in situations all of the same kind.

    What is wrong with all this, of course, is that the concept of needs analysis at least as much as chance does. And, moreover, no analysis seems plausible that does not involve essential reference to chance or, as above, reduce essentially to relative frequency ('tends to yield x' = $_{df}$ 'yields x more often than not'). The former would be viciously circular and the latter simply amounts to a frequency account of chance that we have already rejected.

I settle therefore on the other horn of the dilemma, taking propensity to be a disposition and denying that the result of a chance trial is its display. The advantage is not that dispositions pose no conceptual problems, but that science presents many plain instances which can clearly be accounted for without reference to chance. On the other hand no obvious examples of tendencies present themselves that are not examples of chances. The major scientific concepts to which chance is connected by statistical laws are clearly dispositions.

PROPENSITIES AND CHANCES

The display of a propensity is the chance distribution over the possible results of the appropriate trial. It is the property of the situation, e.g. of the toss of a coin, that characterises the disposition of the persisting entity, e.g. the bias of the coin. The bias of the coin replaces the chance distribution as the feature of the world which warrants some partial beliefs rather than others in events that are outcomes of the toss. The concept of propensity is of a more familiar and intelligible kind than is the chance distribution that may now be regarded as its display. The ordinary physical things that can have propensities are the same as those that have other dispositional properties. Statistical science need no longer add the heterogeneous category of trials to our primitive ontology of things. There will be chance trials of course, just as there are measurings of mass and testings of solubility, but they need not be regarded as the ultimate bearers of statistical properties.

Perhaps things with dispositions should in the end be construed as assemblies of events. I do not believe it, but the thesis anyway bears no more peculiarly on propensities than a wholesale subjectivism does (p. 25). Perhaps also some chance distributions are not displays of any propensity. I have yet to be convinced of examples: certainly not by supposed limits of hypothetical frequencies in arbitrary classes of possible future events. I doubt, though without clear argument, the intelligibility of chances unbacked by propensities (but see chapter 8, p. 173). However this may be, our present subject is propensity and the chances that display it.

One may still ask what is added by introducing the concept of propensity. There are first the constraints remarked on above to which the explanatory postulating of dispositions is subject. Propensities admitted in scientific theory must thereby be connected to other properties in whose terms they admit of explanation. It thus happens that indirect evidence can occur for propensities as for other dispositions. Thus it also happens that traditional gambling examples are not ideal in that their interest lies more in the trial than in the set-up. Serious sciences do not deal with the propensities of coins and dice, although something is known about them. The terminology of trials and chances devised to deal with gambling is not so well suited to describing the rôle of statistical theories. The entities and properties involved are made to seem more different from those of non-statistical theories than they need to be.

Having introduced propensity it is important not to confound it with chance. That the result of a chance trial displays only a tendency gives rise to a peculiar temptation to do this. Popper and Hacking seem at times to yield to it, laying themselves open to Kneale's charge (Körner, 1957, p. 80) of "doing no more than provide a new name for objective probability". The point is that a disposition may in general be character-ised by the feature of a trial that constitutes its display. That feature is often an event, some characteristic result of the trial. But a statement ascribing the disposition does not entail that the characteristic event ever occurs because it does not entail that the disposition is ever displayed. To say that a glass is fragile is not to say that it will break, since it may never be dropped. The temptation to confound propensity with chance arises because disposition statements share this feature with chance statements. A chance statement also deals with an event, for the happening of which it entails that some partial belief is peculiarly warranted. If the strength of this partial belief is less than 1 the statement does not entail that the event occurs, even if the trial does. But a propensity statement, being a disposition statement, further does not entail that the trial occurs. This lack of entailment must not be confused with that shown by a chance statement. For example, if the propensity statement is that a coin is unbiased, it fails to entail that the coin falls heads not only because the chance of heads on a toss is less than 1 but also because it does not entail that the coin is ever tossed at all.

The difference between propensity and chance may be further brought out in this example. The degree of partial belief warranted on a coin landing heads in an interval of time obviously depends on how often the coin is tossed in it. If the coin is not tossed, no partial belief > 0 is warranted; if it is tossed twice or more a stronger partial belief is warranted than if it is only tossed once. The coin's propensity, its bias or unbiasedness, is of course the same in each case. One might suppose a condition that the coin be tossed just once to be implicit in the use of 'chance'; but one could not then identify chance with warranted partial belief. Until I believe the coin will be tossed I have in general no partial belief in it landing heads, although I may predict what my partial belief would then be. The arguments of chapter 2 for measuring partial belief by CBQs both require the gambler to be compelled to bet (pp. 36–7) and exclude conditional bets (p. 49). No doubt 'chance' is often used also of what I call 'propensity', but to explain a confusion is not to condone it.

The point perhaps becomes clearer in a situation like that in chapter 3 where an event can seem to have more than one chance (p. 61). The display of a propensity or of any other disposition is not normally a chance matter. It can be made so, however, if for example we decide to toss one unbiased coin, a, only if another, b, that we toss lands heads. Otherwise a is to be turned tails up. We can make a machine do all this when we press a button, and the chance then of a landing heads is $\frac{1}{4}$, of it landing tails $\frac{3}{4}$. That indeed displays a propensity in the machine; the coin is of course as unbiased as ever. Whatever may be said for ascribing conflicting chances (of $\frac{1}{4}$ and $\frac{1}{2}$) to a landing heads when it does so, no conflicting propensities need be ascribed either to the coin or to the machine.

The trouble that can arise from confounding propensity with chance is best shown in cases where a trial is carried out simply by letting time elapse. Suppose for the moment that a distinct property of a person is displayed by the chance of his dying within a year. (It will be seen in chapter 5 (pp. 83–97) that this is too simple an assumption, but it does not affect the example's illustrative force.) This property is a propensity a person has at any one time. It may change from time to time as his other properties change, such as his state of health, exposure to radiation, etc. Only if there is no such change during a year is the trial carried out that directly displays the propensity to die he had when the year started. In fact the propensity changes continuously with age so that it is never directly displayed. It will of course be indirectly displayed by the display of other dispositions with which it is connected and which in turn connect with the man's propensities to die in shorter periods of time. Then from such chances the chance of death in a given year may be deducible and may well differ from that corresponding directly to any propensity the person had during the year. Suppose a healthy man has, from January to June, a propensity to die in a year that would be displayed directly by a chance of death of 0.05. Suppose now that in June he contracts a disease which changes his propensity to that which would be displayed by a chance of 0.3. It is clear that the chance of the man dying in the whole year, January to December, is between 0.05 and 0.3 and that at no time does he have a propensity of which this chance is a direct display. This is so whatever complication of the sort discussed above may be introduced by assuming that his catching the disease is itself the result of a chance trial (see chapter 5, pp. 90–1). In any case the chance of the man dying during the given year is not a property of the man, ascribable to him at a particular time in the year and capable of changing from time to time, as the propensity is. It is a property of the trial of waiting a year – during which the man's propensity changes. It makes no more sense to locate it temporally within the duration of the trial than it would to ask how the chance of heads changes during the toss of a coin, or what the length of a rod is half way along it.

That Popper and Hacking confound chance and propensity seems to be shown by their unfortunate reform of usage in the literature. We have quoted Peirce (p. 66 above) ascribing something like a propensity to a die. His subsequent account of this "would-be" is unacceptably frequentist but is at least ascribed to the die, just as analogous would-be's are presumably ascribable to coins and atoms. Popper and Hacking, however, seem to be misled by the chance of heads on the toss of a coin depending on how and in what surroundings it is tossed. They thereupon include all these other features in the total "experimental arrangement" (Popper) or "set-up" (Hacking). I have adopted the terminology but wish now to disown some of its connotations.

In bringing about a situation that will display a disposition it is often necessary to add something to the object the disposition is ascribed to. For a solubility to display itself some solvent must be added for the soluble substance to dissolve in. For a glass's fragility to display itself a stone floor, let us say, must be added for the fragile glass to be dropped on. Call the description of what must be added, and how, to bring about the display of a disposition its 'operational definition'. (I don't make the operationalist assumption that each concept has a unique operational definition, but the term is nonetheless useful. Bridgman (1927, chapter 1) may not have introduced the term explicitly of dispositions, but certainly of concepts like length, which I take to be dispositions.) A situation brought about by applying an operational definition to an object has some feature that displays the disposition. The dissolving of the substance in the solvent and the breaking of the fragile glass when dropped are both such features. But these are properties of the situation, not properties of the object; and the dispositions they display are conversely properties of the object, not of the situation. Solubility is not a property of the mixing of a solid and a liquid, and fragility is not a property of the dropping of a glass.

Starting from the situation, or trial, the point may be put by saying that convention picks out some more permanent entity, that could be involved in other trials of the same kind, to bear the disposition displayed in the situation. Although the choice of entity is to an extent conventional, it is by no means arbitrary. The entity must be capable of bearing other dispositions, i.e. of being involved in situations of other kinds, brought about by other operational definitions. The law-like connections between simultaneously possessed dispositions serve thus to explain the features of many diverse situations (see pp. 65–6 above). The physical things with which sciences start their ontological collections are entities of this sort.

The conventional element is well illustrated in the case of solubility. If only one solvent, e.g. water, is in question, the solubilities are ascribed to the different solids whose presence with water gives rise to mixing situations with different features, namely dissolvings of different quantities of the solute. If on the other hand only one solid is in question, the relevant dispositions are ascribed to the various liquids in which it may or may not dissolve. *Aqua regia* is thus notable among liquids for its dispositional ability to dissolve gold. With variety in both solids and liquids a solubility would clearly be ascribed to an ordered pair and express a dispositional relation between them. The dispositions of being hard and soft could similarly be ascribed to a variety of floors as fragile glasses were and were not disposed to break when dropped on them.

The special case of propensity is now clear: Propensity is ascribed to a die or coin rather than to the complete "set-up" present only at the trial displaying it because convention picks out this more permanent entity from others also involved in the trial. There are standard ways of tossing coins and throwing dice that could be specified in an operational definition. They are normally taken for granted, however, just as it is normally taken for granted that solubility is solubility in water and fragility to dropping on a hard floor. The convention could be otherwise. There could be definite varieties of tossing device which systematically affected the chance distributions of coins tossed on them. We should then ascribe bias to a device that gave a biased distribution to a standard unbiased coin. In so doing we should do nothing more exotic than is done in ascribing colours to light that makes white objects look as coloured objects look in white light.

It is true then that the chance distribution over the possible results of tossing a coin is affected by the properties both of the coin and of the tossing device. The propensity displayed may be ascribed to either according to conventions like those governing the ascription of solubility and colour. The convention is unusually arbitrary in this case just because there is no serious science with a network of laws about coins or tossing devices into which the propensity can be fitted. The ascription of a propensity here either way may be taken to express a conviction that such a science is possible. What is clear in any case is that the propensity must not be attributed to the whole assembly of coin, tossing device and environment that is only present when the coin is actually being tossed. To do that is to remove completely the point of ascribing a disposition as something that is present whether or not it is being displayed. It is to confound propensity with the chance distribution that displays it and hence indeed to make 'propensity' no more than a new name for chance.

Hacking seems to suffer from this confusion both in accepting Popper's notion of the set-up and in the example in which he says that "a piece of radium together with a recording mechanism might constitute a chance set-up" (1965, p. 13). On the present account that would be like saying that a thin glass together with a hard stone floor might be fragile, or that a grain of salt with a bucket of water might be soluble, or that a fire together with a thermometer might be hot. I use the term 'set-up' so that a piece or an atom of radium is a chance set-up; a coin is a chance set-up, given standard tossing devices; a tossing device is a chance set-up, given standard coins. The distinction between propensity and chance is as essential as the distinction between a set-up and a trial on it.

DISPOSITIONS AND DISPLAYS

Having emphasised the particular distinction between propensity and chance, I turn again to the general relation between dispositions and their displays. We need to be satisfied that peculiarities of propensity do not make its fit as Procrustean on the dispositional as it is on the frequency bed. It is convenient to start with the operational view of scientific concepts (e.g. Bridgman, 1927, 1938; Dingle, 1950), defunct though that largely is. There is no point in retelling all the objections raised by L. J. Russell (1928), Lindsay (1937), Feigl (1945), Morgenau (1950), Pap (1959), Hempel (1965, chapter 5), Schlesinger (1967) and others. I consider here only what is pertinent to comparing propensities with other dispositions.

The first point is that dispositions are not limited to those that display themselves in situations which can be brought about at will. The class of dispositions is wider than the class of what Carnap (1956, p. 65) calls 'testable dispositions'. The disposition of the sun to bend light rays passing close to it is no less a disposition because it only displays itself during eclipses. It is being able to observe the display of a disposition that matters, not being able to bring it about. The term 'operational definition' adopted above (p. 74) for the procedures by which a disposition is displayed too much suggests contrived displays as opposed to those that occur naturally. The same point has already been made (pp. 59, 67) in the special case of propensity that 'set-up' and 'trial' must be taken to cover natural as well as constructed systems and situations. So the propensity of a radium atom to decay is no less a disposition because its display can be secured merely by the lapse of time; nor does that of a sparrow to die in a cold winter fail to be a disposition because neither we nor the sparrow can control the weather. Nothing here sets off propensities from other dispositions. Hereafter I use 'operational definition', like 'trial' and 'set-up', without implying a restriction to contrived situations.

The next point is that no dispositional concept can be "synonymous with the corresponding set of operations" (Bridgman, 1927, p. 5) precisely because it is ascribed even when the operations are not going on. The whole object of ascribing dispositions is to support subjunctive conditionals about the upshots of trials that may never be carried out (p. 64 above) in the same way that laws support subjunctive conditionals about possible instances. But then, as Hempel (1965, p. 126) observes, "to attribute a disposition of this kind...is to make a generalisation, and this involves an inductive risk". Ascribing a disposition goes beyond what is given by experience in just the way operationalists wish to avoid, even if it is defined exclusively by the results of one kind of operation. It is not safe, "in the same sense in which Bridgman insists it is "not safe" to assume that two procedures of measurement that have yielded the same results in the past will continue to do so in the future" (Hempel, 1965, p. 126). This being so, the motive for operationalist rigour is largely gone. Dispositions such as masses, temperatures and propensities must be admitted whether on the basis of one or of many kinds of operation. Their ascription is no more secure in the former case than in the latter. Yet it is just such unattainable security the operationalist seeks to achieve by excluding the latter case. It is thus not at all a difficulty peculiar to propensity that its true ascription is not entailed by the results of any number, however great, of its displays. Nor do frequentists have any sound operationalist reason here to restrict admissible displays by definition to just one kind, namely frequencies in sequences of single trials.

This leads naturally to the third point, that dispositions normally display themselves in more than one way (cf. Ryle, 1949, p. 44). It is not true of dispositions that "if we have more than one set of operations, we have more than one concept" (Bridgman, 1927, p. 10). There are several issues here, which it is easy to confound. It could be made true, as by Carnap (1956, p. 64), simply by stipulation that a disposition displays itself in only one way. In that case such concepts as mass, temperature and propensity would turn out not to be dispositions but rather, as for Carnap (1956, p. 68), "theoretical" concepts. That however assumes a sharp distinction I do not assume between observable and theoretical properties and, relatedly, the traditional analytic–synthetic distinction. Thus Pap (1959, p. 181) accepts the 'different operation, different concept' stipulation at least for non-quantitative dispositions for the following reason:

This approach has the advantage of avoiding a logically objectionable feature of pairs of reduction sentences for the same disposition term, namely, that a conjunction of analytic statements entails a synthetic (factual) statement. The conjunction of '$Q_1 \supset (D \equiv Q_2)$' and '$Q_3 \supset (D \equiv Q_4)$' entails '$\sim (Q_1.Q_2.Q_3. \sim Q_4)$'; the negated conjunction, . . . however, is logically possible. It is, for example, logically possible that a body which attracts a small iron body should fail to generate an electric current in a closed wire loop through which it moves. But if we put 'D_1' in the first reduction sentence and 'D_2' in the second, we cannot formally deduce the mentioned synthetic (factual) consequence; we should require the further premise '$(x) (D_1 x \equiv D_2 x)$'.

I do not however assume that any statements made by reduction (or related) sentences are analytic in Pap's traditional sense. I take any one such sentence to be rejectable in the face of experience, and whether or not its rejection entails abandoning the concept seems to be more complex than Pap allows for. What Hempel and Carnap admit to be true of theoretical terms I take to be true of dispositions: "Experiential significance is then seen to be a matter of degree. . . and it even appears doubtful whether the distinction between analytic and synthetic sentences can be effectively maintained in reference to the language of empirical science." (Hempel, 1965, p. 133).

What then justifies applying the term 'disposition' to such concepts? First, there are virtually no instances, and certainly no important scientific instances, of "one-operation" dispositions.

The interpretation of scientific terms as pure dispositions cannot easily be reconciled with certain customary ways of using them. . . . a scientist, when confronted with the negative result of a test for a certain concept, will often still maintain that it holds, provided that he has sufficient positive evidence. . . . The scientist will point out that the test procedure. . . should not be taken as absolutely reliable. (Carnap, 1956, p. 68.)

Before any theory of X-rays was developed, X-rays were simply "what you got when cathode rays impinged upon metal surfaces"; and "that which produced photographic images of a certain kind". Only as we advance in discovery and technique such very sketchy definitions are supplanted by fuller qualitative, quantitative, and far-flung relational characteristics. . .(Feigl, 1945, p. 506). Empirical laws enable us to define the same concept by different operational routes. (Feigl, 1945, p. 504.)

The wide range of application of statistical law and theory connects propensity concepts at least as widely as that of an X-ray (see Braithwaite, 1953, pp. 116–17).

The dearth of "one-operation" dispositions leaves us free to apply the term 'disposition' more widely than Pap and Carnap do. To do so is fair because things which have the properties to which I apply it are understood to be thereby disposed to behave in certain ways in certain situations. The list of situations and corresponding ways for a given concept is not fixed. It may be extended and changed as available situations, methods of observation and theoretical connections of the concept change. Consider Newtonian mass, which is a disposition to resist applied forces (cf. chapter 2, pp. 38–9 above). The greater the mass the less the acceleration induced by a given force. The list of Newtonian forces whose application provokes a display of massive inertia has been steadily extended since the concept was introduced. New ways have been found of detecting the resultant display, e.g. in electrically charged masses whose acceleration has electromagnetic effects. Theories of gravitation have proposed an identification of inertial with gravitational mass that makes a weighing as much a display of the former as acceleration is. What Levi (1967, p. 196) observes of temperature is even more plainly true of mass, that "if it is considered dispositional, it [is] a disposition to a great many things". But that fact is no reason not to consider mass and temperature dispositional. It may blur the edges of our concepts and so make life more trying for concept counters. Are there two concepts of mass – gravitational or inertial – or only one? A change of answer to such a question is not of great moment. It transforms an illustration of the present claim that a disposition may be displayed in diverse ways into an illustration of the earlier claim (pp. 65–6) that dispositions must be interconnected by laws, or *vice versa*. Whichever claim a given example illustrates, both claims remain. We shall see in the next chapter how such trivial puzzles of conceptual identity arise with propensity concepts such as radioactive half life and physiological age. Here again we find no cause to doubt propensity's dispositional credentials.

When we take a single disposition to be displayed in different kinds of situation we may apply a common term to the different kinds of display. We may say of a bad-tempered man, whether he is abusing his colleagues or beating his children, that he is in each case indulging in a display of bad temper. Every way his bad temper can display itself is a piece of behaviour to which the non-dispositional property of being a display of bad temper can be correctly ascribed. The concept of the disposition is thus necessarily if trivially linked to the concept of its display. It need not be necessarily linked to any independently characterised kind of situation and behaviour therein, in and by which it is normally displayed.

We rarely have call to distinguish the two concepts. Whatever can be said in terms either of the disposition or of its display can be said differently but equally well in terms of the other. Which one uses depends on whether the thing with the disposition is of more or less interest than the situation displaying it. One might remark on the *bad temper of a man* one knows to be given to anger where most people are not; or one might remark of his behaviour on some suitable occasion that it was a piece or *display of bad temper*. Of a display that comes about naturally it is common to use the same term that is used of the disposition. Both the dispositional colour of a pillar box and its non-dispositional appearance to a standard observer are called 'red'. If one is out in cold weather one may remark that it is cold out, referring to the display of coldness brought on by the operation of going outdoors. From inside one might equally look out at the frost and remark that it is cold out, referring to the disposition of the outside environment to cool a person out in it. The point and normal justification of this usage is the necessary connection of the disposition with its display. It is not at all diminished by there being as many ways of telling in diverse circumstances whether it is cold out or what colour a thing is as there are ways of being bad tempered.

This view of dispositions enables us to resolve apparent conflicts in the literature. Carnap (1956, p. 64) and Pap (1959, p. 181) perceive the necessary connection between a disposition and its display but mistake it for a necessary connection between the disposition and one particular way of displaying it. In particular they tie displays too closely to observation. Then, blurring the distinction between display and disposition makes Carnap (1956, p. 65) uneasy about his own distinction between dispositional and observational terms: 'An observable property may be regarded as a simple special case of a testable disposition; for example, the operation for finding out whether a thing is blue or hissing or cold, consists simply in looking or listening or touching the thing, respectively.' But dispositions do not constitute a half-way house between observable displays and theoretical concepts that are unobservable and so cannot have displays at all. The disposition/display distinction cuts across the observable/theoretical distinction. It has to do rather with the distinction between things and events, and events can be quite hard to observe as things. Once we admit dispositional properties with more varied and less directly observable displays we can reconcile Carnap and Pap more to Popper's suggestion (1957, p. 70) that "all physical (and psychological) properties are dispositional. That a surface is coloured red means that it has the disposition to reflect light of a certain wavelength. That a beam of light has a certain wavelength means that it is disposed to behave in a certain manner if surfaces of various colours, or prisms, or spectrographs, or slotted screens etc., are put in its way." The example shows again how a highly theoretical property like the wavelength of electromagnetic radiation is a "disposition to a great many things" that need not all be necessary for it. Wavelength is indeed normally a good test of colour, yet an observably white light in which a surface looks red to a normal observer may have had the "certain wavelength" that Popper refers to completely removed. Conversely the reflectivity that makes a surface red can be tested quite mechanically without the use of sighted observers.

It needs emphasising that the concept of a display is not that of something especially accessible to direct observation. Displays are not properties of anything like sense-data. For one thing they are not private; displays of colour can as well be recorded by a camera as by a human eye. For another, descriptions of the situations these concepts apply to are given in a full "physical thing" language. Even as public objects they are not stripped of conceptual commitments as Kneale's (1957, pp. 155–7) "views" for instance are. One would be wrong to describe a feature of a situation as a dissolving if one did not take the situation to involve a soluble substance.

These points have been laboured in order to press in two ways the comparison of propensity with other dispositions. (Or, if you please, with mass, temperature, wavelength etc., whether they be called 'dispositions' or no. But I shall use the term.) First no particular objection to chance distributions displaying a disposition can be grounded in their not being directly observable. They need no more be visible or tangible as features of single trials than is the passing of an X-ray. Chance distributions are indeed inferred indirectly and inconclusively from frequencies and from other properties related to them by statistical laws. Such an inference is not less admissible or intelligible than is say the weighing of an inertial mass or a volumetric measurement of a gas temperature.

The other point of comparison is in the necessary connection between disposition and display. It is important on the one hand that this duplication of concepts is practically needless, that whatever can be said in terms of one can be said in terms of the other. Hence in particular

6

to talk of propensity rather than of the chance distribution that displays it is not to change the subject. On the other hand, since not everything *is* said in terms of the disposition, the distinction must be drawn if only to propose a change of usage that might make it redundant. Hence I have had to distinguish from chance the dispositional concept of propensity. To press the comparison I now need to distinguish from other dispositions displays that are not just the results of particular operations. Otherwise the necessary connection between a propensity and its chance display would seem to lack parallels in a non-operationalist account of other concepts.

Some displays of non-statistical dispositions have been referred to already. To take another example, it is necessarily true that an object 30 cm long will yield a "length display" of 30 cm in an occasion of measurement. The particular method used may be inaccurate and so give a misleading result of other than 30 cm. In the same way a green object viewed in what purports to be daylight but is not may not look green to an observer. It is still necessarily true that its "colour display", that which it is disposed to yield on suitable observation, is a "green look". Again, a good method for measuring length may be misapplied or its result misrecorded. Just so may a colour-blind observer be chosen to make a colour judgment in a good light, or a normal observer mistake a colour he glances too carelessly at, or write down 'grue' for 'green'. Admitting all these possibilities of error it is still important to recognise that which the measured object brings to the occasion of measurement, that feature of the situation for which the object, rather than the measurer or his method, is to be held responsible – this is what I mean by 'display'. Display concepts are unfamiliar because they are normally dispensable. To ascribe a length display to an occasion on which an object is measured is neither more nor less than to ascribe a length to the object. In the present account of chance such concepts are not at once dispensable. The present theory is that most if not all chance distributions are displays of propensities. They may be ascribed on the basis of diverse operations, as length and temperature displays may be. Lengths, temperatures and propensities are alike dispositions to yield respectively length displays, temperature displays and chance distributions. Each of these connections is necessary; none is necessary between these properties and the result of any one operation of measurement.

5 Half lives and the force of mortality

ENOUGH HAS BEEN SAID of propensities to excuse an excursion into matters of fact. It is as well to see what sense propensity theory makes of some serious science as well as of gamblers' toys. I take two examples: the elementary theory of radioactive decay and a theory of physiological aging. They are intended to be reasonably realistic without being unreasonably complex. The first is well known as a challenge to subjectivists; the second poses a particularly explicit challenge to frequentists (see p. 53 above). My account of both theories is inevitably rather simplified and dated. The theory of radioactivity has been absorbed in a more comprehensive theory of nuclear activity. It is established but outgrown and by that token expoundable with little risk of scientific controversy. Theories of aging are less secure and more controversial. What I say may make the subject seem more settled than it is, but that does not matter. All parties treat the subject as statistical and deal in the concepts I introduce. We are concerned with the sense of what is said, not with scientific qualms about the truth of details. It is enough that both theories are products of serious and largely successful natural sciences. Either theory may be superseded, but neither is likely to go the way of phrenology or mesmerism. Science's way with its past admittedly foreshadows Orwell's *1984*, but the fact of the Bomb (and the formidably scientific ghosts of Rutherford and others) will surely keep even the falsified remains of radioactivity within the historical pale of science. Concepts of aging have the alternative protection of common usage. Some men are known to age, to grow old before their time. That is the sort of thing we would all know even if medical science had not presumed to make statistical sense of it.

DEATH RISK AND PHYSIOLOGICAL AGE

Consider the trial of waiting to see if an individual a of age w dies in a further stretch of time t. Assume that this trial has a chance distribution over the alternative results that a dies and that he survives. Let the chance of a dying in the stretch of time t be p. For short stretches we assume that p is roughly proportional to t. The chance of a man dying in two days is about twice that of his dying on one. To get a quantity more characteristic of the individual we therefore divide the chance p by the time t, and take the limit of this fraction as t decreases. Thus the individual's *death risk* μ at age w may be defined as

$$\mu = \operatorname*{Lim}_{t \to 0} \frac{p}{t}. \qquad \text{(Taylor, 1961, p. 349)}.$$

The evil influence of frequentism has made the term 'death rate' almost synonymous with 'death risk', and values of μ are usually given in such units as 'deaths per 1000 per year' (e.g. Jones, 1961, p. 274). Statistical usage is not consistent, but we shall see that death risk is best regarded as a propensity of individuals. I reserve the term 'death rate' hereafter for some frequency of deaths in a population, which might be used to measure a member's death risk.

The death risk of individuals is taken to be a function of environment and state of health as well as of age. In a constant environment and state of health, however, the death risk of an adult increases steadily and sharply with age. On the long standing theory (Gompertz, 1825) I am taking as exemplar, "the relative annual increase in the death [risk] as a consequence of aging is a constant fraction which depends upon the species concerned" (Jones, 1961, p. 270). For a number of species (including men, mice and flies) the fraction is proportional to the life span of the species. If we take the life span as the unit of time we can therefore superimpose the graphs of death risk against age for members of these species, as shown in figure 1 (from Jones, 1961, p. 271). In figure 1 "curves A, B, and C represent successively better states, whether with respect to genetic factors, overt disease, or environment" (Jones, 1961, p. 271). That is, an individual whose death risk is given by A has seven times the death risk at any given age of an individual whose risk is given by C.

From such general relations as those shown in figure 1, relations of death risk to age for particular species follow immediately. Figure 2 shows the relations for men that follow from A, B and C if we assume a life span of 100 years. I have also superimposed on figure 2 a plot of death rates against age for white U.S. men and for Swedish men in 1955. (From Taylor, 1961, p. 352; World Health Organisation, 1958, pp. 54–7.) The comparison is not strict, for two reasons. First, actual death rates calculated for such five-year age-spans are not identifiable with death risks; they are in effect death risks averaged over that age range. Secondly, the death rates of Swedish and U.S. men are averaged over many individuals in different environments and states of health and with consequently different death risks. The plots may neverthe-

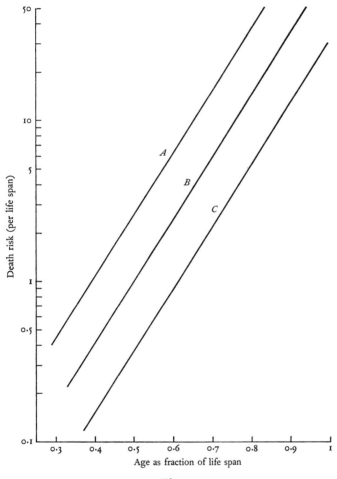

Figure 1.

less reasonably be taken within limits of experimental imprecision to represent the death risks of typical members of these two populations.

The characteristic rate of relative increase in death risk with age for members of a given species is often referred to as its 'force of mortality'. It may be expressed in terms either of the rate constant or of the time taken for the death risk to double (Jones, 1961, p. 271). Figure 2 shows that the force of mortality for men is given by a "doubling time" of eight years. The time is the same on all three theoretical graphs; whatever one's environment and state of health, provided it stays the

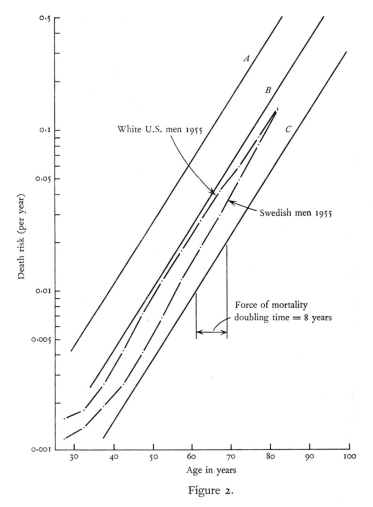

Figure 2.

same, one's death risk goes up about ten per cent a year for most of one's adult life.

Men cannot live long at the same age, and the exponential increase of death risk with age must be allowed for in general when deriving chance distributions from the theory. However, the effect on the distribution in an extended trial of the increased death risk towards its end is reduced by the chance that the man may die before then. Allowing for these factors, chance distributions for various extended trials derived from

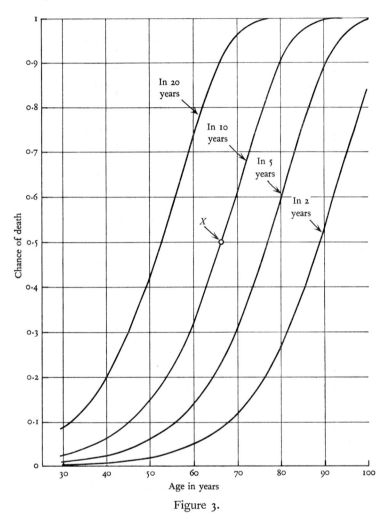

Figure 3.

graph *B* of figure 2 are given in figures 3 and 4. The general relation is

$$p = 1 - \exp \frac{\tau}{\ln 2} \left[\mu(w + t) - \mu(w) \right].$$

Figure 3 shows the chances of death in trials of two, five, ten and twenty years duration as functions of age. Figure 4 shows the chances of death as functions of duration for extended trials on men aged thirty, fifty, seventy and ninety. Thus point X on figure 3 shows a fifty–fifty chance that a man aged 66 will live another ten years; point Y on figure 4 shows a chance of 39 in 40 that a man of thirty will do the same.

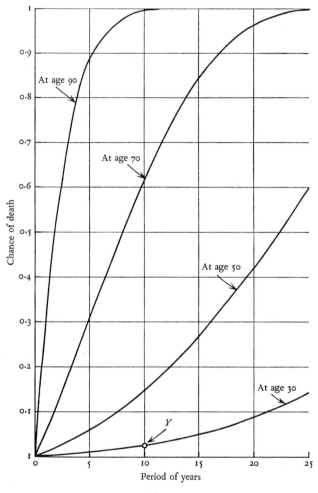

Figure 4.

It is of course assumed in figures 3 and 4 that the risk of the man whose death is in question continues to be represented throughout the trial (or as much of it as he survives) by graph B of figure 2. I have expressed this assumption by saying that the man's environment and state of health remain constant. The first condition has been difficult to satisfy in Europe and the United States during the last hundred years, as rising hygienic standards have shown themselves in steadily falling death rates. The derivation of chance distributions for extended trials in these conditions is more complicated although not different in principle. We ascribe to the environment a variable propensity to induce death in people of various ages and states of health. The chance distribution in a given trial displays this propensity as well as the death risk of the individual. If its variation with time were known quantitatively as is that of death risk in a constant environment, the chances of death in extended trials would again be derivable.

The complexities of this example make two things very plain. First the need to distinguish propensities from chances. Secondly, the conventional element remarked on in chapter 4 (pp. 74–6) in assigning dispositional properties. With a variety of people in similar environments we take their different chances of death to display different propensities in them. With similar people in a variety of environments we take their different chances of death to display different propensities in the environment.

Consider a journeying motorist who maintains an invariable ability and vigilance. The chance of his dying in the next minute (say) still varies with the state of the road and traffic. A stretch of road on which this chance is particularly high we call 'dangerous'. The term denotes a propensity of individual roads which traffic engineers put much effort into removing. They do so by altering other properties of the road connected to it, such as its surface, its gradient, its width, its lighting, its markings and its road signs. What they are doing is exactly analogous to removing the colour of a paint by changing its chemical composition with a bleach, or the fragility of glass by changing its stress distribution in annealing it.

Equally, of course, the chances of two drivers dying in similar cars on the same stretch of road may differ widely. A driver whose death has a particularly high chance we call 'dangerous'. The term again denotes a propensity, this time in him, with which other properties are known to be connected, such as the level of alcohol in his blood. Cars too can be dangerous in the same sense. It is invariably held, as it is with roads and men, that dangerousness is a function of a car's other properties. It must be possible to make a car less or more dangerous by changing it in some other respect.

We see illustrated here the general regulative principle of connectivity (Schlesinger, 1963, chapter 3), of which we shall say more hereafter. The principle is used to settle the ascription of dispositions on the basis of other properties connected to them. Suppose a glass breaks on a floor. Does this display unusual fragility in the glass or hardness in the floor? It depends on whether relevantly similar glasses break on relevantly different floors, and whether relevantly different glasses break on relevantly similar floors. Without an array of other properties of glasses and floors, and a network of laws to tell us which are relevant to fragility and hardness, we cannot settle the question. It is the same with propensities. Their ascription on the basis of measurements of chance requires an effective ontology of things like men, cars and roads or coins and tossing devices (p. 75), variable in other respects to which the ascribed propensities may be connected.

Death risk must be distinguished from the chances that display it if specious objections are not to be raised. A man may obviously be so assassinated that his death is not a matter of chance at all. A biased coin may equally be so lowered to the ground that its landing heads is not a matter of chance (p. 60). Or a radioactive atom may be split by deliberate bombardment. That these are not chance trials does not count against the things involved being chance set-ups. The assassinated man still had his death risk, the lowered coin its bias and the bombarded atom its half-life.

The propensities of the person must similarly be distinguished from those of the environment. Consider the radioactive analogy. A bombarding environment may not certainly hit an atom in it but only have a propensity to do so. And a hit atom may not certainly decay but only have a higher propensity to do so than an unhit atom has. We can calculate from these data what the chance of decay in a given time is for an atom placed in such an environment. It will be higher than the chance decay in that time of an unhit atom which is not being bombarded. We might put this by saying that the environment has raised the "decay risk" of the atom, but it would be misleading. It would suggest that merely by entering the environment the atom acquires a new propensity to decay, intermediate between those of hit and unhit atoms. This is not the case. No change in the properties of the atom takes place unless and until it is hit (see pp. 99–100 below). The third propensity needed to calculate the chance of decay is a property of the environment, not of the atom.

Similarly with the death of people. There are statistical theories of epidemics which credit human environments with propensities to give people dangerous diseases. Suppose for example that the greater the proportion of people in a community with an infectious disease, the greater the chance of an uninfected person catching it (e.g. Feller, 1957, p. 110). Someone with the disease moreover has a greater death risk than a similar person without it. Now the chance of an uninfected person dying is clearly increased by his entering the epidemic area. But he acquires no new propensity to die unless and until he actually catches the disease. To say that his death risk increases on his merely becoming exposed to infection is to confound propensity with chance.

The terms 'death risk' and 'death rate' have been loosely used in this respect to cover chances of death displaying propensities both of people and of their surroundings. Thus Jones (1961, p. 286) asserts that "the single, heavy-smoking male, sedentarily employed in a large United States city, may be compared [in death risk] with a married, non-smoking female living in rural Scandinavia". This heterogeneity has not worried workers in the field because frequentism, adopted *faute de mieux*, has led them in any case to suppose that death risk "cannot be determined for an individual; it is a measure associated with a population" (Taylor, 1961, p. 349). We can, however, confine ourselves to the extra death risks of those who have contracted specific diseases. These are undoubtedly propensities of people rather than of their environments. Nor, despite frequentist protestations, is there any doubt that these concepts are specifically applied to individuals. Thus Jones (1961, p. 289): 'Individuals having malignant tumours are known to have particularly high death rates...such death rates characterise all such patients.' Jones considers the various established causes of such high death risks and whether they can be reversed. In the table on his p. 287 he classifies these causes accordingly. Of the risk of death from heart disease he concludes (p. 285) that "reduction of the heart disease risk appears practicable, using dietary methods for lowering the disturbed elevations of serum lipoproteins". A man on such a diet is not worried about "a measure associated with a population"; he is concerned to change that property of himself which would otherwise be displayed in an excessive chance of his death during the years ahead.

As a more convenient and perspicuous measure of such death risks from specific diseases, the concept of physiological aging has been introduced. It has been observed that "not only does the death [risk] from all causes for a given population increase at a constant relative rate with age, but also the [risk] for almost any selected cause of death increases at about the same pace" (Jones, 1961, p. 271). The immediate effect of contracting a disease of which this is true is to produce a sharp rise in the death risk, e.g. from graph *B* to *A* on figure 2. Thereafter the death risk of the person with the disease remains on graph *A* as he grows older. The overall effect therefore is to shift his whole death risk/age curve a number of years to the left. His death risk at any chronological age is the same as he would have reached that number of years later had he not contracted the disease. A disease may therefore be characterised, in its effects on death risk, in terms of the number of years of "physiological aging" it produces (Jones, 1961, p. 287). Figure 5 shows this effect for the diseased bodily state that smoking twenty cigarettes a day induces, which Jones (p. 287) cites as aging a man seven years. If in a given environment we use the death risk of a healthy individual as a standard, we can define not merely increases but absolute values of physiological age. A man's physiological age is the age of a healthy man with the same death risk.

So much serves to introduce the concepts of death risk and physiological age. More needs to be said in support of interpreting them as propensities of individuals. Death risks and physiological ages are of course directly measured by frequencies *via* derived chances such as those in figures 3 and 4. But not every frequency of death among an arbitrary class of people measures a chance. Frequency of death in a class of "man-years" only measures chance directly when all the members of the class have the same chance. In particular, the chances will be equal if all the men involved have the same physiological age and are in similar environments.

This account requires that pairs of unknown chances, death risks and physiological ages can yet be known to be equal. There is no vicious circularity in such an assumption; it is a logical commonplace that two classes of unknown size can be known to be equinumerous (Russell, 1919, chapter 2). More pertinently, the measuring of many physical quantities requires similar assumptions. Consider a scientist using a thermometer to measure the temperature of an object. He must first satisfy himself that the thermometer is at the same temperature (*ex hypothesi* unknown) as the object. Only then is he justified in ascribing to the object the temperature he reads off the thermometer. Similarly when a length is measured with a pair of calipers or when a bridge method is used to measure differences of electrical potential (Astbury, 1962). There is thus nothing peculiar in our assumption; but it needs showing how it can be known to be satisfied in the case of death risks (and hence chances).

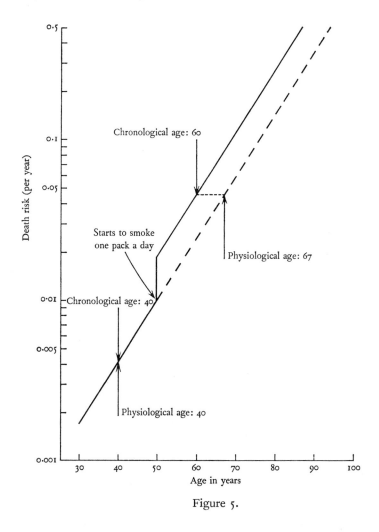

Figure 5.

I have remarked that propensities, like dispositions generally, are admitted only as being connected by laws with other properties. When such proposed laws are established they can be used to ascribe death risk and physiological age on the basis of measurements of connected properties. We have seen a man's age to be the property most notably connected to his death risk. Hence the age of a person in a fixed state of health is a measure of his death risk, just as the volume of a fixed mass of a given gas at a fixed temperature is a measure of its pressure. Two such samples of gas of the same known volume are thereby known to be of the same, even if unknown, pressure. Similarly two people of the same age in the same known state of health are thereby known to be of the same, even if unknown, death risk and physiological age. Hence the frequency of death in some time interval among a class of such persons in relevantly similar environments is a good measure of the chance of their death. If the environment is suitably standard this chance is in turn a display of the physiological age of the people involved; once we know some physiological ages we can take such chances to display the "dangerousness" of non-standard environments. The case is exactly like that of using frequencies in coin tosses to ascribe bias alternatively to the coin or to the tossing device (chapter 4, p. 75).

Where physiological age is a known function of some "cause of death", a frequency of death among a quite different class can be a good measure of the chance of death. Figure 5 shows the aging of seven years caused by smoking twenty cigarettes a day. Call such people 'smokers' and those who do not smoke at all 'non-smokers'. Then the physiological age of a smoker of 35 is the same as that of a non-smoker who is 42 but in otherwise similar health. Hence the frequency of death among 42 year-old non-smokers is a good measure of the chance of a similar smoker of 35 dying in the same period. Analogously, the effect on the pressure of an ideal gas of doubling its volume V is exactly cancelled by doubling the absolute temperature θ. A reading of the pressure of a gas sample at $2V$ and 2θ is therefore a good measure of the pressure of an otherwise similar sample at V and θ. So indeed would an average be of readings of samples, some at V and θ and some at $2V$ and 2θ. In the same way frequency in a mixed class of smokers of 35 and non-smokers of 42 provides a perfectly good measure of their common physiological age.

Thus a frequency in a class of people some of whom are dissimilar in a relevant respect can give a good measure of man's physiological age. Conversely, a frequency in a class of people who are all similar, but in an inadequate number of relevant respects, can give a bad measure. So far from the frequency of death among smokers (of all ages) being the only acceptable measure of "a smoker's chance of dying" (as on the frequency definition), there may well be *no* smoker of whose chance of dying that frequency is an acceptable measure. Death risk is a pronounced function both of age and cigarette consumption. Frequency in a class of smokers of all ages is a bad measure of the death risk of a smoker of 35, as is frequency in a class of 35 year-olds many of whom are non-smokers. In the same way an average of pressure readings of gas samples all of the same volume as a given sample but of widely varying temperatures is a bad measure of the pressure of the given sample.

The appeals above to people and gas samples being "otherwise similar" do not beg the question at issue. We are not given *a priori* the respects in which other things must be equal, nor are they forced on us directly by observation. It is a matter for "conjecture and refutation" (Popper, 1963). If we suspect relevance in a previously unregarded property it can be tested for in the ways I have illustrated. It is true that gases are less complex than people, and we can be surer of having satisfied '*ceteris paribus*' clauses about them. But this is a difference of degree, not of principle. The "relevant respects" other than volume and temperature in the case of gas pressure are known to be mass and chemical composition. In the case of physiological age the relevant respects other than smoking and age are a finite number of personal properties. Some of them are established, others still under investigation. "Thus, radiation effect, genetic constitution, physical injury, and some of the infectious diseases produce through their action the equivalent of advancing of physiological age" (Jones, 1961, p. 269).

Physiological age is not only affected and explained by other physiological properties with which it is connected. Once established it is itself used in physiological explanation. Thus Jones (1961, p. 272) suggests that "many of these causes [of death] – cancer, vascular disease, diabetes – are linked to the quality of internal metabolism.... It is reasonable to assume that these deaths are the result of aging in the sense that decay of functional vigor somehow underlies the onset of these functional failures." And on the other hand there are "metabolic events known to be associated with aging... the risk of recurrence of a vascular disease accident was shown to be dependent upon the patient's serum lipoprotein level" (Jones, 1961, pp. 284–5). The law-like status of these generalisations is further shown in such counterfactual inferences as the one to the conclusion (p. 91 above) that dietary methods would reduce a patient's heart disease risk *via* their effect on the serum lipoprotein level. The same criterion is used to distinguish relevant from irrelevant factors affecting heart disease risk. Investigations

suggest that blood pressure has about equal importance with serum lipids in the estimation of heart disease risk...Blood pressure and blood lipids are only very slightly correlated, so that their usefulness in predicting the risk is additive. On the other hand, overweight...may not supply additional information beyond that contained in the lipid and blood pressure data, because of the strong positive correlations between overweight and either blood pressure or serum lipids. (Jones 1961, p. 286.)

In other words, the data suggest the counterfactual inference that if a person's weight were changed without changing his blood lipid or pressure levels, his death risk from heart disease would be unaffected. Weight is thus not a property independently connected to heart disease risk.

I have given this example in perhaps excessive detail, and laboured elementary facts of measurement, to show how much less mysterious death risk and physiological age appear on a propensity than on the received frequency view. They are quite commonplace attributes of individuals, dispositions admitted on the basis of their law-like connections with other properties that in turn provide many alternative non-frequency measures of them. Physiological age serves in the deductive explanation of hosts of statistical laws about the effects of bodily causes on the chances of a person's death. It is in turn explained by its correlations with such other of his properties as age, genetic constitution, blood pressure, etc. That these correlations are not as complete and certain as those enshrined in the gas laws shows merely that the medical sciences still have work to do. It is endlessly possible that the work will reveal further relevant factors and falsify existing statistical law statements. So it is with deterministic laws. Meanwhile, we have a rational account of why life insurance companies investigate some properties of a client and ignore others. They are not making mysterious prudential or methodological decisions about how much ignorance is worth dispelling before settling on a relative frequency, or logical probability relation, or purely subjective partial belief. They interest themselves in the properties currently established as connected to their client's physiological age, of which they thereby hope to make an indirect measurement. (They of course enquire similarly into the dangerousness of his environment, which also affects the chances of his death.) And there is nothing more obscure or irrational in the indirect measurement of physiological age than there is in the indirect measurement of any other disposition.

I suppose incorrigible determinists, whether frequentist or subjectivist, may still object that all the given statistics reflect is ignorance of the
cause of each person's death. To any two people differing in life span
some other explanatory difference, they might claim, must (and hence
doubtless can) be ascribed. The statistical data then result from a
merely accidental mixture of such different kinds of person in the
population. The long answer to this is given in chapter 8. The short
answer is that these alleged explanatory differences between people who
die at different ages are not known in all cases, and existing theory does
not provide for them. The claim that they must nevertheless exist and
that neither people nor environment can "really" have propensities is
based on an assumption of determinism that is the very point at issue.

HALF LIFE

If physiological theory does not provide deterministic differences
between individuals who pass away at different ages, the theory of
radioactive disintegration positively excludes them. It does not postu-
late differences between radium atoms that decay at different times and
then lay down measures for our ignorance. It asserts identity of
properties between them, and especially of a property whose display is
the equal chances of their decay in equal times. On this theory a radioactive atom is a chance set-up. "A radioactive atom...is in an unstable
condition. In any interval of time it will have a certain definite probability of disintegrating" (Delaney, 1962, p. 45). The "unstable condition" of an atom is the propensity to decay, of which the chances of
decay in various times are the displays. The chances of decay are
derivable from the theory as they are from the theory of physiological
aging. The set-up here is simpler than a person, and so the derivation is
simpler, involving fewer independent variables. "The probability λ
that any particular atom will disintegrate in unit time is constant and
independent of the age of that atom" (Collinson, 1962, p. 44). A trial on
this set-up consists of waiting for a finite time t, in which there is a
finite chance p that the atom will decay, where p is given by

$$p = 1 - \exp(-\lambda t). \quad \text{(Delaney, 1962, p. 45).} \tag{1}$$

The decay constant λ is commonly given in terms of the half-life
$T(= \ln 2/\lambda)$, which is the duration of a trial in which the chance of
decay is $\frac{1}{2}$. The half-life is the same for all atoms of the same "radio-

element", a radioelement being a (radioactive) isotope of a chemical element (Brown, B., 1962, p. 60). The half-life of the most common isotope of radium, for example, is 1622 years (Myerscough, 1962, p. 168).

This is a case in which the same propensity is equally displayed in trials of any duration, with consequently diverse chance distributions. The same is true of physiological age, but the situation is further complicated there by several propensities being displayed in any given trial. The point is seen more clearly in the austerer context of radio-activity. We thus do not distinguish radioactive trials as differing in kind merely because they differ in their chance distribution (see chapter 3, p. 61). Such trials only differ in kind where they involve atoms of different radioelements. To say this is merely to say that equation (1) is very analytic to the radioactive disintegration theory. There is no doubt that statistical measurement of T for a given radioelement on trials of one duration would be subject to correction *via* equation (1) by statisti-cal measurement of the chance distribution on trials of other durations. Hence these constitute only one kind of trial and the atom's single propensity to decay is that expressed in the value of its half-life, which it shares with all other atoms of the same kind, namely of the same radioelement. The half-life is the single property of a radioactive atom, as physiological age is of a person, that enters into the law network connecting it with other properties.

It may be thought a peculiar feature of statistical dispositions to be capable of display in trials of many apparent "kinds", but it is not so. Analogous situations arise with many other properties, as has been generally urged in chapter 4 (pp. 76–82). Young's modulus, an elastic property of materials of which Hooke's law is true, is equally displayed by any stretching of a wire made of the material within its elastic limit. Less obviously perhaps, consider whether the vapour pressures of a substance at various temperatures constitute as many different proper-ties of it, or whether measurements at these temperatures are all equally displays of a single property. The question obviously turns on how analytic is the function involved, i.e. the extent to which it would be used, like equation (1), to combine data taken indifferently at various temperatures. A typical relation between vapour pressure P and temperature θ is an exponential relation of the form

$$P = \exp (A - B/\theta), \tag{2}$$

where A and B are constants for a given substance. Such a relation may be so analytic to a new (e.g. a synthesised organic) substance that its vapour pressures at all temperatures are calculated from just enough measurements to fix the values of A and B (see Armstrong, 1962, p. 587; Othmer and Gilmont, 1955). This is particularly likely when, for example, knowledge of vapour pressure is needed for investigating chemical reactions at temperatures at which the substance's instability makes direct measurement impossible. In such circumstances the characteristic values of A and B in equation (2) express just a single property of the substance. Vapour pressures at different temperatures, where measurement at one temperature is thus subject to correction *via* equation (2) by measurements at others, are not taken to be independent properties. They are of course all derivable from equation (2), just as the chances of many individual outcomes in a chance trial are all derivable from the one chance distribution (see chapter 3, p. 59). Equation (2) is capable of such analyticity largely because it is derivable with simplifying assumptions from thermodynamic theory. (In this context, and that of similarly derived equations of state, the use of such expressions as 'semi-empirical' is an excellent indication of the status of a proposed generalisation (see Thewlis, 1962, volume 3, p. 4).)

Construed as a disposition, then, half-life is not peculiar in being displayed in many different chance distributions. All this commonplace fact gives us reason for is repeated insistence on the distinction between propensity and chance.

The obvious differences between the concepts of half-life and physiological age are immaterial to their status as dispositions. It is true for example that half-life cannot change continuously as physiological age can. The half-life of an atom is nevertheless a property of it which is connected with its nuclear properties although independent of its state of chemical combination. Nuclear structure is not as readily and is not continuously changeable as are the properties with which physiological age is connected. This is not an important difference. Nuclear structure *is* changeable: the radioactive disintegration theory postulates that the *same* atom is transformed, when decay occurs, from one structure to another. In the thorium series an atom of thorium-232 passes by decay through twelve successive stages to the stable lead-208. In each stage the atom has a distinct half-life, ranging from 10^9 years (thorium-232) to 10^{-7} seconds (tolonium-212) (Brown, B., 1962, p. 60). Thus a numerically identical atom undergoes over a period of time a series of drastic changes in its propensity to decay, these changes being connected with and explained by changes in its nuclear structure. Such changes may occur naturally or may be brought about artificially, for example by bombarding stable elements with neutrons, protons or deuterons (Brown, B., 1962 *a*).

The case is therefore quite closely analogous to that of physiological age, in which a person's propensity to die may change naturally, increasing with increasing age, or be changed artificially by taking or giving up smoking, exposure to radiation, physical injury etc. Like physiological age, half-life explains on the one hand a host of derived statistical laws about disintegration in various quantities and mixtures of radioelements. On the other, it is in turn explained by its correlations with the other physical properties that distinguish different isotopes of the same chemical element. And here too, indirect measurement of half-life, *via* that of the disintegration rate of a sample of the radio-element, is a commonplace. "There are four main methods of measurement [of disintegration rate], namely counting, calorimetric, loss of charge and ion chamber", of which only counting ("normally only suitable for weaker sources" (Collinson, 1962, p. 41)) is anything like a frequency measure. But this frequency measure is certainly not so much more analytic than the other methods, relying on correlations of half-life with other properties, that the concept would be retained if the other methods failed to correlate. The correlations are direct consequences of the radioactive disintegration theory which alone provides employment for the concept of half-life. Frequencies of decay in arbitrary classes of atoms would no doubt continue to be measurable without such a theory, but not the explanatory propensity, of which such frequencies now measure only one of a large number of alternative possible displays.

6 Imprecision and inexactness

THE PREVIOUS CHAPTER supplied examples of respectable scientific propensities. I now resume the quest for cause or just impediment why these quantities may not be joined together in the conceptual category of dispositions. In so doing I shall be led to deal further with dispositions in general, the results being applied specifically to propensities in chapter 7.

I consider first whether any peculiar logic of measurement in propensity marks it off from other dispositions. Propensities are obviously quantities. Their values are given by those of the chance distributions that display them. Where many distributions display one propensity the value is that of the parameters of the analytic relation between them, such as the half-life and doubling time in the examples of the last chapter. Such values are generally capable of continuous variation on at least an interval scale (Stevens, 1959; Ellis, 1966, pp. 58–67) of rational (Braithwaite, 1953, p. 130) or, in general, of real numbers.

It has been widely if tacitly supposed that a true quantity must be capable in principle of having precise values ascribed to individuals. No doubt tiresome but trivial "errors of measurement and other forms of experimental error" may have to be discounted before "our attention can turn to the logico-mathematical structure" of relations between these quantities (Sellars, 1961, p. 73). Even the discussion provoked by exceptions apparently implied by the Uncertainty Principle serves to emphasise the otherwise general assumption.

Precise values of chances, and hence of propensities, are notoriously not ascribable even in principle. On any recognised theory of testing statistical hypotheses (e.g. Neyman, 1952, chapter 1) all that can ever be shown is that a chance lies in an interval of values. Even this assertion will be subject to a finite probability of falsehood. Not only can precise values of chance not be ascribed, it cannot even be shown conclusively that a value lies in any interval less than [0, 1]. This all stems not from errors of measurement but from the very nature of chance. Does this apparent distinction show that propensity is not after all a true quantity?

The distinction in fact is only apparent. Chance values can be shown to lie in intervals less than [0, 1] as conclusively as measurement can show anything dispositional. Values of propensities can be shown to be in significantly restricted intervals even if they cannot be given precisely. And contrary to common belief, nothing more can be shown in the case of other dispositional quantities. Imprecision is just as inevitable in measurements of other quantities as it is in measurements of propensity, and just as inherent to the quantities measured.

Consider first the propensity statement that a coin *a* is unbiased, which we may symbolise as

$$p_a (H) = 0.5. \tag{1}$$

No doubt (1) cannot be tested directly, only statements derived from (1) of the form
$$k < p_a (H) < l, \tag{2}$$

where $0 \leqslant k < 0.5 < l \leqslant 1$. Any test criterion will moreover leave a finite probability of rejecting a true statement of the form of (2) or accepting a false one (apart from the degenerate case $k = 0, l = 1$).

Chwistek (1948, p. 256) has observed that this is just as true of statements assigning particular values of any other quantity measurable on a continuous interval scale. Take temperature as a typically respectable dispositional quantity. Consider the statement that the temperature of a coin *a* is 21 °C, which we may symbolise as

$$\theta_a = 21. \tag{3}$$

Again, all that thermometers of varying precision can test directly are derived statements of the form

$$k < \theta_a < l, \tag{4}$$

where $-273.2 \leqslant k < 21 < l \leqslant$ melting point of *a* in °C. Any given test criterion (i.e. operational definition prescribing a method of applying and reading a thermometer) will leave a finite probability of rejecting a true statement of the form of (4) or accepting a false one (apart again from the degenerate case $k = -273.2, l =$ melting point of *a* in °C).

To this parallel two objections might be raised. The first is that the probabilities of error in testing (1) are calculable from the original statement and indeed intrinsic to its meaning (Braithwaite, 1953, pp. 151–5), whereas this is not true of (3). In reply to this we observe that *incidental* sources of error are as possible in tests of propensity statements as in tests of temperature statements. It is as possible to make a mistake in counting the number of heads in a sequence of tosses as it is to misread a thermometer. It is also as possible for a particular sequence of trials to fail to display the propensity (e.g. the coin is warped by a temperature change during the sequence) as for a particular surface reading to fail to display the temperature (e.g. chemical action sets up temperature gradients inside the coin). Doubtfulness in the value of a dispositional quantity introduced in this sort of way I call 'operational imprecision'.

Conversely, what I call 'conceptual imprecision' is inherent in temperature measurement just as it is in that of propensity. Its existence is recognised in current theories of temperature. Fluctuating molecular velocities limit the precision of any possible temperature measurement. No refinement of measuring technique could warrant ascribing a precise value of a temperature as opposed to an imprecise ascription in the form of (4). This is inherent to the present concept of temperature; the probability of a supposedly precise reading deviating from the "true" mean value by any given amount is calculable from its theory. The same is true of lengths, pressures, electric currents, and the magnitudes of fields, electromagnetic, gravitational etc. connected with particles in indeterminate motion.

The second objection that might be raised is that the concept of a probability of error has been introduced. This concept seems to have a connection with propensity that it lacks with other quantities (see e.g. Braithwaite, 1953, p. 155). But this is not so. Measurement of any quantity is subject to error as well as to imprecision, and error is often an outcome of a chance trial. The set-up is the measuring device and the trial consists of making a measurement prescribed by an operational definition of the quantity measured. The possible results are the possible readings the device gives of the quantity. Its propensity is displayed in the chance distribution over these possible readings. If this propensity is not known it may itself be measured. Thus estimates are made of the reproducibility of thermometer readings and the results of statistical trials alike. And doubtless the devices used in *these* measurements have a propensity to err, of which further measurements could be made. There is an endless regress, but it is neither vicious nor mysterious. In the special case of frequency measurements, indeed, Braithwaite (1953) has made it the basis of his definition of chance. I decline the definition, but not because it involves a regress. That devices for measuring propensity resemble devices for measuring temperatures in having propensities to err reinforces rather than diminishes the similarity between them. It certainly discloses no distinction in their logics of measurement (see Mellor, 1967a, pp. 325–6).

What is controversial in this field is not chances of error given the true value of a quantity, but using the concept of probability in inverse inferences from a reading to the true value. Despite the strictures of the Neyman–Pearson school (e.g. Neyman, 1952, p. 235), scientists certainly do make such inferences from readings and interpret error distributions in terms of probability. On the other hand it is certainly not clear what kind of trial could have true values of a quantity as possible results nor what kind of set-up could have a propensity to produce such true values. It is not even clear how bets on the results of absolutely conclusive measurements could ever be settled (cf. chapter 2, p. 31). If probabilities are involved, therefore, they seem not to display propensities nor even to be interpretable as CBQs. They are the concern of confirmation theory rather than of statistical science. The probability that a dispositional quantity lies in a certain interval, given a reading of it, is thus a questionable concept. But it is quite immaterial to its legitimacy whether the quantity being measured is a propensity or a temperature.

Whether or not they are interpreted probabilistically, there are as established criteria for accepting statements like (2) as there are for accepting statements like (4). Neither acceptance is secure against inductive doubt, which cannot therefore be invoked peculiarly against propensity. It is endlessly possible for future measurements, both of propensity and of temperature, not to correlate with past ones. It is endlessly possible for temperatures and propensities alike no longer to correlate as they have previously done with other dispositions. The traditional problems of induction bear on the present topic not at all, since they are posed equally by the ascription of any disposition. Measurement can show as conclusively that a coin's propensity to fall heads is between 0.45 and 0.55 as it can show its temperature to be between 20.5 and 21.5 °C.

It remains to discuss why imprecision is as inherent to other dispositional quantities as it is to propensity. I have emphasised already that constraints are imposed on explanatory dispositions in science (chapter 4, pp. 65–6). For a term denoting a disposition to convey information it must be applicable on the basis of more than one operational definition. It must be usable in stating a law not entailed by its method of application. "If the linear expansion of a mercury column in a glass tube of even width furnishes the basis of an operational definition of 'temperature', then the question whether mercury expands in linear proportion to temperature (so defined) must be answered 'yes' as a matter of logical necessity" (Feigl, 1945, p. 504). Defining temperature by a mercury thermometer would say nothing about the world until the defined concept was related to others in a logically distinct way, for example in the laws of thermal expansion of other liquids and gases. But then these laws in turn can be made to provide alternative operational definitions of temperature. In fact any sufficiently well established law into which a disposition enters, whether a quantity or not, can be invoked in an operational definition. Whatever the historical order of their discovery, once others are accepted no one law about such a concept remains analytic in the traditional sense. Science has no conservative regulative principle, that concepts should be permanently enshrined in the oldest known general truths about them. There is no one uniquely privileged operational definition of a dispositional quantity. So a chemical substance can be identified in analysis by any suitable set of its properties – melting point, solubility, chemical reactions, colour, hardness. Similarly a length can be measured from the period of a pendulum, the flow of a viscous fluid, the extension of a rod on heating or under stress, by sundry optical and mechanical means; in short, by invoking any applicable law into which the concept of length enters. To be acceptable a scientific disposition must enter into at least two laws well established enough to provide alternative operational definitions. Normally indeed it will enter into a whole "law-cluster" of them (Putnam, 1962). This is the feature that gives rise to conceptual imprecision in quantities.

Various reasons of theory and convenience determine the choice of operational definition on different occasions and for different values of a dispositional quantity. The thermocouple and the pyrometer become the standards of high temperature measurement, as the micrometer and interferometer replace the metre rule for short lengths. In the same way calorimetric and charge loss methods replace counting as a measure of radioactivity for strong sources, and age becomes the measure of death risk for a healthy man (see chapter 5 above). Nevertheless, the continued use of a single term through all these shifts of operational definition is not just a typographical accident. It signifies a presupposition that all the sufficiently well-established laws the disposition enters into hold, whether they are invoked in the particular operational definition or not. Identifying a chemical substance permits an immediate inference to any of its established physical and chemical properties, not just to those by which it happened to be identified. Similarly, however any length or half-life is in fact measured it is invariably implied by the use of the term that invoking any other applicable law would give a consistent reading.

As refinements of measuring technique decrease operational imprecision, different operational definitions may fail to correlate as they used to do. This is the valid point on which operationalists have insisted. "It is not *safe* to forget [that] the equivalence of two operations is established by experiment, and we must always adopt the attitude that the results of such an experimental proof may be subject to revision when the range or accuracy of our experience is increased" (Bridgman, 1938, pp. 121–2). Such failure of correlation generates conceptual imprecision, since to assert the value of the quantity too precisely is then to falsify at least one established law into which it enters. Whereas if one says merely that the value lies in an interval containing both readings, neither law is falsified. I have called the shortest such interval (or its length, according to context), containing readings by all accepted methods, the 'imprecision' in a dispositional quantity (see Mellor, 1965, 1967, where this topic is explored in more detail). *Operational* imprecision arises from requirements of reproducibility in applying any one operational definition; *conceptual* imprecision is a measure of the discrepancy between readings produced by two or more definitions, equally well established. As all dispositions have at least two operational definitions conceptual imprecision can be revealed in any dispositional quantity by sufficiently precise measurement.

The distinction between and mutual independence of conceptual and operational imprecision may be illustrated by two of many possible examples:

(i) The height of the atmosphere is conceptually imprecise. Its operational definition could be given much greater precision as the height to some arbitrary density level. But then fluctuations in temperature (for example) would lead to a failure of this to correlate with height defined by pressure at sea level, so that inferences drawn from one to the other with such precision would not be reliable.

(ii) There are various ways of measuring size distributions of collections of small particles: with a microscope, by wet or dry sieving, by settling in still or moving air or liquid, by using various centrifugal devices. Each method is operationally precise to a few per cent, but they correlate to only 10–20 per cent. Thus only a "settling size" or "wet-sieve size" distribution can be established with any precision. Values of the single quantity denoted by 'particle size' as used in all these contexts can be given to a precision no better than ten per cent.

There is not a major dispositional quantity in the physical sciences which is conceptually precise. The dimensions and mass even of the most rigid, inert and involatile solid are conceptually imprecise on an atomic scale, and most dimensions and masses have much greater imprecision than that. There is conceptual imprecision similarly in the pressure and temperature of even the most stable and isolated equilibrium system. These facts we have seen above (p. 103) to be recognised and accounted for in physical theory. And what is true of physical quantities is as true of psychological ones. I have had occasion (chapter 2, p. 33) to insist that imprecision should not disqualify partial belief as a quantity. If it did, science would have few quantities.

The world no doubt might have been such that only precise dispositional quantities were needed in its description (Swinburne, 1969). It could equally have been finite and deterministic, so that only precise frequencies were needed to give objective application to the probability calculus. The point however is that the quantitative concepts science in fact applies to the world, rightly or wrongly, are inherently imprecise, propensity no more so than any other.

The view that imprecision in measurement is trivial and incidental to the quantities measured (e.g. Pap, 1963, chapter 3) seems to have two sources. The first is a line of reasoning of the sort that leads to the Sorites paradox (Cargile, 1969). Since it is certainly not inherent in quantitative concepts to have any specific imprecision, it is tempting to suppose that they need have none. In the same way Fellows of Cambridge Colleges have been known to argue that since any specific rent for their rooms would be arbitrary they should pay no rent. Such reasoning may be persuasive but it is not sound. It need not be arbitrary that the rent of a room, the number of grains in a heap of sand, and the imprecision in a quantity should all exceed zero, however arbitrary their precise values may be.

The other source of the view of quantities as precise is the failure of most philosophers of science to distinguish conceptual from operational imprecision. Bridgman (1927, pp. 33–4) for example accounts for the "approximate character of empirical knowledge" in terms of a "penumbra of uncertainty... to be penetrated by improving the accuracy of measurement". Nagel (1961, p. 84) does indeed note "the tacit assumption underlying the use of... diverse procedures [for measuring electric current]... that they yield concordant results" and (p. 99) how one "theoretical notion is made to correspond to two or more experimental ideas". But he does not consider these sources of conceptual imprecision in discussing the "haziness" and "lack of sharp contours" of experimental ideas, as when (p. 100) "what is experimentally identified as a spectral line corresponds, not to a unique wavelength but to a vaguely bounded range of wavelengths". Some of the examples in which Duhem (1914, p. 134) contrasts "theoretical facts" with imprecise "practical facts" suggest conceptual rather than operational imprecision: 'the body is no longer a geometrical solid; it is a concrete block. However sharp its edges none is a geometrical intersection of two surfaces; instead these edges are more or less rounded and dented spines'. But he refers explicitly (p. 172) only to operational imprecision, to "the degree of approximation... [increasing] gradually as instruments are perfected".

With such analyses it is not surprising that imprecision in quantities has been treated as a trivial matter of discountable error. Yet this mistaken view has had consequences in the philosophy of science far beyond the expected bounds of chance and the theory of measurement. Defenders of deductive explanation have been curiously insensitive to the weakness of their treatment of imprecision and to the attacks to which this exposes them. Hempel (1962, p. 101) has a dismissive footnote for Duhem's attack on deductivism, in which he admits that "the explanation of a general law by means of a theory will usually show [that]... the law holds only in close approximation, but not strictly". He is here considering Duhem's example (1914, p. 193) of the inconsistency between Kepler's laws and Newton's theory of gravitation. Hempel's implied concept of "approximate but not strict" deductive explanation seems to me unsatisfactory. Deducibility does not come by degrees (except arguably in inductive logic, which is not here in question); either one proposition follows from another or it does not. Popper (1957a) takes the same example to illustrate a "sufficient condition for depth" in a theory, that "it corrects [laws] while explaining them", and hence avoids "circularity" by "deducing something better in their place". But he gives no account of the sense in which the "something" can at once be better than and yet explain the laws. Similarly in the case of quantities, Brodbeck (1962, p. 244) admits that "there is no deduction...of a single, exact value. There is instead a strict deduction, by the probability calculus, of a so-called "chance" variable, that is, a frequency distribution, which is quite another thing." But the probability calculus provides no deductive step either way between a finite number of data points and either a chance or a limiting frequency distribution. In short, a notion of conceptual imprecision such as I develop in my (1965) paper is necessary, if not sufficient, to a defence of deductivism against the attacks of Feyerabend (1962, p. 48), "based upon the fact that *one and the same set of observational data is compatible with very different and mutually inconsistent theories.* This is possible...because the truth of an observation statement can always be asserted within a certain margin of error only."

Conceptual imprecision cannot then be as readily discounted as operational imprecision; it is the attempt to do so that creates an illusory distinction between propensities and other quantitative dispositions. Consider the following example. A small piece of a short-lived radioelement is left to disintegrate. A functional law relates its mass to its initial mass and the time of decay. Readings are scattered about the line relating precise values of these quantities which is taken to represent the functional law. The scatter of imprecise data points is "discounted" as an effect of experimental error, the discount growing in relative importance as the mass decreases. At some point the whole precise-functional-deterministic-law-plus-error scheme is suddenly exchanged for a statistical description from which experimental error has disappeared as a separable concept. This abrupt change in the description of an obviously continuous process is absurd. The scatter of results inherent in the statistical law cannot be just incidental to the functional law it explains. It will not do to dismiss it as error, nor need we reject the functional law. All we need do is admit imprecision in the concept of radioactive masses that are subject to decay laws, just as we do in the concept of propensity.

Imprecision then affords no ground of distinction between propensities and other dispositional quantities. A person has a physiological age even though its value cannot be truly given to a minute just as a table has a width even though its value cannot be truly given to a thousandth of an inch (Wittgenstein, 1958, part 1, §88). Where I give or refer to precise values of quantities in what follows, it is only because the complications introduced by imprecision do not affect the argument, not because I suppose the quantities really to be precise.

INEXACTNESS

Requiring alternative operational definitions leads to conceptual imprecision in quantitative dispositions. The same requirement gives rise to a related quality of inexactness in dispositions generally. From criteria for resolving inexactness a so-called "principle of connectivity" (Schlesinger, 1963, chapter 3) can be extracted. The present relevance of the principle is its use in the next chapter to derive some classical propensities from non-frequency evidence without appeal to indifference arguments. Connectivity has reasonably been advanced as a primitive regulative principle in its own right; it is still worth showing how the principle relates to others.

It is convenient to consider a simple fictional example, that of the concept of a tributary. Suppose for simplicity that this concept enters into the minimum of two well established laws I have taken to be necessary for an explanatory disposition. Its "law cluster" (p. 105 above) thus has just two members. Suppose that these are

L_1: a tributary is the shorter of two river branches,

L_2: a tributary has the smaller volume flow of two river branches.

These are taken to be statements of equivalence, not just of implication. Being the shorter river branch and having the smaller volume flow are criteria for applying the term 'tributary' to river branches. I assume that there are no problems in applying these criteria themselves. (There obviously could be: e.g. it might make a difference which bank the length of a branch was measured along. All we need, however, is that it does not make a difference; Mellor, 1966, pp. 351–2). Now suppose a deductive theory of tributaries prescribes either L_1 or L_2 as a definition and derives the other as a law. Consider how such a theory would be assessed against various possible observations.

First we need some more terminology, which I derive from Tarski (1944) and Körner (1964; 1966, chapters 2, 12). Corresponding to L_1 and L_2 we have a pair of sentential functions:

$Q_1(x)$: 'x is shorter than the other river branch',

$Q_2(x)$: 'x has a smaller volume flow than the other river branch'

in which river branches are values of x. A river branch *satisfies* the sentential function $Q_1(x)$ provided the statement made by the sentence derived from $Q_1 (x)$ by substituting the name of the river branch for 'x' is true. Similarly for $Q_2 (x)$. Then a *positive instance* of the concept of a tributary is a river branch that satisfies both $Q_1 (x)$ and $Q_2 (x)$. A *negative instance* of the concept is a river branch that satisfies neither $Q_1 (x)$ nor $Q_2 (x)$.

Now although L_1 and L_2 are supposed to have been equally well established before the construction of the theory, neither is supposed to have entailed the other. There would be no contradiction in describing a river branch as satisfying $Q_1 (x)$ but not $Q_2 (x)$, or *vice versa*. Of such a river branch it would be misleading either to assert or to deny without qualification that it is a tributary, since the inferences sanctioned by L_1 L_2 would in either case lead to contradiction. Such a river branch I call a '*neutral candidate*' to the concept (Körner, 1966, p. 26). The possibility of such neutral candidates arising constitutes the *inexactness* of the concept. The appearance of actual neutral candidates compels the construction of a deductive theory to resolve the conflicts of criteria by creating an *exact form* of the concept.

I should note that I need not follow Körner (1966) in his three-valued logic of inexact concepts. Of every river branch it may be true that it is a tributary or true that it is not (Cargile, 1969). The trouble is that we have possibly conflicting criteria for applying the term. There could be river branches where the criteria not only do not tell us whether they are or are not tributaries, but prevent us from saying either. So we might have to change the criteria for the term. Whether and in what sense the concept is then changed, or was ever subject to other than classical two-valued logic is a moot point. It is not a point on which I commit myself by calling a concept 'inexact'.

It is also convenient to note here that the conceptual imprecision discussed above is not a form of inexactness. There conflicting criteria, operational definitions prescribing alternative methods of measurement, yield different values of a quantity all accommodated in an interval of imprecision. Neutral candidates do not arise in the same way. (This point is made more fully in Mellor, 1967, pp. 1–4.) The bounds of intervals of imprecision and of imprecise readings may be taken to be precise. There need not be conflicting criteria for a reading being contained in an interval of imprecision. There must nevertheless be limits to admissible imprecision, prescribed by theory or otherwise, if quantitative theories are to be testable (Mellor, 1965, §§4–5). Two readings of a quantity given by well established methods of measurement may differ by more than any admissible imprecision in it. The conflict of criteria in that case is exactly analogous to that of the tributary example. It calls for the same sort of reconstruction of the concept's criteria. To this extent quantities are inexact as well as imprecise.

With this preamble we return to our tributaries and consider how a theory of them copes with neutral candidates. Suppose to start with that the theory prescribes L_1 as the definition and derives L_2 as a law. There are two sorts of possible neutral candidate:

(i) River branches that satisfy $Q_1(x)$ but not $Q_2(x)$. These are positive instances of the theory's exact form of the concept, since they satisfy its definition. But the law L_2, derived in the theory, is not true of them. Hence they refute the theory.

(ii) River branches that satisfy $Q_2(x)$ but not $Q_1(x)$. These are negative instances of the theory's exact form. Because they do not satisfy the theory's definition they are not tributaries so far as the theory is concerned and hence do not refute it. Equally they are unexplained by it. The theory does not explain why these river branches have the smaller volume flow, since it does not apply to them at all.

Suppose now that only neutral candidates of the first sort are found. (There is a defect in this example, which is not general, namely that the two sorts of neutral candidate go together. If the left hand branch of a river is a neutral candidate of the first sort, the right hand branch is a neutral candidate of the second sort, and conversely. The example being merely illustrative this feature can be ignored; or it can be removed by applying the theory only to left hand river branches!) For a theory of tributaries to remain unrefuted in that case, it must take L_2 as its definition. It thus excludes the neutral candidates as negative instances of its exact form of the concept. But if a sizeable proportion of river branches consists of neutral candidates which are thus left unexplained, the theory will be held to be *inadequate*. In changing the exact form of the concept from that defined by L_1 to that defined by L_2, the theory has been kept from refutation at too great a cost in scope of application. The extension of the exact form of the concept of a tributary has been shrunk to the extent of making the theory trivially true. Indeed no longer, given its widespread flouting of the pre-theoretical criterion L_1, can it plausibly claim to be a theory of tributaries as previously understood.

To meet the *criterion of adequacy* invoked here some feature needs to be discovered that explains, in a reconstructed theory, why so many river branches have the greater volume flow while being shorter in length. This might happen in one of two ways. The first would involve discovering some further property G possessed by no neutral candidates and by all positive instances of the inexact concept. G might for example be the property of having a particularly hard and inerodable river bed. We can then replace the unrefuted but inadequate implication that having the shorter volume flow (F_2) implies being the shorter river branch (F_1):

$$(x)\ (F_2 x \to F_1 x) \tag{1}$$

by the unrefuted and adequate equivalence:

$$(x)\ (F_2 x \leftrightarrow F_1 x\ \&\ G x). \tag{2}$$

This involves replacing L_1 in the law cluster of the concept of a tributary by the stronger statement

> L*: a tributary is that one of two river branches which is the shorter and has a bed of hardness $> s$,

where s is a specified mean value of hardness on some agreed scale. Whether such a theoretical reconstruction of the law cluster is acceptable naturally depends on how strongly science needs an adequate theory of river branches. The fictional example is unconvincing here just because there is no pragmatically indispensable theory of tributaries to force us to revise our pre-theoretical usage. But that again is no objection to the example's illustrative use.

The second way to making the theory more adequate would be opened by a theory that introduced geological concepts accounting for the formation and change of river branches. In such a theory a glacial valley, say, could be a chance set-up with propensities to produce river branches of varying lengths and volume flows. With such concepts available one might replace L_2 in the law cluster with the weaker statistical statement

> L_2^*: there is a chance p of a tributary developing (and having thereafter) the smaller flow of two river branches,

where $0.5 < p < 1$. A similar statement would be available in a theory which catered for fluctuations of volume flow from time to time. The river branch itself could then have a propensity to yield the smaller instantaneous volume flow on a trial measurement. I take the latter example for simplicity, since it enables the relevant propensity F_2^* to be attributed to the river branches over which x ranges. Suppose then that we obtain on this basis the unrefuted and adequate equivalence:

$$(x)\ (F_2^*x \leftrightarrow F_1 x). \tag{3}$$

We have again an incentive to carry out the corresponding reconstruction of the concept's law cluster. And again, whether this weakening of the concept and its theory (L_2 is no longer derivable) is acceptable depends on other than theoretical considerations. If it did not the construction of adequate theories would be trivially easy.

The next thing to note is that both ways of making the theory adequate result in the assertion of equivalences. This is a consequence of two exact forms of the concept in adequate and unrefuted theories having the same extension, i.e. the reconstructed inexact concept of a tributary has in fact no neutral candidates. This is not an accidental feature of the example. It is true in general that an adequate characterisation of a system shows itself in the full statement of its laws as equivalences and not just as implications. For otherwise a system which satisfies the consequent of the law need not satisfy the antecedent. Its difference from those systems that do satisfy the antecedent is unexplained, and although it does not refute the law it shows the law to be inadequate.

CONNECTIVITY

The requirement that any adequate law when stated fully must be expressible in symmetrical form as an equivalence is Campbell's (1920, chapter 3) version of the principle of connectivity. The term 'connectivity' comes from Schlesinger (1963, chapter 3). Campbell does not use it, but enquires instead whether laws, expressed as "dual relations" of "uniform association" are always symmetrical. "That is to say, if the relation between A and B is such that, if A can be observed, B can be observed, then is it also such that, if B can be observed, A can be observed? The common sense answer...that it is not...is certainly incorrect; it is based simply on the neglect of the qualifying conditions" (Campbell, 1920, p. 74). This view of laws is perfectly compatible with recognising that what are normally used and tested are not fully stated symmetrical laws, but rather derived statements of implication. For example the incomplete asymmetrical law (1) of the last section is derivable from the complete symmetrical law (2). Hence it is that laws are usually represented as being of this asymmetrical form.

The principle of connectivity has been extracted from an anti-operationalist account of dispositions and an appeal to criteria of adequacy in deductive explanation. Those who do not find this an acceptable basis can still accept the principle on its own merit as one that in fact governs science's explanatory use of disposition terms. I restate it now in the more perspicuous and useful form in which it has been expounded by Schlesinger (1963, chapter 3). Consider its application to the properties of some physical system, for example a chance set-up such as a coin. The principle requires the set of scientifically connected (and thereby explainable) properties of the system to be divisible into two subsets, such that possession of all members of either implies possession of all members of the other. The necessary and sufficient condition for this is clearly that laid down in Schlesinger's version (1963, p. 73), namely that "two physical systems never differ in a single aspect only". It is readily seen in the tributary example that the process of satisfying this version of the principle is just that of devising an adequate and unrefuted theory. For a system here (i.e. a river branch) may be characterised as a tributary, on the theory of which (2) is a consequence, either because it has both properties F_1 and G or because it has the property F_2. Having all members of either of the subsets $\{F_1, G\}$ and $\{F_2\}$ of the set $\{F_1, F_2, G\}$ is taken to imply and explain having all members of the other. Either subset can provide an operational definition for the concept of a tributary as occasion requires. If a theory prescribes either it will be whichever was previously taken to be the better established. Similarly on the weaker statistical theory, of which (3) above is a consequence, with the pair of properties F_2^* and F_1.

A mathematical example of connectivity is implicit in Lakatos'(1963) discussion of the history of Euler's theorem. It will serve here to illustrate the wide application of the principle. The inexact concept is that of a polyhedron and the problem is to prove Euler's theorem:

$$V + F - E = 2,$$

where V is the number of vertices, F the number of faces and E the number of edges of the polyhedron. Lakatos calls the theorem the 'main conjecture' in order not to beg the question of a proof's validity. In the present terminology it is a well established law about polyhedra. The problem is to explain it by derivation in a theory from a defining set of other well established laws. These other laws are the lemmas of suggested proofs. (One proof for example invokes the lemma that any polyhedron can be stretched flat, after having one face removed, by a distortion that does not affect V, E or F.) The set of lemmas invoked in any one proof defines an exact form of the concept of a polyhedron.

A neutral candidate of the first sort (p. 112 above) that refutes the theory (i.e. a supposed proof of the main conjecture) is a figure of which all the lemmas are true but of which the main conjecture is false. This Lakatos calls a 'global (but not local) counter example'. A neutral candidate of the second sort that does not refute the theory but rather demonstrates its inadequacy is a figure of which the main conjecture is true but one or more of the lemmas false. This Lakatos calls a 'local (but not global) counter example'. Such figures show inadequacy in the theory because they are figures of which the theorem is true but to which the proof does not apply, since they are negative instances of that particular exact form of the concept. Thus their Eulerianness is left unexplained by the proof.

Lakatos' historical discussion illustrates admirably the way in which the exact form of the concept of a polyhedron, as embodied in the various proposed proofs, is continually changed in the face of new counter examples to try and fit the inexact concept as closely as possible. Success in the enterprise would be an unrefuted and adequate theory in which the proof applied to all and only Eulerian figures. That would yield in turn a statement of equivalence in that satisfying the lemmas not only guaranteed but was guaranteed by the Eulerianness of the figure. Consequently any Eulerian figure would differ from any non-Eulerian figure in at least two properties (since the latter would also fail to satisfy at least one of the lemmas), thus fulfilling the principle of connectivity.

One of the main points this example brings out is that deductivist accounts have laid too little stress on the need for theoretical explanation to be adequate as well as unrefuted. Observed inadequacy can lead as urgently as observed refutation to theoretical reconstruction. One doubtless puts up with an inadequate theory if nothing better is available. Equally one may have to put up with a refuted theory, with no less equanimity.

Moreover, if a certain number or proportion of apparently observed neutral candidates is needed to show inadequacy in a well established theory, the same is true for refutation. The very fact that an observation would refute such a theory casts doubt on its authenticity. The point is made in Mellor (1965, pp. 113–14) in giving a probabilistic interpretation to limits of imprecision. A proportion of apparently discrepant readings can be discounted as having more probably arisen from some mistake in carrying out the operational definition. The third member of the following series of purported readings of a length would certainly be rejected on this ground alone:

$$25, \quad 27, \quad 2, \quad 26, \quad 26, \quad 29.$$

The general point is made by Hume (1777, p. 113) that where "the fact, which the testimony endeavours to establish, partakes of the extraordinary and the marvellous...the evidence, resulting from the testimony, admits of a diminution, greater or less, in proportion as the fact is more or less unusual". The particular point is made in a published lecture on the design of experiments (Royal Institute of Chemistry, 1961, pp. 11–12):

One immediate application of the error function is its assistance in deciding whether an individual result falling well away from the main group of results can be legitimately rejected from a series.... Correlation of rejected results with major physical disturbances or serious personal mistakes should be used as confirmation of the rejection of poor results.

Explaining away a proportion of apparently discrepant results by a "mistake hypothesis" conflicts with Bennett's theory (1963, pp. 116–19) of the matter. He reckons that scientists' treatment of discrepant data is better accounted for by assuming that they tacitly treat laws as only "weakly quantified" (i.e. not 'all...' but 'nearly all...'). He denies the assumption scientists often explicitly make that such reports must be rejected as false if the law in question is to be preserved. I think the mistake hypothesis explanation the more plausible, but Bennett's being right would if anything improve the case against the exaggerated ease and importance of refutation. It is in any event agreed that not every fleeting glimpse of an off-white swan or greying raven suffices to refute a well-founded law.

The requirement for provisional or continued explanatory use of a theory, that it should not have been refuted, might profitably be treated as a regulative principle on a par with that of connectivity rather than as an exceptionless rule. Certainly a refuted theory cannot be true, but its explanatory use *faute de mieux* need be no more deplorable than that of an inadequate one.

The regulative status of the principle of connectivity perhaps needs further emphasis. It is perhaps clearer in Schlesinger's formulation of the principle than in Campbell's. If two physical systems ever did differ only in a single property, the difference could not be explained by correlation with any other. This is so whatever view – positivist, instrumentalist or realist (Nagel, 1961, chapter 6) – one takes of theoretical explanation. To construct – or employ, or seem to discover – a theoretical entity that accounts for just one isolated difference is to restate the difference rather than to explain it. That a theoretical entity detectable in just one way is unacceptably *ad hoc* is a corollary of connectivity that is probably better recognised than the principle itself.

It is plain enough that the principle of connectivity does not make a straightforwardly empirical assertion. As Schlesinger observes (1963, p. 88), "we are not given a clear, detailed and generally applicable definition of what constitutes a single aspect" or property of a system. Any proposed counter example to the principle could apparently be dealt with in one of two ways:

(i) One could refuse to recognise the observed difference as exhibiting a real property or physical state at all. Thus Schlesinger (p. 78): 'In general, according to the principle of connectivity, if two physical systems have different properties or the same property to a different degree, this is bound to manifest itself in more than one way.' Clerk Maxwell's view is similarly expressed that "if a quantity is connected to other effects that are independently defined then it is a physical state; if not, then it is a mere scientific concept" (Turner, 1955, p. 231). I have already argued (pp. 65–6) that dispositions satisfy this condition.

(ii) One could deny the observed difference to be really in just a "single aspect"; "we could always break up the ostensibly single property into more elementary ones" (Schlesinger, 1963, p. 90). Suppose we were confronted with Poincaré's example (1913, p. 333):

When I say: Phosphorus melts at 44°, I mean by that: All bodies possessing such or such a property (to wit, all the properties of phosphorus, save fusing point) fuse at 44°. . . . Doubtless the law may be found to be false. Then we shall read in the treatises on chemistry: "There are two bodies which chemists long confounded under the name of phosphorus; these two bodies differ only by their points of fusion".

We would deal with this situation by denying that melting point was a single property. "Melting point alone may be exhibited as a complex property; it is the property of becoming liquefied at a certain temperature but also the property of discontinuously assuming a different specific heat at the very same temperature" (Schlesinger, 1963, p. 91).

This latter example is unconvincing just to the extent that the connections between the different properties that characterise a melting point are very well established. There is much direct evidence for them, and they have become deeply embedded in our structure of physical laws and theories. Hence they have become very analytic to the major concepts of a *solid* and of a *liquid* that are built into this structure. To this extent the concept of a melting point that embodies these connections *is* regarded as a single real physical property. It is to be explained by being connected through the law network with other properties, not explained away as an unexplained coincidence of its diverse symptoms. It is the same with the connections between the logically distinct propensities to decay in different times that are embodied in the concept of the half-life of a radioelement. These connections are so analytic to the theory of radioactivity that the half-life is treated as a single real physical property. It too is to be explained by its connections with other (nuclear) properties of the radioelement, not explained away as an unexplained coincidence of its diverse symptoms. One would refuse equally to evade the application of connectivity to melting point and to half life and insist that an observed difference in either must correlate with some other physical difference. Only after the most strenuous investigation had failed to disclose such another difference might we conceivably be prepared to resort to reconstructing the conceptual scheme and "deny that a pure substance had always a constant melting point" (Campbell, 1920, p. 76) or a radioelement always a constant half life.

But one way or the other the principle of connectivity would be preserved. It appears then as a regulative criterion for the adequacy of a scientific description and explanation of a physical system. Not every minute detail of the system need be supposed subject to it, but certainly all the major physical states, the properties linked by the network of established laws that apply to it. Conversely, to point to some feature of a system as a significant scientifically explainable property is to require *inter alia* that the principle of connectivity be applied to it.

This conclusion has been denied, oddly enough, even in its plainest applications. It has been denied, for example, that colour need be an explainable property of physical things. At least, it has been denied that the principle of connectivity need apply to colours of things. In this respect colour has been contrasted with moral and aesthetic properties to which connectivity has been applied under the name 'descriptive universalisability'.

> It is a peculiarity of moral predicates, it is suggested, that if you apply one to any subject you are also, by implication, applying it to anything that is like that subject in the relevant respects. . .if you say that a picture is good, and I produce another picture exactly like the first (or at least like it in the relevant respects), you cannot deny that it is also good. . . . There can be little doubt that this is true: the objection to it is simply that it would seem to apply to any term at all, or almost any. If you say for example, 'this piece of cloth is yellow', you are certainly implying that another piece like it in the relevant respects is also yellow. There is indeed one important difference. . .the "relevant respect" in which the second piece of cloth is like the first will be simply its yellowness. The other characteristics of the cloth may be quite independent of its colour.
>
> (Monro, 1967, pp. 155–6; see also Hare, 1963, p. 141).

In fact there is no difference between 'good' and 'yellow' in this respect. Two pieces of cloth cannot just differ in that one is yellow and the other is not. The question 'what makes it yellow' is just as inadequately answered by 'its yellowness' as is the question 'what makes it good' by 'its goodness' (*pace* Monro, 1967, p. 156). We do not just use colour terms as inexplicable labels for sensations and for objects of our merely passive and incurious gaze. It is also part of our usage that things can be made and kept yellow by processes for which there are intelligible recipes. If something could cease to be yellow without changing in any other way there could be no such recipes. It is contingent that the recipe is what it is (a matter of chemical composition) and that we know what it is. But the idea of I.C.I. Paints Division making every Dulux colour out of one otherwise identical stuff is more than a contingent absurdity. Imagine I.C.I. blenders trying to change Dulux colours without making any other changes in it. Imagine retailers trying to keep it the same colour when their preserving all its other properties would be of no avail. All this would presumably have to be done by incantation, by magic. . .

Even if the colours of things are magical, their propensities are not. Propensities are not such directly observable properties that they could be forced inexplicably on our senses. They are self-consciously postulated as part of the scientific attempt to make the world intelligible. They share with other dispositions the crucial feature of entering into distinct laws with other properties, by none of which are they uniquely defined. Nor does their imprecision mark them off in any relevant way from other dispositions or save them from inexactness. I conclude therefore that propensity shares with the other dispositions of a chance set-up a subjection to the principle of connectivity. In the next chapter I put this conclusion to use; the plausibility of what follows from it that is not otherwise explainable I take to be a further recommendation of the present view.

7 Connectivity and classical propensities

IN EARLIER CHAPTERS I have taken it for granted that the bias of a coin (or its unbiasedness) is a propensity. This is in fact an illuminatingly moot point. Consider the universal proposition S expressed by the sentence

'The chance of heads on a toss of an unbiased coin is $\frac{1}{2}$.'

Is S contingent or not? There seem to be two obvious possibilities:

(α) Bias is defined in terms of other physical properties of the coin without reference to its propensity to land heads when tossed. Then S is a law, if true. It could have a counter example, namely a coin which was unbiased in its other physical properties yet gave unequal chances of heads and tails on a standard toss. Confronted with such a coin we would reject S, perhaps with regret, but at least without a sense of conceptual outrage.

(β) S is necessarily and trivially true, since bias is defined in terms of the coin's propensity to fall heads when standardly tossed. Any coin that gives a chance of heads other than $\frac{1}{2}$ on such a toss is, by definition, biased and so not a counter example to S.

Taking bias to be a propensity commits one to (β), but neither alternative appeals as an adequate account of our use of the terms 'bias' and 'unbiased'. S does not seem to be trivially analytic in the definitional sense of (β), yet it would surely not be given up as readily as (α) suggests. Here in fact is a clear case of the apparently *a priori* knowledge of objective chance of which the classical Laplacean analysis is so plausible. (And frequency analyses so implausible: the claim that our confidence in S on (α) is either based on or reducible to confidence in the results of millions of tosses of unbiased coins is barely even specious; or on (β), for our confidence that a given coin is unbiased.) I now set out to show how propensity theory can account naturally for such knowledge without using classical arguments from ignorance. In so doing I show how the individual propensity expressed in the distribution

$$p_a (\text{H}) = p_a (\text{T}) = 0.5$$

(chapter 6, p. 101) can be established within the limits of conceptual imprecision.

Suppose we have a standard tossing device on which coins may display their propensities. It is an auxiliary measuring device in the way a thermometer is. So we ascribe the displayed propensity to the coin rather than to it (chapter 4, pp. 74–6). We take the coin to be a chance set-up with a propensity displayed in the chance distribution over heads, tails and any other possible result (such as landing on edge) of tossing it on the standard device. Let the determinable chance be $p(H)$, $p(T)$ and $p(E)$ respectively, with determinate values p_a (H), p_a (T) and p_a (E) for the coin a (see Johnson, 1921, chapter 11). Then

$$p_a (H) + p_a (T) + p_a (E) = 1.$$

The coin's propensity D_a may be represented by the ordered triple

$$\langle p_a (H), \quad p_a (T), \quad p_a (E) \rangle. \tag{1}$$

D_a will, on the present account, be connected to the coin's other physical properties. The coin's being magnetised in a particular direction may affect the chance of it falling heads. Warping the coin by heating it may affect the chance of it falling tails.

We may suppose the other properties connected to D_a to be known, even if the details of the connections are not all known. It may be known that magnetisation and temperature alone affect D_a but not exactly how they affect it. This is a very common situation with other quantities. The volume of a fixed mass of a given non-ideal gas, for example, is known to be a function only of temperature and pressure, even though it is not known what this function is. Each function moreover is understood to apply only in circumstances restricted in some natural way. It will be taken for granted that the coin is not heated to its melting point or put under a pile-driver; it will be taken for granted that the gas is not put in a vessel with which it reacts chemically.

To the connected properties the principle of connectivity applies. Two coins, a and b, known to be similarly magnetised and at the same temperature are thereby known to have the same propensity. Two equal masses of the same gas known to be at the same pressure and temperature are similarly thereby known to have the same volume. The conclusion in each case, that the pairs of coins and masses of gas have respectively equal propensities and volumes, is of course contingent. It is contingent both that the coins and gases have the other properties ascribed to them and that these are all the connected properties. But the principle of connectivity that warrants the inference is, as a regulative principle, not contingent. We have seen how it would be preserved, and used to judge the adequacy of any scientific characterisation of physical systems such as coins and samples of gas.

Now the statements asserting that just such-and-such properties are connected to a propensity, although not logically necessary, may be very well established. Just so are the corresponding statements connecting pressure and temperature with the volume of a gas. That these are the connected properties is much better established than is the statement of any specific functional relation between them. More to the point, however doubtful it may be whether some properties *are* connected to a propensity or to a gas volume, there is no doubt that some properties are not connected. It is even more sure that the colour of a gas is not connected to its volume than that its viscosity is not so connected. It is similarly implicit in the use of coins as chance set-ups that those of their surface features that serve to label one side 'heads' and the other 'tails' are *not* among the properties connected to their propensities. Of coins used in gambling it is known that labelling does not introduce bias (in sense (β) above); coins of which this was known not to be true would not be acceptable gambling devices.

In particular, therefore, reversing a coin's labelling would affect its propensity merely by interchanging the values of the chances of heads and tails. It follows that the application of connectivity would be unaffected by relabelling one of our two coins a and b – say a. Suppose every true proposition ascribing connected properties to b becomes true of a when 'tails' is substituted for 'heads' in the sentence expressing it: connectivity requires the proposition ascribing the propensity D_b to become true of a under a similar substitution.

More precisely, we may express the two applications of connectivity relating the coin b respectively to the labelled and relabelled coin a as follows. Let S_b be the conjunction of all true propositions ascribing to b properties connected to D_b, and let S_a be the proposition obtained from S_b by substituting 'a' for 'b' throughout the sentence expressing it. Then the principle of connectivity asserts that

$$(S_b \equiv S_a) \rightarrow (D_b = D_a). \tag{2}$$

It follows trivially from (1) and (2) that

$$(S_b \equiv S_a) \rightarrow (p_b(H) = p_a(H)). \tag{3}$$

Let S_a^* be the proposition obtained from S_a by carrying out the described substitution of 'tails' for 'heads' and 'heads' for 'tails' throughout the sentence expressing it. The same substitution in the sentence stating that a's propensity is D_a yields a sentence stating that a's propensity is D_a^*, where D_a^* is obtained from D_a by interchanging a's values of $p(H)$ and $p(T)$, i.e.

$$D_a^* = \langle p_a(T), \quad p_a(H), \quad p_a(E) \rangle. \tag{4}$$

Applying the principle of connectivity to a and b after a's labelling has been reversed yields the assertion that

$$(S_b \equiv S_a^*) \to (D_b = D_a^*). \tag{5}$$

It again follows trivially from (1), (4) and (5) that

$$(S_b \equiv S_a^*) \to (p_b(H) = p_a(T)). \tag{6}$$

Now suppose that (3) is exemplified by a and b, i.e. that

$$S_b \equiv S_a. \tag{7}$$

From (3) and (7) we have immediately that

$$p_b(H) = p_a(H). \tag{8}$$

Suppose further that $\quad p_a(H) \neq p_a(T).$ \hfill (9)

(e.g. $p_b(H) = p_a(H) = 0.7$; $p_a(T) = 0.2$).

Then from (8) and (9) $\quad p_b(H) \neq p_a(T).$ \hfill (10)

From (6) and (10) $\quad S_b \not\equiv S_a^*.$ \hfill (11)

From (7) and (11) $\quad S_a \not\equiv S_a^*.$ \hfill (12)

Thus, if (i) a coin b exists related to a by (7) and (ii) a's propensity is such that the chance of heads on a standard toss of it differs from the chance of tails, *then* the truth-value of the conjunction of true propositions ascribing connected properties to a is changed by the substitution of 'tails' for 'heads' and 'heads' for 'tails' throughout the sentence expressing it. In other words, under these conditions connectivity requires an asymmetry in some non-propensity property of a; i.e. roughly, some other property truly ascribed to heads in a must be falsely ascribed to tails.

Condition (i), the existence of the coin b, is guaranteed by the existence of a, since the latter is itself such a coin, whose self-identity entails the necessary truth of (7). Connectivity thus requires any asymmetry in a coin's propensity to land heads and tails to be connected to an asymmetry in some other property. Conversely, if the coin is unbiased in the sense (α) that there is no such asymmetry, connectivity asserts that there is no asymmetry either in the propensity. If heads and tails are in fact the only possible results (i.e. if p_a (E) $=$ 0) we arrive at the proposition S: the chance of heads on a toss of an unbiased coin is $\frac{1}{2}$.

The sense in which S can be stronger than a natural law without being trivially analytic is now clear. Bias may indeed be defined in terms of other properties of the coin, namely those connected to its propensity. It is taken for granted that the properties serving to distinguish heads from tails are not so connected. From this premise, heads and tails being the only possible results, S follows necessarily by the principle of connectivity. Apparent counter examples would be explained away, although not with the trivial ease of (β). A coin with unequal chances of heads and tails is thereby shown to be biased in some other property. If it is unbiased in all known properties, then there must be some other as yet undetected. The independent detection and identification of the unknown property is not, of course, a trivial matter.

It might be objected here that I have claimed to establish a proposition ascribing a precise value of a propensity, despite the account of imprecision given in the last chapter. This is not so. While S is indeed established with an absolutely precise value, the proposition

$$p_a \text{ (H)} = 0.5$$

cannot be so established. (I avail myself here of a convention of imprecision in the scientific use of decimal notation. A quantity is normally given to so many "significant" figures, and an imprecision of 1 in the last unit given is understood. Thus to say that a temperature is 25.3 °C is to say that it is in the interval (25.25, 25.35) °C; if less imprecision is intended the extra digit is put in, thus: 25.30 °C. The convention is not rigidly adhered to; I adopt it here only to indicate that *some* imprecision is implied when '0.5' is used in place of '$\frac{1}{2}$'.) To apply S to a named coin we must show the coin to be unbiased in all its connected properties. Apart from the possibility that some such property has been overlooked, unbiasedness in any one quantity can only be established within limits of imprecision. Suppose we can show the centre of gravity of a coin to be within 0.01 cm of its geometrical centre. Suppose it is known that shifting the centre of gravity 0.01 cm changes the chance of heads by not more than 0.005. Then to know that a coin is unbiased in its mass distribution to within 0.01 cm is to know (setting aside other sources of bias) that the chance of heads lies in the interval (0.495, 0.505). Where several imprecise quantities are involved the relevant laws give imprecision in propensity as a function of that in each of them, as illustrated in Mellor (1965). There is what I there call an 'acceptable interval' of propensity readings consistent with the assumed truth of the laws and the estimated imprecision in each quantity.

So symmetrical propensities of individual coins are established only within intervals of imprecision, and with no more surety than that of the particular laws invoked in their indirect measurement. But that neither detracts from the status of S nor imposes imprecision on the propensity value in it. It remains a regulative principle that *any* deviation from equality, however slight, in the chances of heads and tails is to be explained by asymmetry in other properties.

One might still feel that deriving so classical a propensity must involve principles peculiar to chance. In particular an appeal to classical indifference principles of ignorance, or "insufficient reason", may be suspected of lurking behind the symmetry arguments. To show that this is not so I use an exactly analogous argument to derive the value of a non-chance quantity. I follow this up in the next section by analysing the case of a biased coin, further to point the contrast with classical analysis.

Imagine a rigid air-tight vessel a divided into two parts, called 'heads' and 'tails', by a flexible but impermeable partition. The total volume is known; suppose it to be 1 unit. We wish to know the volumes of the two parts, v_a (H) and v_a (T), when each part is filled with equal masses of the same gas. It is very well established that the volume in each part is a function only of its pressure and temperature. In particular it is taken for granted that the surface features by which we distinguish heads from tails are not connected to their volumes. Let us define an unbiased vessel as one in which the two parts are the same in their connected properties, specifically in pressure and temperature. The principle of connectivity immediately warrants the conclusion that the volumes of heads and tails are equal, i.e.

$$v_a \text{ (H)} = v_a \text{ (T)}.$$

Since we already have that

$$v_a \text{ (H)} + v_a \text{ (T)} = 1$$

if the volume v_a (E) of the partition is neglected, it follows at once that the volume of heads in an unbiased vessel is $\frac{1}{2}$, which is an exact analogue of the propensity proposition S. If the laws relating volume, pressure and temperature of the gas are known, the imprecision in v_a (H) for a particular vessel may similarly be derived from the imprecision in measurements of pressure and temperature.

I have contrived this case to present the most blatant analogy with the standard coin tossing example. Its more artificial features are quite incidental. For example, the total volume may not be known. Then connectivity merely shows the equality of v_a (H) and v_a (T). A reading of one is equally a reading of the other. Similarly the chance p (E) may be finite of a coin landing on its edge. Connectivity then merely shows the chances of heads and tails to be equal. Frequency of heads in a sequence of standard tosses then affords as good a measure of the chance of tails. The main point is that there is no need for all the chances in a distribution to be equal. The present account makes no appeal to ignorance, to carving up the range of possibilities into "a certain number of cases equally possible, that is to say, to such as we may be equally undecided about in regard to their existence" (Laplace, 1819, p. 6). In the case of a die, for instance, one may quite well know that although it is biased towards six, it is not biased between two and five. The chances of two and five, whatever they may be, are equal, even if both are irrational.

We need to recognise the widespread use in measurement of connectivity arguments to show equality of a known with an unknown quantity. To take a simple example, the direct current flowing through an electrical resistance is a function only of the applied potential difference and the determinate value of the resistance. A common method of measuring this value is to vary a known resistance to which the same voltage is applied until the same current passes through each: it then follows by the principle of connectivity that the known and unknown resistances are equal and so a reading of the latter is obtained. This is a special case of the "Wheatstone bridge method [which] is perhaps the most widely used for measurement of d.c. resistance" (Brown, R., 1962*a*, p. 287), where the balancing resistors are equal. In general they are in a known variable ratio which the unknown resistance then bears to the known variable resistance. This complication does not affect the application of connectivity. Similarly with voltage measurement: "the potentiometer [which] is one of the most fundamental instruments of electrical measurement...[measures] an unknown potential difference by balancing it...by a known potential produced by the [known] flow of current in a resistance net-work of known value" (Gall, 1962, p. 613). (For the use of such "null" methods in electrical measurement see Astbury, 1962.)

The present application of connectivity to measuring propensities *via* readings of other quantities merely instances a common technique for indirectly measuring all sort of physical quantities. It is surprising only that propensity should for so long have been thought peculiar in this respect; in particular that inferences to it should be thought to depend on principles of indifference not needed elsewhere. Certainly the inference is fallible. One may be wrong for a number of reasons in thinking a coin unbiased. It may not after all be symmetrical in the supposedly connected properties. The assumed laws connecting the properties may in fact be false; or the conditions for their application may not be satisfied. The coin may be asymmetrical in some unsuspectedly connected property. The prediction that a coin is unbiased is never absolutely certain.

But there is nothing peculiar to propensity in all this. Consider a prediction that a liquid will boil at θ °C because it is of substance X and the pressure is U atmospheres. The prediction may fail: if the pressure in fact is not U atmospheres; if the substance has been wrongly identified; if the assumed vapour pressure law for X is false; if some unknown circumstance is also connected to the boiling point. It would evidently be perverse to conclude either that our faith in the prediction is warranted simply by ignorance of these possible falsifying factors or that it is not warranted at all. And so it is with predictions about propensities based on measurements of other quantities.

BIAS AND IGNORANCE

Suppose we know a coin *a* to be biased but do not know whether its bias favours heads or tails. According to Laplace (1819, p. 56), our ignorance warrants our assigning equal probabilities to heads and tails on our first toss of it:

If there exist in the coin an inequality which causes one of the faces to appear rather than the other without knowing which side is favoured by this inequality, the probability of throwing heads at the first throw will always be $\frac{1}{2}$; because of our ignorance of which face is favoured by the inequality the probability of the simple event is increased if this inequality is favourable to it, just so much is it diminished if the inequality is contrary to it.

9

With probability interpreted as warranted partial belief, the conclusion still seems plausible. Can propensity theory account for it?

The difficulty facing a propensity account in this case is obvious. Whatever true proposition is expressed by the sentence 'The probabilities of heads and tails on the first toss of coin *a* are equal', it is not the proposition that

$$D_a = \langle p_a (\text{H}), \quad p_a (\text{T}), \quad p_a (\text{E}) \rangle$$

is such that

$$p_a (\text{H}) = p_a (\text{T})$$

since the latter proposition is known *ex hypothesi* to be false. The coin is known to be biased, and hence such that either

$$S_1: \ p_a (\text{H}) > p_a (\text{T})$$

or

$$S_2: \ p_a (\text{H}) < p_a (\text{T}).$$

What is taken to be true is that S_1 and S_2, as composite hypotheses about the propensity, have equal probabilities before any tosses of the coin. (A "simple" statistical hypothesis is one that completely specifies a chance distribution; a "composite" hypothesis is a disjunction of simple ones. See Neyman, 1952, p. 22.) These equal probabilities are taken to be objective. I now show that where they exist they display propensities, although not of the coin.

Neither S_1 nor S_2 *prima facie* asserts that an event occurs which is an outcome of a trial on a chance set-up. In fact each does assert this in the relevant sense that the occurrence of such an event is empirically necessary and sufficient for its truth. Equal partial beliefs on the truth of S_1 and S_2 can be warranted by knowledge of the relevant propensity of the set-up in question. I postpone to the last chapter (pp. 165–7) a consideration of when these equal partial beliefs are warranted. Let us waive the question for the present and assume that they are so.

To avoid confusion we have to elaborate our terminology. I represent these "initial" probabilities of S_1 and S_2 by '$P(S_1)$' and '$P(S_2)$' respectively. These are numerically equal to chances of outcomes on a chance set-up yet to be identified. The equal probabilities of heads and tails on the first toss are $P(\text{H})$ and $P(\text{T})$ respectively. They are to be distinguished of course from the unequal chances of heads and tails on that (or any other) toss ($p_a (\text{H})$ and $p_a (\text{T})$) which display the unknown bias of the coin. We have here a case of events seeming to have two objective probabilities, of the sort discussed in chapter 3 (p. 61). We shall see that there is no inconsistency in this; meanwhile it is essential not to mix the probabilities up. I represent conditional probabilities in the usual notation and interpret them for the time being in a Bayesian way (see chapter 2, pp. 47–9).

The claim as to what is taken to be true in this case needs qualifying. To give the required conclusion that P (H) and P (T) are equal, it is in general neither necessary nor sufficient that P (S_1) should equal P (S_2). Consider the special case where S_1 and S_2 are such that on S_1

$$p_a \text{ (H)} = 0.82, \quad p_a \text{ (T)} = 0.18, \quad p_a \text{ (E)} = 0;$$

and on S_2 $\quad p_a \text{ (H)} = 0.43, \quad p_a \text{ (T)} = 0.57, \quad p_a \text{ (E)} = 0.$

S_1 and S_2 are now exhaustive simple hypotheses on which

$$P \text{ (H, } S_1) = 0.82; \quad P \text{ (H, } S_2) = 0.43;$$
$$P \text{ (T, } S_1) = 0.18; \quad P \text{ (T, } S_2) = 0.57.$$

Then, by an elementary theorem of the probability calculus (Feller, 1957, p. 106, equation (1.8)), since S_1 and S_2 are exclusive and exhaustive,

$$\left. \begin{aligned} P \text{ (H)} &= P \text{ (H, } S_1) \, P \text{ (} S_1) + P \text{ (H, } S_2) \, P \text{ (} S_2), \\ P \text{ (T)} &= P \text{ (T, } S_1) \, P \text{ (} S_1) + P \text{ (T, } S_2) \, P \text{ (} S_2). \end{aligned} \right\} \tag{13}$$

The assumption that $\quad P \text{ (} S_1) = P \text{ (} S_2) = \frac{1}{2}$ $\qquad\qquad$ (14) here yields the result

$$P \text{ (H)} = 0.625; \quad P \text{ (T)} = 0.375.$$

Hence the assumption is not sufficient for P (H) to equal P (T). The same special case also shows the assumption to be unnecessary, since the result

$$P \text{ (H)} = P \text{ (T)} = \frac{1}{2} \tag{15}$$

here follows from the incompatible assumption

$$P \text{ (} S_1) = 0.4; \quad P \text{ (} S_2) = 0.6.$$

But the knowledge assumed in this case is extremely esoteric. It is not known which way the coin is biased, but it is known that if it is biased towards heads the bias is greater than if it is biased towards tails. This curious blend of knowledge and ignorance is indeed not explicable on the present account. It does not follow from knowledge of any propensity. But equally it is not the case intended by Laplace, nor is it one in which assumed knowledge of the objective probabilities P(H) and P(T) has any intuitive plausibility. There is nothing obviously objective here to account for.

Laplace clearly supposes that whatever knowledge there is of the bias is symmetrical between heads and tails. In the simplest case, the extent of the bias would be known. It might be known that the chances of heads and tails, respectively, are either o.6 and o.4 (S_1) or o.4 and o.6 (S_2). If the precise extent of the bias is not known, it is still assumed that whatever is known of the chance of heads on hypothesis S_1 is known of the chance of tails on hypothesis S_2. Strictly, we assume that each of a pair of sentences expressing S_1 and S_2 may be obtained from the other by substituting 'heads' for 'tails' and 'tails' for 'heads' throughout. This excludes all such special cases as the one just considered, and now assuming equal probabilities for S_1 and S_2 *is* both necessary and sufficient for equality between P (H) and P (T).

On these assumptions, a convenient measure q_a of the coin's bias is the magnitude of the difference between the chance of heads and the chance of tails. That is,

$$q_a = |p_a (H) - p_a (T)| \tag{16}$$

which is invariant under the permitted transformations between S_1 and S_2.

We have excluded pairs of hypotheses differing in the extent of the bias they ascribe to the coin. Even so, there is oddity in claiming both to know, however imprecisely, the bias of a coin and not to know which way it is biased. (I exclude the uninteresting special case where a better informed person simply fails to pass on all his knowledge.) Knowledge of a coin's bias comes directly from statistical evidence for the coin's propensity or indirectly from knowledge of its other connected properties. These must evidently relate peculiarly to one side of the coin if they are to provide knowledge of bias. In these circumstances, not to know which way the coin is biased is just not to know how its sides are labelled. This is a perfectly intelligible state of ignorance. There is no need for the sides of a coin to be labelled when it is made or when its propensity is fixed. A coin may become biased by bending, for example, after it is labelled; the labelling could be reversed subsequent to its biasing.

It may be taken as well established in current British society that a coin of the realm will not have been relabelled since it was minted. Everyone is equally convinced, rightly or wrongly, that British coins as minted are unbiased (within limits of conceptual imprecision). Bias is introduced into coins later, if at all, by some quite independent process.

Let us again exclude cases of concealed knowledge that a coin has been deliberately biased towards heads; nothing is to follow merely from ignorance. We appeal instead to our earlier assumption (p. 124) that the surface features of a coin that distinguish heads from tails are not among the properties connected to its propensity. Any natural process by which a coin becomes biased would be quite unaffected by reversing the labelling of the coin. The same bias would simply have been imparted towards heads instead of tails or *vice versa*.

Consider a coin that is in fact biased. Call the side with the greater chance of falling uppermost in a standard toss 'the likely side' and the other side 'the unlikely side'. These are determinate sides of the coin, detectable by measurements of its propensity while it is biased and reidentifiable by surface features at any time. At some time, before or after becoming biased, the likely side will have been labelled either 'heads' or 'tails'. A device for doing this is kept at the Royal Mint; let us hereafter call it 'the Mint'. There is only one Mint, while there are many natural biasing processes. We consequently ascribe to the processes rather than to the Mint a propensity to make heads (say) the likely side of a biased coin. But this, as we have seen with such other dispositions as solubility, is a matter of convention (chapter 4, p. 74). Let us instead for expository convenience assume a standard repertoire of biasing processes and settle the propensity on the Mint. Let us further assume that the Mint is in other respects standard and that its variable propensity is a function only of properties of the coin being labelled. It is conceivable for example that a magnetised coin would be more likely to have its "north face" labelled 'heads' than 'tails', or that a bent coin would be more likely to have 'heads' stamped on its convex than on its concave side.

In these terms our pious convictions about biased British coins come to this: the properties distinguishing the likely from the unlikely sides (i.e. which *are* properties connected to the propensity displayed in a coin toss) are *not* connected to the propensity displayed in its labelling. The Mint is *not* more likely to label 'heads' the "north face" of a coin that subsequently becomes biased by being magnetised. Nor is a subsequently bent coin more likely to have 'heads' stamped on what will be its convex side. (When labelled, in fact, British coins have not yet acquired the asymmetrical properties connected to their propensities to land heads. So it is hardly surprising that they are unconnected to the Mint's labelling propensity.) A connectivity argument like that of the last section can now be applied. Let C_a be the determinate propensity expressed by the ordered pair

$$\langle p_a \text{ (L)}, \; p_a \text{ (U)} \rangle,$$

where p_a (L) and p_a (U) are the determinate values for coin a of the determinable chances p (L) and p (U) of the likely and unlikely sides respectively of a biased coin having been labelled 'heads' by the Mint. Clearly

$$p_a \text{ (L)} + p_a \text{ (U)} = 1.$$

Similarly for another coin b.

Now let R_b be the conjunction of all true propositions ascribing to b properties connected to C_b. Let R_a be the proposition obtained from R_b by substituting 'a' for 'b' throughout the sentence expressing R_b. Then connectivity asserts that

$$(R_b \equiv R_a) \rightarrow (C_b = C_a)$$

and hence, trivially,

$$(R_b \equiv R_a) \rightarrow (p_b \text{ (L)} = p_a \text{ (L)}).$$

Let R_a^* be the proposition obtained from R_a by substituting 'the likely side' for 'the unlikely side' and *vice versa* in the sentence expressing R_a. The same substitution in the sentence stating that the Mint's propensity to label coin a is C_a yields one stating that its propensity is C_a^*, where C_a^* is obtained from C_a by interchanging p_a (U) and p_a (L), i.e.

$$C_a^* = \langle p_a \text{ (U)}, \; p_a \text{ (L)} \rangle.$$

The features distinguishing the likely from the unlikely side are not connected to the propensity displayed in labelling the coin. So the application of connectivity to a and b is unaffected by this transformation and yields the assertion

$$(R_b \equiv R_a^*) \rightarrow (C_b = C_a^*);$$

whence, again trivially,

$$(R_b \equiv R_b^*) \rightarrow (p_b \text{ (L)} = p_a \text{ (U)}).$$

From here the argument goes exactly as in the last section, yielding the conclusion that, for any coin a, connectivity requires a difference between p_a (U) and p_a (L) to be explained by a change in truth value of R_a under the transformation to R_a^*. But the properties distinguishing the likely from the unlikely sides are not connected to the labelling propensity. Hence the terms 'the likely side' and 'the unlikely side' need not occur in the sentence expressing R_a. In which case the prescribed transformation cannot change the truth value of R_a since it leaves the sentence expressing it completely unaltered. R_a and R_a^* will be materially equivalent for the conclusive reason that they are identical. Thus the chances of the likely and the unlikely sides being labelled 'heads' are equal; these being the only possible results, the chance of each is $\frac{1}{2}$.

But the proposition that the likely side of the biased coin a is heads is the proposition S_1, which says that

$$p_a (H) > p_a (T).$$

Similarly for proposition S_2. We thus have

$$P(S_1) = p_a (L) = p_a (U) = P(S_2) = \frac{1}{2}$$

which is assumption (14) above (p. 131) that the initial probabilities of S_1 and S_2 are equal. Under the conditions there assumed it follows at once that the probabilities $P(H)$ and $P(T)$ are equal. Let the coin's bias be q_a, given by equation (16) above. For all q_a and $p_a(E)$ we have

$$
\begin{aligned}
&S_1: p_a (H) = \tfrac{1}{2} (1 - p_a(E) + q_a); \; p_a (T) = \tfrac{1}{2} (1 - p_a(E) - q_a); \\
&S_2: p_a (H) = \tfrac{1}{2} (1 - p_a(E) - q_a); \; p_a (T) = \tfrac{1}{2} (1 - p_a(E) + q_a).
\end{aligned}
\quad (17)
$$

From (17) we have at once

$$P(H, S_1) = P(T, S_2) = \tfrac{1}{2} (1 - p_a(E) + q_a),$$
$$P(H, S_2) = P(T, S_1) = \tfrac{1}{2} (1 - p_a(E) - q_a).$$

Applying equations (13) above,

$$
\begin{aligned}
P(H) &= \tfrac{1}{2} (1 - p_a(E) + q) \times \tfrac{1}{2} + \tfrac{1}{2} (1 - p_a(E) - q) \times \tfrac{1}{2} \\
&= \tfrac{1}{2} (1 - p_a(E)) = P(T). \quad (18)
\end{aligned}
$$

If there is no chance of the coin falling on its edge (18) reduces to (15)

$$P(H) = P(T) = \tfrac{1}{2}.$$

Thus equal probabilities of the propositions that a tossed coin will fall heads and tails display a propensity in the labelling set-up. Where the conclusion of Laplace's classical argument from ignorance is correct it follows from empirical knowledge of propensities displayed in coin labelling situations. The further frequency evidence of coin tosses relates directly to the bias of the coin. How it should affect the initial probabilities we have established is a matter for Bayesian argument. We are concerned only that the initial probabilities are neither *a priori*, subjective nor warranted merely by ignorance. Their objectivity is a consequence of their displaying a propensity. We thus escape the dilemma of having to accept a classical analysis because of the obvious existence of classical probabilities, or of having to deny their existence because of the equally obvious defects of classical analysis. In the last two sections of this chapter I examine the views of Kneale (1949), who has taken the former course, and of Hacking (1965), who has taken the latter.

THE CLASSICAL ARGUMENT

Lady Bracknell: Ignorance is like a delicate exotic fruit; touch it, and the bloom is gone.

Wilde, *The Importance of Being Ernest*, Act I

I have used connectivity arguments to derive some classical propensities from empirical, though not frequency, evidence. Similar arguments will obviously establish other classical propensities: for example, an equal distribution of chances over throwing the faces of a die known to be "true" in its connected properties. The argument nowhere appeals to ignorance, and the notorious paradoxes (see, e.g. Keynes, 1921, part 1, chapter 4) are easily avoided. 'Throwing a 6' and 'throwing an odd number' are not equiprobable alternative outcomes; nor does ignorance of the bias in connected properties between them suffice to make them so.

In general, the use of connectivity to justify assigning equal probabilities is restricted to systems whose other properties are known to be symmetrical in the relevant respects. In the games of chance to which classical probability was originally and is appropriately applied, this symmetry is deliberately contrived. Even so positive empirical evidence is needed to show that the contrivance has been successful in a given instance. One does not need to know exactly what would bias a die or a coin; it suffices to know it to be unbiased in every property suspected of being connected to its propensity. Still, one may overlook something, and it is not the overlooking that makes the chances equal. It is even more necessary to insist on this point in investigating the uncontrived natural phenomena that concern science most, especially since Kneale (1949, part 3) has made an influential attempt to extend an essentially classical analysis to such cases.

The classical element in Kneale's account of probability is the insistence that probabilities are to be understood in terms of numbers of equiprobable alternatives. In the language of the probability calculus this means that the sample points must be assigned equal probabilities. If two apparently simple events (i.e. results of chance trials) differ in probability, this shows at least the more probable event to be in fact a compound event, an outcome containing more than one result (see chapter 3, pp. 58–9 and Feller, 1957, p. 14, for this terminology). Kneale does not claim to give an *a priori* method of finding equiprobable alternatives and hence chance distributions: 'The range theory...is wrongly conceived as a method for determining probabilities *a priori*' (p. 185). What he claims is that every distribution is to be interpreted as a distribution over equiprobable results. We must take this to be stronger than the trivial claim that any quantity can be understood in terms of some number of its units (which is all that Keynes' assertion (1921, p. 41) that "in order that numerical measurement may be possible, we must be given a number of *equally* probable alternatives" seems to amount to). A volume can be regarded as a number of equal unit volumes, and a temperature difference as a number of equal centigrade degrees. Kneale's claim cannot be the unremarkable one that every chance, say 0.3, is a number N of chances each $0.3/N$. It must be that there really are in every case ultimate alternative results each with such equal chances: 'The *chances* of which gamblers and theorists alike have spoken so often in the plural are simply equipossible alternatives' (Kneale, 1949, p. 181).

Every outcome of a chance trial must on Kneale's account contain an integral number of these ultimate chances. The number need not be finite; statistical probabilities are not restricted to rational values (cf. Braithwaite, 1953, p. 130):

Although primary sets of equipossible alternatives are basic in the theory of chance, we cannot safely define the probability of an α thing's being β as the proportion of the alternatives in such a set under α-ness which involve β-ness. For we have no guarantee that even the principal set under α-ness with reference to β-ness will be finite. On the contrary, we have good reason to believe that in very many cases this principal set must be infinite. (Kneale, 1949, p. 181.)

Kneale introduces the concept of a *range* of equiprobable alternatives to deal with non-finite cases. I discuss such an example later; but first we need to ask why, even in the finite case, *equal* probabilities are supposed to be so much more intelligible than unequal ones as to provide an acceptable analysis of them.

Kneale's term (above) is 'equipossible', not 'equiprobable', but for the desired conclusion to follow the terms must be taken to be synonymous. The question remains: on what principle must results (as opposed to outcomes) of trials always be assigned equal rather than unequal chances? Although Kneale disclaims any intention of providing a method for settling chance distribution, I can only take him to suppose that equal chances are easier to establish than unequal ones. To this extent he subscribes to a principle of indifference. It is true that he rejects it in the form he attributes to Laplace:

We may call alternatives equiprobable if we do not know that the available evidence provides a reason for preferring any one to any other. (Kneale, 1949, p. 173.)

Kneale's own position is stated thus:

We are entitled to treat alternatives as equiprobable if, but only if, we know that the available evidence does not provide a reason for preferring any one to any other.

But this is still too weak, as is Jeffreys' (1961, p. 33) formulation:

To say that the probabilities are equal is a precise way of saying that we have no ground for choosing between the alternatives...if we do not take the prior probabilities equal we are expressing confidence in one rather than another before the data are available, and this must be done only from definite reason. To take the prior probabilities different in the absence of observational reason for doing so would be an expression of sheer prejudice.

– but no more so than to take them equal in the same circumstances. We had occasion to remark in chapter 1 (pp. 6–7) that lack of belief does not entail partial belief. Equally, a lack of different partial beliefs on two topics does not entail equal partial beliefs in them. And the same goes for chances, which are the objective grounds of partial belief. Available evidence, when seriously incomplete, may provide reason neither for preferring nor for not preferring one alternative possibility to another. The sufficiently strong formulation is:

> 'We are entitled to treat alternatives as equiprobable if, but only if, we know that the available evidence provides a reason for not preferring any one to any other.'

On this formulation it is clear that evidence may as well provide reason for a preference as for a lack of it. There is nothing more fundamental in the latter that warrants its use to explicate cases of the former. I have indeed produced connectivity arguments from evidence of symmetry in other respects to equality of chances; but evidence of symmetry is no more profound or easier to come by than evidence of asymmetry. Incomplete evidence may equally suggest symmetry where there is asymmetry and suggest asymmetry where there is symmetry. '*Ceteris paribus*' clauses are as much needed in the one case as in the other. I have in any case been at pains to show that equal chances established by connectivity arguments are nothing like Kneale's "ultimate alternatives". A coin may be unbiased in that its chances of landing heads and tails are equal, but there may still be a smaller, finite chance of it landing on its edge. What the ultimate alternatives are in this case is as unclear as in the case of a biased coin.

When we turn to infinite "primary sets of equipossible alternatives", a classical approach becomes even less plausible. Kneale considers the chance that an α-thing is also β, and tries to meet the difficulty that there may be more than one equally fundamental measure of a range of α-ness, leading to conflicting values of the chance. That Kneale feels it essential to meet this difficulty is shown by his assertion (1949, p. 183) that "to admit two different ways of measuring the range would be to abandon all hopes of formulating an objectivist theory of probability".

Part of Kneale's argument is perfectly acceptable, since he is prepared to use empirical information about a set-up to exclude certain measures as inappropriate. He shows for example how the "puzzles of Bertrand's paradox disappear when a practical method for selecting a chord at random is specified" (p. 185). This well-known paradox (discussed also in Neyman, 1952, pp. 15–18) concerns the chance that a chord drawn "at random" to a circle will be longer than the side of an equilateral triangle inscribed in the circle. If the angle the chord makes to a given line is taken to measure the range of possibilities, the chance is $\frac{1}{3}$ (figure 6); if the distance between the centres of the chord and circle is taken as the measure, the chance is $\frac{1}{2}$ (figure 7); if the area of a concentric circle to which the chord is a tangent, $\frac{1}{4}$ (figure 8). Not more than one measure is appropriate to a particular set-up. Drawing the chord along the line of a previously spun pointer whose axis is on the edge of the circle excludes the distance and area measures; letting its centre be fixed by the first drop of rain to fall within the circle excludes the angle and distance measures. So far so good, but it is not enough. An infinite number of non-linear measures remain of each of angle, distance

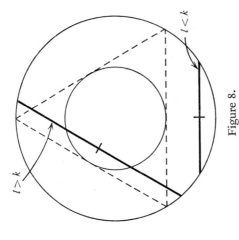

l > k

l < k

Figure 8.

The area of the circle is A.

For $l > k$: the mid-point of the chord lies in an area of magnitude $A/4$, i.e. within the inner circle.

For $l < k$: the mid-point of the chord lies in an area of magnitude $3A/4$, i.e. outside the inner circle.

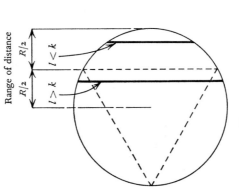

Range of distance

$R/2$ $R/2$

$l > k$ $l < k$

Figure 7.

The radius of the circle is R.

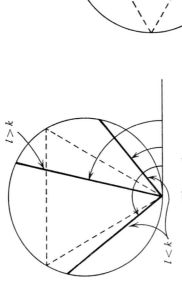

l > k

l < k

Figure 6.

For $l > k$: the range of angles from the tangent is 60–120°, i.e. the chord lies within the angle of the triangle.

For $l < k$: the range of angles from the tangent is 0–60°, 120–180°, i.e. the chord lies outside the angle of the triangle.

In each figure l = length of chord (———); k = length of side of inscribed triangle (– – –).

and area. Only positive empirical information justifies our excluding them and so arriving at the requisitely unique measure. As before, it is not sufficient for the available evidence to give us no reason for preferring any one equal area (say) of the circle to any other: it must give us reason not to have such preference. To know enough about a chance set-up to choose the right measure of the range of possible results is to know directly the chance distribution the measure is supposed to establish. The general point has been made by Will (1954, p. 23). But the flaw in Kneale's answer (p. 188) to this anticipated objection has not been sufficiently exposed.

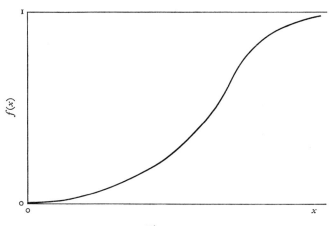

Figure 9.

Kneale needs to show that, where there are apparently distinct and equally fundamental measures of the same range of possibilities, they will nevertheless yield the same chance distribution. He relies (pp. 142–4) on generalising a theorem of Poincaré's (1913, p. 403). Poincaré takes the example of a spinning pointer and considers the chance $f(x)$ that it will travel an angular distance x before stopping. He assumes reasonably that this cumulative chance is a continuous and everywhere differentiable function of x. Figure 9 shows a sketch of a plausible function f; figure 10 sketches its derivative f' with respect to x. Then, for any such f, if a and b are two *sufficiently close* values of x, it follows that the chance of the pointer stopping between a and $\frac{1}{2}(a+b)$ differs from the chance of it stopping between $\frac{1}{2}(a+b)$ and b by less than any stipulated amount, however small. For sufficiently close a and b the

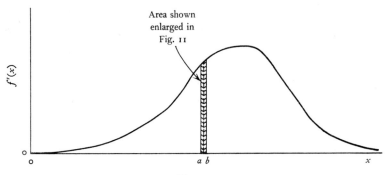

Figure 10.

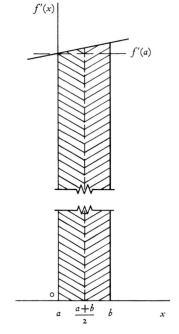

Figure 11.

◫ Area = chance of pointer stopping between a and $\dfrac{a+b}{2} \doteq \tfrac{1}{2}\,(b-a)f'(a)$;

▨ Area = chance of pointer stopping between $\dfrac{a+b}{2}$ and $b \doteq \tfrac{1}{2}(b-a)\,f'(a)$.

chance is simply $\frac{1}{2}$ $(b$-$a)f'$ (a) as shown on figure 11. Kneale then argues that if the pointer is spun hard enough these "sufficiently close" values a and b may be taken to differ by 2π. So whatever the overall shape of the function f there is an effectively equal chance of the pointer stopping in any equiangular sector of the circle. This further inference is invalid. The trouble lies in the words 'sufficiently close'. That a sufficiently small interval (a, b) *exists* is true; that this interval includes any interval of interest (in this case one of length 2π) does not follow at all, however short the interval of interest may be.

Consequently, the general conclusion Kneale draws (p. 189) from Poincaré's theorem, and which his theory admittedly requires, is false:

> If, as seems reasonable, it can be assumed (*a*) that of any two connected variables [*x* and *y*] which are equally fundamental each is a continuous analytic [i.e. every-where differentiable] function of the other and (*b*) that by either scale of measurement the range of α-ness is a small part of the configuration space in which it lies, we are entitled to say that metrical relations *within* the range of α-ness will be approximately the same, whether the variation of x or that of y be chosen as a dimension of the configuration space.

It is not enough to know that "the range of α-ness is a small part. . .": it must be a *sufficiently* small part for the degree of approximation (i.e. imprecision) required. To know this is already to know the conclusion it is desired to establish. The same objection holds against Kneale's further analogy from map-making (p. 189):

> When two maps of a continent are made according to different projections, regions represented by equal areas in one map may be represented by markedly unequal areas in the other. If, however, we consider only those part of the same two maps which correspond to a single county, we find that the differences introduced by different methods of projection are negligible; parishes which are represented in the one by equal areas are represented also in the other by approximately equal areas.

Again the problem remains: given the degree of approximation, to show that particular pairs of parishes or counties are *sufficiently* small to be represented by equally equal areas on both projections. Knowledge that this is so is no more easily come by than knowledge that it is not so.

The invalidity of the classical argument and the proper application of connectivity may be illustrated in Kneale's own example. Let x be the angular distance travelled by a spinning pointer, and let another measure of the range be

$$y = x + m \sin x, \tag{19}$$

where $0 < m \leqslant 1$ is a constant. Then x and y satisfy Kneale's criteria

(p. 187) for being equally fundamental and "each is a continuous analytic function of the other". Then if the cumulative chance function $f(x)$ is continuous and everywhere differentiable, so is its counterpart $g(y)$.

Now suppose $g(y)$ to be such that any interval of length

$$y_1 - y_0 = 2\pi = x_1 - x_0$$

is "sufficiently small". That is, the chance p of the pointer stopping in any small interval (a, b) whose measure Δy is less than 2π is directly proportional to Δy:

$$p = k\Delta y, \qquad (20)$$

where k is a constant. In particular this is true for a sub-interval small enough for its measure δy to be given by

$$\delta y = \frac{dy}{dx} \delta x. \qquad (21)$$

Hence from (19), (20) and (21)

$$p = k\,\delta y$$

$$= k\frac{dy}{dx}\,\delta x$$

$$= k\,(1 + m\cos x)\,\delta x$$

The chance that the pointer will stop in a small sector of angular width δx is thus *not* directly proportional to δx. It varies between

$$\left. \begin{array}{lll} k\,(1 + m)\,\delta x & \text{at} & x = 2n\pi, \\ \text{and} \quad k\,\delta x & \text{at} & x = (2n+1)\pi \end{array} \right\} \quad (n = 0, 1, 2, \ldots).$$

Any one of an indefinitely large number of measures y (corresponding to different values of m) of the range of possible stopping places of the spinning pointer could satisfy the condition (20). To each corresponds a cumulative chance function $f(x)$ of which Kneale's conclusion is false. The derivative of one such function is sketched in figure 12. It could easily express the propensity of a magnetised pointer spun in a magnetic field. However hard the pointer is spun there are substantially unequal chances of it stopping in equiangular sectors of a circle. Such a pointer shows also how more information is needed to resolve Bertrand's paradox than Kneale admits. Suppose its stopping place were used to fix the angle of the chord. The chance of the chord being longer than the side of the inscribed triangle depends on where its axis is placed. The chances will differ if it is placed on the west and north sides of the circle, and neither is likely to be $\frac{1}{3}$.

In this case as in every other such a propensity can only be excluded by positive evidence that the connected properties – e.g. magnetic properties – of the set-up are absent. It is of course possible that no connected property of the pointer discriminates between some pair of sectors of the circle. If so, connectivity will require that the propensity

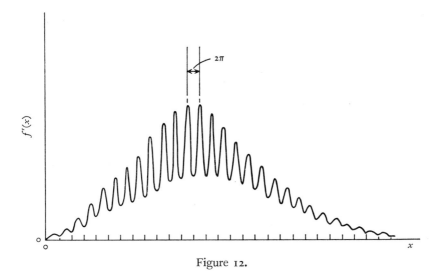

Figure 12.

of the pointer to stop there does not do so either. In a particular case this might be true of every pair of equiangular sectors.

(The analogy between spun pointers and tossed coins can be pushed further. There is an analogue of Laplace's biased coin. Consider a magnetised pointer in a known magnetic field. The two opposite ends of the pointer are labelled 'heads' and 'tails' respectively; it is not known whether heads or tails is the north pole of the pointer. Mark off a semicircle round the pointer symmetrically disposed about a line through the pointer's axis in the direction of the field. Say the pointer 'lands heads' if it stops with heads within this semicircle. We know that the chance of this is either greater or less than $\frac{1}{2}$ – the pointer is biased, but we do not know which way. There may then be equal objective probabilities of the pointer landing heads and tails on its first spin. If so, the propensity displayed is that of a labelling or magnetising device: the chance of the north pole being labelled 'heads', or of heads being made the north pole, is supposed to be $\frac{1}{2}$.)

I conclude that there is no easier or more *a priori* knowledge to be had of equal than of unequal chances, and therefore that there is no justification for analysing the latter in terms of the former. True conclusions of classical arguments can be established by applying connectivity to empirical knowledge of related symmetries in some set-up. Equality of chances can be shown in this way, but no more readily than inequality of chances.

THE FIDUCIAL ARGUMENT

I have shown the empirical basis of some seemingly *a priori* probabilities and rejected classical arguments for them. I now consider Hacking's fiducial argument (1965, chapter 9) for corresponding posterior probabilities in Laplace's case of the biased coin, relating its assumptions to those of the connectivity argument. The term 'fiducial' is taken from the work of Fisher (e.g. 1959, pp. 51–7), of which Hacking claims (p. 140) to have given a consistent reconstruction: 'Fisher invented the fiducial argument. At any rate, I suppose that what he called the fiducial argument must, if it has any validity, take something like the course described above.' Both the connectivity and the fiducial arguments apply under the same conditions, namely that the hypotheses S_1 and S_2 ascribe the same (perhaps unknown) bias q_a to the coin. The fiducial argument then yields the posterior probabilities of S_1 and S_2 that follow by conditionalisation from the prior probabilities given by the connectivity argument. Since Hacking claims to assume nothing about prior probabilities, this calls for explanation.

Hacking's general thesis about inductive support may be granted at once. If scientists need a measure of inductive support for hypotheses it will always be of inductive support on some evidence. If the measure is probabilistic, what scientists need are posterior probabilities, not prior ones. The problem of measuring support is that of finding a consistent method of assigning posterior probabilities. This can either be done directly, or indirectly by assigning prior probabilities and conditionalising. The objection to classical methods is not that they assign prior probabilities but that they are inconsistent. Indifference principles can be used to assign incompatible prior probabilities to the same proposition. It is equally an objection to the fiducial argument as used by Fisher that it can be used to assign incompatible posterior probabilities (Hacking, 1965, p. 151).

It is no objection to a method which yields consistent posterior probabilities that it does so *via* prior probabilities. Still less is it an objection that Bayes' theorem can always be used to derive prior from posterior probabilities. There is no need to interpret prior probabilities as measures of inductive support at all if the concept of support by no evidence is found objectionable. This point needs making to cover cases where prior distributions fail to satisfy the probability axioms (Hacking, 1965, pp. 192–4; Jeffreys, 1961, §3.1). It needs making also to meet the following objection to Bayesian methods: any posterior probability can be derived from some prior probability; there can be no objective basis for assigning one prior probability rather than another, since they are probabilities relative to no evidence; hence there can be no objective basis for assigning one posterior probability rather than another. (See Kyburg (1963, p. 198) in the discussion of Braithwaite (1963) who showed that *any* statistical decision strategy is equivalent to *some* Bayesian strategy of assigning prior probabilities and then settling for the hypothesis with the highest posterior probability.) The apparent virtue of the fiducial argument is that it assigns posterior probabilities independently. It assumes no prior distribution. Prior probabilities may then be derivable from Bayes' theorem, but they are redundant. No sense need be made of them.

Whether there could be any consistent and compelling method of assigning absolutely prior probabilities seems to me an open question. The connectivity argument applied to Laplace's coin is certainly not such a method. The probabilities it establishes are prior only to the frequency evidence obtained from coin tossing. They are not prior to all evidence.

Hacking (pp. 136–45) only deals with the special case

$$p_a(E) = 0; \quad q_a = 0.2;$$

where the competing hypotheses S_1 and S_2 become

$$S_1: \quad p_a(H) = 0.6; \quad p_a(T) = 0.4;$$
$$S_2: \quad p_a(H) = 0.4; \quad p_a(T) = 0.6.$$

His argument applies however to any pair of hypotheses S_1 and S_2 that satisfy equations (17) of p. 135 above. It is convenient to consider the more general argument in order to see why it applies just when connectivity also applies. Hacking starts by defining a new kind of derivative trial, of which the two possible results are

o   if   H occurs and S_2 is true

or T occurs and S_1 is true;

1   if   H occurs and S_1 is true

or T occurs and S_2 is true.

The chance distribution over the results of this trial is known because it is independent of whether S_1 or S_2 is true. From equations (17) we have

$$p_a (0) = \tfrac{1}{2} (1 - p_a(E) - q_a);$$
$$p_a (1) = \tfrac{1}{2} (1 - p_a(E) + q_a).$$

It is essential to the fiducial argument that the chance distribution of the derivative trial should be fixed in this way. Such trials are called 'pivotal' (Hacking, 1965, p. 140). The necessary and sufficient condition for this derivative trial to be pivotal is obviously that the chances of heads and tails on hypothesis S_1 equal respectively the chances of tails and heads on S_2. This we have seen (pp. 131–2) to be precisely the case to which the connectivity argument applies.

In this case it follows at once from Hacking's "frequency principle" (see p. 67 above) that the probabilities of the propositions that o and 1 respectively will occur at the first trial, relative to this evidence, are

$$P (0) = \tfrac{1}{2} (1 - p_a(E) - q_a),$$
$$P (1) = \tfrac{1}{2} (1 - p_a(E) + q_a). \tag{22}$$

Now suppose the trial occurs and the result is tails. How does this extra evidence affect the probabilities of o and 1? On Hacking's *principle of irrelevance* it affects them not at all. Without fully developing his terminology we can say that, for Hacking, extra evidence is irrelevant to a choice of hypotheses if it leaves their relative likelihoods unaltered (Hacking, 1965, p. 141). In terms of his logic of support he shows that this condition is satisfied here. In an earlier passage he argues informally (pp. 138–9):

It may seem that. . .occurrence of tails. . .is simply irrelevant to whether or not o has occurred. This may appear from considerations of symmetry in the definition of o and 1. Or you may reflect that occurrence of o means that either heads or tails occurred, and whichever it was, the odds were in favour of what actually happened; occurrence of 1 means that either heads or tails occurred, and that the odds were against what actually happened. . . . Learning that tails happened is no help at all to guessing whether o happened.

Hence the probabilities of o and 1, relative to the extra evidence that tails occurred, remain at the values given in (22). "But as o is defined, occurrence of tails implies that o occurs if and only if S_1 is true. Hence by the logic of support" (p. 139)

$$P\,(S_1,\,T)\ =\ P\,(o)\ =\ \tfrac{1}{2}\,(1-p_a(E)-q_a),\Big\}$$
$$P\,(S_2,\,T)\ =\ P\,(1)\ =\ \tfrac{1}{2}\,(1-p_a(E)+q_a)\ \Big\} \qquad (23)$$

and similarly if heads is the result.

Thus Hacking derives posterior probabilities for S_1 and S_2 on either possible result, heads or tails, of a single toss of the coin. It is elementary to show that these probabilities derive by conditionalisation from the prior probabilities

$$P\,(S_1)\ =\ P\,(S_2)\ =\ \tfrac{1}{2}.$$

Of this connection with the classical prior probabilities Hacking observes (p. 147):

It is true that there is a residual, if unformalisable, intuition that if the chance of heads must be either 0.4 or 0.6, then, lacking other information, each of the alternatives is equally well supported by the feeble data available. So it is pleasant that our theory should not conflict with this tempting alleged intuition. But mere lack of conflict with something so nebulous cannot be taken as evidence that our foundations are correct.

We have seen that the intuition is not so unformalisable, and the data are not so feeble, as Hacking here supposes. Where the connectivity argument applies, it is not merely pleasant but essential that Hacking's argument should yield a compatible conclusion. But the connectivity argument rests on empirical data of which the fiducial argument seems to take no account. It is worth enquiring whether the latter has implicit empirical premises equivalent to those the connectivity argument employs explicitly.

The applications of Bayes' theorem and the relation of chance to degree of support have not been in question on either theory. What is in question is Hacking's application of his principle of irrelevance, which he claims (p. 140) to be essential to consistent use of the fiducial argument. What the principle of irrelevance claims in this case is that "learning that tails happened is no help at all to guessing whether o happened". Now in our earlier terminology what happens if o occurs is that *the unlikely side* of the coin comes up – the side, whether heads or tails, with the lesser chance. If 1 occurs what has happened is that *the likely side* has come up. That a particular side comes up is manifestly not irrelevant to whether or not *that side is the likely side*. What Hacking claims to be irrelevant is that *that side has been labelled 'heads'*. It is surely obvious that this information is irrelevant if and only if the likely and unlikely sides had equal chances of being so labelled. To know that the result tails is irrelevant to the hypothesis that the result o occurs is to know that those chances are equal. This is just the knowledge derived by the connectivity argument from empirical evidence of the independence of coin labelling and coin tossing set-ups. But relative to this evidence we have directly equal prior probabilities of S_1 and S_2. Lacking this evidence, the principle of irrelevance cannot be known to apply and the fiducial argument for the corresponding posterior probabilities fails.

Thus, while the fiducial argument does not assume prior probabilities directly, it does assume facts about propensities which equally warrant them. The objection to prior probabilities, that they are relative to no evidence, is here seen to be misplaced. It is a virtue of the connectivity argument to make explicit the extra propensity evidence tacitly assumed in the fiducial argument.

It must be said that the fiducial argument is far more general; in such other applications as the theory of errors and cases where the prior distribution is not probabilistic, there is no obvious connectivity counterpart of it. The convergence of the two arguments in the biased coin case may thus be a coincidence. If so, it is at least as curious as it is gratifying. What their general relationship may be I do not know, but the following observations seem to me pertinent. The connectivity argument makes no use of Bayesian inference in deriving from propensities what here count as prior probabilities. Nor does the fiducial argument use Bayesian inference in deriving its posterior probability after one toss. But Bayesian inference is needed to relate the two, and we have noted in chapter 2 (pp. 47–9) a distinct lack of rationale for it. The apparent fortuitousness of the agreement in this case may merely reflect that fact. But the lack of rationale for Bayesian inference affects the fiducial argument more than the connectivity argument. There is not much point in having a probability posterior to one toss that cannot be conditionalised to probabilities posterior to many tosses. Whereas it is no matter to propensity theory if there are no objective probabilities relative to evidence between full knowledge of a labelling propensity and full knowledge of a coin's bias.

8 Determinism and laws of nature

IF PROPENSITIES are ever displayed, determinism is false. Every event may still have a cause; in particular the results of chance trials may have causes. But their trials cannot be their causes either directly or indirectly. Roughly speaking, "causal chains" end in chance trials. Causal talk is not really illuminating in statistical contexts. It is unprofitable to ask whether "the outcome or the result of a trial" is "in any way due to the trial" (Watling, 1969, p. 41). Chance is not a sort of weak or intermittently successful causal link. I have avoided causal concepts in my account of chance. Still, something should be said of its relation to determinism.

On the present account a statistical law asserts of *each* trial of a certain kind that on it there is the stated chance p of some outcome. Where a statistical law is put in some such common form as

$$\text{'}100\,p\%\text{ of } F \text{ are } G\text{'}, \tag{1}$$

this sentence must be taken to state that

$$\textit{all } F \text{ have a chance } p \text{ of being } G. \tag{2}$$

It is as much a universal proposition as it is that

$$\text{all } F \text{ are } G. \tag{3}$$

The common distinction between "universal laws" and "statistical generalisations" can be misleading if it is taken to imply that the latter are either not universal or not lawlike.

Suppose the sentence (1) above refers to an outcome of kind G on a trial of kind F on what is taken to be a chance set-up. Suppose also that standard statistical criteria, applied to observed relative frequencies of G and F, leave no reasonable doubt of its truth. It could still be claimed (e.g. Ramsey, 1926, pp. 207–8) that (1) could still fail to state a statistical law in our sense. (1) would fail, it is argued, if there is another difference between the F-trials of which the outcome is G and those of which the outcome is $\sim G$. Suppose the former are all F^* and the latter all $\sim F^*$. A causal explanation could then be given of the result of each trial on the basis of deterministic (and, moreover, causal) laws

$$\left. \begin{array}{l} \text{All } F \text{ and } F^* \text{ are } G, \\ \text{All } F \text{ and } \sim F^* \text{ are } \sim G. \end{array} \right\} \qquad (4)$$

Since each trial is either F^* or $\sim F^*$ the "chance" of it being G is either 1 or 0. In particular, of no trial is the chance of G p. So (1) does not state the statistical law (2). It is thus argued that the possibility of deterministic explanation of G-events, i.e. the existence of an F^* such that (4) are laws, is incompatible with (1) ascribing chances to single trials. Conversely for (1) to do so requires that there is no such F^* – a fact of non-existence that can never be known.

The argument is persuasive but it begs the question. It is agreed that (1) expresses a true proposition; what is in question is its status. Is it a law or a statistical accident? Whichever it is, the true proposition expressed by (1) will not be derivable from the laws (4) unless a further premise is added, namely that made by the sentence

$$` 100 \, p\% \text{ of } F \text{ are } F^* \text{'}. \qquad (5)$$

But what is the status of this proposition? It is perfectly compatible with everything so far supposed that (5) expresses a statistical law. If it does, so does (1). Statistical law neither requires the absence of deterministic explanation of the events it refers to nor does it just express ignorance thereof.

As usual, it is the confusion of propensity with chance that makes this conclusion seem puzzling and tempts one to deny it. A fluctuating propensity can be ascribed to a temporally persisting set-up from time to time. So it is tempting to ascribe a fluctuating chance from time to time to a temporally extended trial. Consider the chance that the temporally extended process of conception and delivery of a human child (F) has the outcome that the child is male (G). Immediately before delivery there is an explanatory difference between all those trials that have outcome G and those that have outcome $\sim G$; namely that the *unborn* child is either male (F^*) or not ($\sim F^*$). Of each class it is observed that the chance of any member yielding outcome G is either 1 or 0. Hence, it is argued, in no case was the chance ever other than 1 or 0. The only objective feature of the trial is that the child is either G or $\sim G$. All our statistical speech expresses is suitably quantified ignorance of the outcome.

We have already (chapter 4, pp. 72–3) remarked the fallacy of locating a chance at some temporal point within a trial. It can only seem plausible to do so because the corresponding propensity can be so located. But the latter signifies something quite different. If *per impossibile* a second child were conceived before the first was born, it too would have a definite chance of being born male. The attempt to locate a chance within a trial shows only that on a quite different kind of trial the sex never changes. The chance of an unborn child changing sex during delivery is 0. This well known fact does bear on the original trial to a limited extent. It shows that the chances of born and of unborn children being male are the same. So the outcome G or $\sim G$ of the original trial might be indirectly settled, by determining F or $\sim F^*$, earlier than it could be settled directly.

One might still urge that it must be possible "in principle" to predict the sex of an embryo. There "must" be some prior difference between acts of conception giving rise to such different outcomes. Similarly for coin tosses that give rise to outcomes as different as heads and tails. But the problem simply recurs: what is the status of true statistical propositions about the occurrence of acts of conception or of coin tossing of these two alleged kinds? However far back sequences of causally connected events are traced, it is still "in principle" possible for the happening of one, F^*, or other, $\sim F^*$, event to be itself the outcome of a chance trial. But the principles here invoked on either side are *a priori* principles of determinism and indeterminism respectively, and the matter is not to be settled *a priori*.

In the case of conception we do not suppose that the causal chain ending in a male birth can go back endlessly in time. The number of its members may be unlimited but we take them all to follow the act of conception. The causal antecedents of a coin landing heads likewise all follow the act of tossing it. Of that act none is a causal effect, although the act may well have other effects.

I take this much at least to be entailed by a coin toss being a chance trial, and I take determinism to deny it. A determinist will suppose a more detailed description to distinguish the trials that result in heads from those that result in tails. The result heads, when it occurs, is taken to be a causal effect of the act of tossing under some more detailed true description (e.g. Sklar, 1970, p. 360).

To avoid our earlier regress the determinist must suppose the occurrence of coin tosses of the two kinds he distinguishes not to be itself a chance matter. He must decline to explain the observed relative frequencies with which tosses of the two kinds occur. (1) and (5) he must take to state merely "brute frequencies" in the world – any true propositions they express he must suppose to be accidental, not lawlike. No subjunctive conditionals follow from them. Nothing follows about the prospects of being F^* or G an entity would have if it were F. Nothing follows even about the proportions of items that would be F^* or G if they were all F. The inadequacies of this account of (1) and (5) are those of the frequency accounts of chance discussed in chapter 3 above. No sense is made of applying statistical law to single cases. No explanation is given even of observed frequencies of heads and tails. They must be supposed to result from a purely accidental mixture of two kinds of deterministic trial – i.e. a mixture governed by no law at all, and certainly not by statistical law. No principles of inference can be provided either way between observed frequencies and those in the world as a whole. A determinist could have no intelligible basis in observation for accepting (or rejecting) (1) or (5) of an open class of F. Nor could he rationally infer from them anything about frequencies he does observe.

Not all observed frequencies are the inexplicable brute facts the determinist must suppose them to be. Some statistical sentences like (1) and (5) are accepted as true and treated as lawlike. They are used to explain frequencies and they plainly support subjunctive conditionals. So I take determinism to be contingently – but quite adequately – false.

I do not distinguish in this conclusion between statistical laws and so-called "initial conditions". It is often held that classical statistical theories, like the kinetic theory of gases, are compatible with determinism. Classical gas particles move by deterministic laws. If their velocities and places relative to the boundaries of the containing vessel are given at any time, those at any later time are thereby determined. The gas laws appear statistical only because the initial velocities and places are not known. They are given a statistical distribution and this is understood in a frequency sense. Such-and-such proportions of particles have velocities and places in such and such intervals of values. The initial condition of the gas is thus described statistically; the laws connecting it to later conditions are deterministic. This is supposed to suffice for determinism, because the statistical initial conditions merely express ignorance of more detailed determining conditions.

We have met this argument already in the coin tossing case, and the reply to it is the same. The distribution of particle velocities prescribed by kinetic theory is not accidental. It is taken to be a law of nature that every sample of gas is subject to it, and the theory plainly supports subjunctive conditionals. If anything were a sample of gas the prescribed statistical distribution would apply to it. The subject matter of the theory is not in fact the velocity and place of gas particles. From those alone the macroscopic gas laws would not follow that the theory purports to explain. Its subject matter is the chance distribution over possible places and velocities at any time, from which the gas laws do follow (within limits of conceptual imprecision – see chapter 6, pp. 103–107). It is immaterial that velocities and places are deterministically linked to velocities and places earlier and later. That signifies no more than does the existence of causal antecedents of male births and coins landing heads. It shows merely that earlier and later gas particle velocities and places also have chances. And their having chances is as compatible with their also having determinate (not determined) values as the chance of radioactive decay is with its actual occurrence. The frequency account of these chances, on which the determinist relies in dismissing statistical initial conditions as accidental, is no more adequate here than it is elsewhere.

The gas case may seem puzzling because the deterministic chain of antecedents of a given velocity or place distribution could be temporally endless. It does not end in any analogue of the acts of tossing a coin or conceiving a child. If one thinks of chance as a sort of weak causal link between trial and result, it is hard to see what the trial could be. There seems to be no event to which chance can link particle velocities and places in the way the result heads is linked to the toss of a coin. I have however remarked already (p. 151 above) that chance is not a sort of weak causal link. Heads is in no way causally "due to" the coin toss; the decay of an atom in no way "due to" its having a certain nuclear structure for a certain time. We shall have cause to see again (p. 158 below) that causal talk must be eschewed if chance is to be understood. There is no need to look for something like a cause of gas velocity and place distributions in order to find a chance trial. The trial is simply the gas sample being in a determinate state of volume, pressure and temperature at a given time. In any of a wide range of such situations the theory warrants a distribution of partial beliefs over the possible velocities and places of single gas particles, and over possible frequency distributions among the velocities and places of numbers of gas particles.

Kinetic theory ascribes to gases standing propensities which are equally displayed by the chance distributions of particle places and velocities in diverse states of volume, pressure and temperature. Like radium atoms and mortal men and unlike coins, gases continuously display their propensities in one chance distribution or another. This perhaps explains a confusion of propensity with chance (and thence with frequency) in this case, although it hardly excuses it. The dispositional insolubility of a rock on the sea bed is also continuously displayed; but it is still not the same as the fact of the rock not dissolving.

In a deterministic world there would be no propensities. (There is a slightly frivolous borderline case: an otherwise deterministic world with biased coins that were never tossed would have propensities but no chances). We might still find use for false statistical theories in a deterministic world and thus a use for fictional propensities. Chemical engineers for instance habitually work with continuum theories of fluid mechanics that are convenient although known to be false. The theories ascribe to fluids uniform point densities, viscosities and other mechanical and thermal properties which they are known not to have. One cannot therefore argue directly from the successful use of these theories to a continuous distribution of fluid matter. Can a determinist properly object to the similar inference to indeterminism from the successful use of statistical theories?

The determinist argument here could not rely on a general instrumentalist view of laws and theories (see Nagel, 1961, chapter 6). The doctrine cuts both ways that laws and theories are neither true nor false and so lack ontological consequences. Instrumentalism does not favour discrete over continuum theories of matter, nor deterministic over statistical laws. On it, if the continuum is a merely useful fiction, so are atoms; deterministic dispositions such as fragility are no more real for instrumentalists like Ryle (1949, pp. 119–20) than propensities would be.

I adopt a realist view of laws and theories, while recognising that many false theories continue to be usefully employed. Their falsity however deprives their use of any ontological implications. The force of the continuum example comes from our accepting as true an alternative atomic theory. That theory shows the continuum theory to be false. It also shows what makes the continuum theory useful. It shows in what circumstances the consequences of the continuum theory are true. The circumstances are most common, and in them the desired results are much more readily derived from the continuum theory. It is only our acceptance of an underlying atomic theory that warrants our declining the inference from this widespread use to a real continuum; and only because it commits us instead to real atoms.

It is the same with statistical laws and theories. The inference from them to real chances and propensities can only be resisted if an accepted underlying deterministic theory shows their use to be merely instrumental. It is not enough that such an underlying theory is conceivable. The determinist must put up a better supported deterministic alternative to every statistical theory. The indeterminist need not do as much because his claims are more modest. He need not claim that all laws are statistical, merely that not all laws are deterministic. I hope propensity theory may induce determinists to similarly moderate their claims and reconcile themselves to a world that science shows to be deterministic in some respects and statistical in others.

NATURAL NECESSITY

I turn now to a constraint propensity theory is alleged to place on one's view of natural law. Professors Kneale and Mackie have privately objected that it imposes a non-Humean view of natural necessity. My enquiry here is not exegetical. I do not know what Hume would say of propensity theory. The sequel will make it clear what views I take to be Humean; they are compatible at least with such accounts of natural law as Braithwaite (1953) and Ayer (1963) have given.

The argument I dispute may be put as follows in terms of the coin tossing example. Suppose a given coin always lands heads and hence that all coins of some independently specified kind do so. There could be a natural law to this effect. For a Humean it would assert the constant conjunction of events of these two independent kinds, namely coin tossings of the specified kind and landing heads. There is assumed to be no logical connection; being a toss of the specified kind is no criterion for the result being heads. And there is for the Humean no further connection in nature which could somehow necessitate the result heads on each toss.

Returning to the statistical case, we have again a conjunction of events of two logically independent kinds, but no longer a constant conjunction. Sometimes a suitable and suitably tossed coin lands heads, sometimes not. Yet the propensity theory seems to assert that nature contains more than the two events. It contains also objectively, empirically, in each single case, something of which chance is the measure that makes it reasonable to expect (to a greater or less extent) the one event to follow the other. In the extreme case of the chance approaching or equal to 1 it has precisely the rôle of that necessary but non-logical connection which a Humean denies to exist. That is, a chance 1 is a feature of nature over and above the events it conjoins which necessitates their conjunction. Chances less than 1 then appear on the propensity theory, it is alleged, as similarly non-Humean connections. They do not in general necessitate a conjunction of events, but exercise a sort of "partial compulsion" on the result event to follow the trial event.

It is thus argued that a propensity theorist has to accept non-Humean necessary connections as the extreme cases of chance as it tends to 1 or 0. Even if this alleged consequence were acceptable in itself the propensity theory's probabilistic extension of it would not do. The idea of "partial compulsion" is quite unintelligible – of a connection which is, in the relevant natural law sense, "necessary" but which does not always work. This is the idea of chance as a weak or intermittent causal link that I have already had occasion to reject (pp. 151, 155), and it would be fatal for propensity theory to be saddled with it. The connection would have to be there in every coin toss, yet what (when the coin lands tails) would it connect and what would it explain? At least in the extreme case it can always connect the toss to the landing heads and could be supposed to explain the constancy of the conjunction. In the statistical case *no* other invariable consequence of the toss exists for this alleged probabilistic link to connect and thereby explain.

The propensity theory seems on this account to be unacceptable even to a non-Humean. To a Humean it seems directly unacceptable because its extreme deterministic case is a non-logical necessary connection. Mackie takes a frequency theory of chance (and *a fortiori* of statistical law) to be the natural extension of a Humean view of deterministic law. Just as the one expresses invariable conjunction between events of two kinds, so the other is to express merely a frequency of conjunction between events of two kinds. Now it makes no sense to say of a single instance of a deterministic law that in it the antecedent is "invariably" conjoined with the consequent event. Of an instance of a statistical law it equally makes no sense to say (e.g.) that *this* toss of a given coin is "frequently" conjoined with this particular instance of the result heads. The frequency theory of statistical law, like the Humean theory of deterministic law, allows it to assert nothing about the single case, only about the set of all cases instantiating the antecedent. The propensity theory differs from the frequency theory on precisely this point, which is consequently taken to show its incompatibility with the Humean outlook.

It is not, however, true that propensity theory has all the consequences here drawn from it. Consider again what it really commits one to when the chance is 1 or 0. I assume that deterministic laws about events can be identified with universal conditionals ascribing these extreme chances. The assumption is not trivial, since it rules out some widely held frequency theories. In particular the limiting frequency of heads in an endless sequence of coin tosses may be 1, even though an indefinitely large number of tails occurs in the sequence. Thus on a limiting frequency theory one occurrence of tails would not show the chance of heads to be less than 1, whereas it would refute a deterministic law. The propensity theory, however (like such non-limiting frequency theories as Braithwaite's, 1953), need not leave this implausible logical gap between deterministic law and the extreme cases of statistical law. In any case, if there were such a gap, the propensity theory of chance would imply nothing about the status of deterministic laws. Chances of 1 and 0 would not be identifiable with necessary connections; the argument I am disputing would not get started.

I take it then, that a deterministic law ascribes a chance of 1 to an occurrence of one event (of kind B, say) given the occurrence of another (of kind A). What does this amount to on the present theory? We have that, assuming the law, upon each occurrence of an A-event the reasonable partial belief to adopt on the occurrence of a B-event is of degree 1. This entails that it is in these circumstances unreasonable to put any money on a B-event not happening, whatever odds are offered. The question is: for this to be unreasonable does the assumed deterministic law have to be given a non-Humean force? Must it assert some necessary connection between the A-event and the B-event? The answer is plain: a Humean constant conjunction is quite good enough. If I know that every A-event, past, present and future, is accompanied by a B-event, I know that this one is. It would be unreasonable of me in this assumed state of knowledge to put any money on the B-event not happening, since I know in advance that I would lose it.

This truth about an event, that being of kind A and given the deterministic law, the chance is 1 of its being attended by a B-event, is not of course the same as the truth that it *is* so attended. The latter does not entail the former. A coin may land heads even though the chance of heads is not 1. Where the chance *is* 1, that is a fact about the toss over and above the fact of it landing heads. A Humean constant conjunction suffices to establish this extra fact. No further connection is needed between pairs of events of kinds *A* and *B*.

Similarly in the statistical case. It is an extra fact about an *A*-event that some degree of partial belief *p* is more reasonable than others on its being accompanied by a *B* event. This extra fact is established by the truth of the relevant statistical law. The question is whether statistical laws can be given a Humean interpretation on the propensity theory. The answer is not quite clear. We certainly cannot take a statistical law to assert merely a constant, or indeed any specifically frequent, conjunction of *A*-events and *B*-events. If that is to be non-Humean, so be it. But I suppose it sufficient to deny any statistical analogue of a nonlogical necessary connection, and to accommodate Humean scepticism about induction. That much propensity theory can do.

The relation between frequency and a degree of partial belief being reasonable is obvious in the deterministic case. It is unreasonable to put any money on a *B*-event not attending an *A*-event because that money would always be lost. The facts of the statistical case that make some partial beliefs reasonable and others not are doubtless more complex. We need to show that they are nevertheless still merely about occurrences and non-occurrences of *B*-events and *A*-events.

I argue that a partial belief is reasonable if the gambler can know he would break even after some repeated bets at the corresponding CBQ and unreasonable if he cannot know this. To say an event has a chance is to assert this possibility of knowledge for some, but not for all, partial beliefs in the event. (It may also be possible to know of any CBQ that the gambler will fail to break even on some number of repeated bets at it; but this will give no reason to prefer one degree of partial belief to any other). A sense is thus given to a partial belief being "reasonable" that both gives content to the propensity theory and is Humeanly acceptable. The argument appeals to the so-called "strong law of large numbers" (e.g. Feller, 1957, pp. 189–90). In it I need to show how that law can provide knowledge that a gambler will break even. I need further to show what makes it reasonable to prefer a CBQ for which this knowledge is available to one for which it is not.

The betting situation is the one specified in chapter 2. The constraints there put on it are needed to ensure that the choice of betting quotient measures the gambler's partial belief and nothing else. Its salient features are that (i) the gambler has to bet, (ii) he chooses the betting quotient, and then (iii) his opponent chooses the stake size and the direction of the bet.

If a gambler can be made to bet once, he can be made to bet again. If one trial has a chance distribution, any trial sufficiently similar in its connected properties has the same distribution. That means on the present view that a CBQ warranted on one such trial is warranted on all. It is reasonable to avoid certain loss in a compulsory bet on one trial, by making one's betting quotients coherent. It is also reasonable to try to avoid loss in compulsory bets on many such trials by a suitable choice among coherent quotients.

We shall not want to set a limit to the possible number of repetitions of the trial. On the other hand our gambler cannot be credited with both unlimited cash and a serious interest in winning more; so we set up the following situation. The gambler and his opponent devote a fixed stake to a complex bet whose result is the net result of a sequence of N bets on single trials. The bet on every single trial is at the same CBQ, r, chosen by the gambler. The fixed total stake, chosen subsequently by his opponent, is divided equally among the N bets. All N bets are the same way round, the direction again being fixed by the opponent on learning the value of r.

Suppose the frequency of B-events in the sequence of N trials is f. The net profit per unit stake is the difference between the frequency and the agreed CBQ, $|f - r|$. In the prescribed situation the gambler cannot apply any knowledge he has about these events to ensure that he, rather than his opponent, gets whatever net profit the sequence yields. He can on the other hand try so to choose r as either to maximise his profit (hoping to win) or to minimise his loss (fearing to lose). The former policy will evidently never give him cause to choose a CBQ other than 1 or 0. In any case, our man has to be supplied with enough money to put up any stake his opponent may set; for such a man winning more will matter much less than not losing what he has; and there is a nontrivial policy he can apply to minimise his losses.

The gambler, we suppose, holds there to be a chance p of a B-event on each occasion of the bet. If he is right then the strong law of large numbers shows of p alone that there is an arbitrarily high probability $1 - \epsilon$ that after some sufficiently large number of bets, N, the frequency f will differ from p by less than some arbitrarily small amount δ. This is on the present account to say that some partial belief of strength p, and no other, is such that an arbitrarily strong partial belief $1 - \epsilon$ is reasonable on the bet that $|f - p| < \delta$.

The arbitrarily small constant δ plainly explicates the concept of breaking even. The gambler breaks even if and only if the net profit on the sequence is less than δ. Various considerations – monetary units, the size of stake, personal utilities of winning more or less – may set upper or lower bounds to δ in a given situation. δ can take any required positive value. For a finite stake in a discrete currency, δ can always be made small enough to stop any net transfer of cash being compatible with breaking even.

The problem is to avoid begging the question in accounting for reasonableness in the single case CBQ. We want to say that the reasonable single case CBQ, r, to adopt is the one, p, to which the strong law of large numbers applies. But the law refers in turn to a CBQ, $1 - \epsilon$, being reasonable on the many-case bet. This reference must be accounted for without further appeal to chance, if our explication of the single case is not to be viciously circular.

I rely here on an asymptotic property of very high reasonable CBQs. The property is roughly that the better a very good bet is, the more circumstances there are in which the gambler may act as if he knew it was won. In chapter 1 I argued that increasing partial belief must merge into full belief. In particular (pp. 6, 15), as one's partial belief in a proposition increases, it must in the end amount to belief in the proposition. So a reasonable degree of partial belief which tends to 1 implies eventually that the corresponding full belief is reasonable.

There need not be a fixed degree of partial belief at which this always happens. The common view of knowledge as reasonable true belief, indeed, entails that there cannot be. The reasonableness of any particular partial belief, however strong, cannot be identified with knowledge that the bet will be won. Any such identification falls foul of a lottery paradox. For let the reasonable partial belief be of degree $1 - \epsilon$, with ϵ arbitrarily small. Suppose a one-prize lottery with S equal tickets, where $S \geq 1/\epsilon$. The chance of each ticket not winning is not less than $1 - \epsilon$, yet we cannot claim, on pain of contradiction, to know of each, and hence of every, ticket that it will not win.

One might argue that it is reasonable to believe of each ticket that it will not win. It is just that one such reasonable belief will fail to be true and so fail to be knowledge, and we do not know which. But we do not need these complications. All the lottery paradox shows in any case is that in some circumstances a claim to knowledge is not adequately supported by the reasonableness of any particular partial belief however strong. If the reasonable partial belief is raised in strength from $1 - \epsilon$ to $1 - \epsilon'$ (where $\epsilon' < \epsilon$), the number of these circumstances is reduced, by eliminating those lotteries with numbers S of tickets such that $1/\epsilon' > S \geqslant 1/\epsilon$. In the present case, any sceptical challenge whatever, expressed by a lottery of any number of tickets S, however great, can be met. The strong law of large numbers entails the reasonableness, for *some* number N of single bets, of a many-case partial belief strong enough to make that lottery unparadoxical. Although it is true it is not pertinent that against any knowledge claim based just on this partial belief a further paradoxical lottery could be produced. It is enough that in any given circumstances a strong enough partial belief can be warranted to support a knowledge claim. It is immaterial to point to other circumstances in which a still higher reasonable degree of partial belief would be needed; and even if it were material, the stronger reasonable belief can always be produced.

Nothing in the lottery paradox counts against the asymptotic claim made for very strong reasonable partial beliefs. The strong law of large numbers can be used to meet any sceptical challenge. On the strength of it the gambler can properly be said to be able to know that he will break even after some number of bets at a CBQ p. He cannot know this for any other CBQ. Now conditions (i) and (iii) above of the betting situation compel the gambler to bet and prevent him aiming for a profit as opposed to avoiding a loss. So breaking even is the best result the gambler can possibly hope to know of. This obviously makes it uniquely reasonable to set his CBQ r equal to p. The reasonableness is that of betting behaviour in a situation of a kind tailored to the measurement of partial belief. No further appeal is made to the concept of chance.

The objective chance p the gambler supposes to exist is thus the measure of the partial belief he should have in a B-event accompanying an A-event. Of course a gambler may not know what the value p is, or he may know only that it lies in some interval. But his claim that an objective chance exists, about which more or less may be known, still has the sense propensity theory needs. Ignorance does not make other CBQs as reasonable as p. At no other CBQ can the gambler know that he will avoid losing in repeated compulsory bets the indefinitely large stake his opponent can make him put up. Should these bets ever be enforced, it would be unreasonable to remain in any avoidable ignorance of the value p.

The sense thus given to the gambler's claim, that an A-event has a chance p of being attended by a B-event, should be entirely acceptable to a Humean. It is that the gambler can know that after some number of repeated bets at CBQ p he will break even. His knowledge here is of nothing but facts about occurrences of A-events and B-events, since these suffice to determine whether he does break even. No non-Humean connections in nature are needed to establish the fact that this A-event, by virtue of being of kind A and of the truth of the statistical law, is such that it is reasonable to prefer a partial belief of degree p to any other on its being attended by a B-event. And that is, on the propensity theory, just what it is to say that p is the chance – the objective, empirical, single case probability truly ascribable to the situation.

A couple of defensive remarks may be needed here. Suppose the world lacks enough A-events for the gambler to break even on. We seem then to appeal to counterfactuals about what *would* happen were there more A-events than there (tenselessly) are. Do not these go beyond Humean facts about actual A-events? No more so, I think, than when a Humean denies equivalence in meaning to a deterministic law and the conjunction of its instances, while insisting that no other facts about events in the world are needed for it to be true. It is debatable whether a Humean can so distinguish lawlike from accidental universals. But he has no special problem with statistical laws. If Humean deterministic laws can support counterfactuals so can Humean statistical laws. If they can't, Humeanism is false anyway, and it will not matter whether propensity theory is compatible with it.

The second remark defends the emphasis above on repetition in justifying the reasonableness of a CBQ. I might ascribe a chance with no interest at all in repetitions of A-events. I might even, on some principle, refuse any offers of repeated bets. One might object that it can't be what *would* happen in a sequence of bets that makes my CBQ in such a single bet reasonable, if such a sequence can be explicitly ruled out. Here one must recall that ascribing a chance is not, on the propensity theory, the same as betting. CBQs are only one measure of the partial belief I claim is warranted. And all I say is what CBQ I would adopt *if* I were made to bet in the curiously specified circumstances laid down by the theory. And in those circumstances I could be made to bet again and again on events of the same kind. In claiming my CBQ on each of these events to be reasonable I merely claim the events to be such that repeated bets at my CBQ *would* leave me breaking even in some long run. I no more have to be prepared actually to repeat the bet than I have to make it in the first place.

One might still ask how any reasonable, i.e. rationally justified, measure can be placed on the expectation that a *B*-event will attend an *A*-event. There being no logical connection between the events, is it not the essence of Humeanism that no measure of expectation can be rationally justified?

Now, on the propensity theory, the truth of some law-statement, deterministic or statistical, is necessary for the truth of a singular statement ascribing a chance, 1 or less, to an event. The consequence of Humean arguments is merely that we can have no rationally justified measure of our degree of belief in the truth of these law-statements. And without them we cannot derive singular statements of chance, in the sense of reasonable partial beliefs, from non-probabilistic singular statements alone.

All that may be granted. Hume may have shown that a probabilistic account cannot be given of our uncertain knowledge of natural laws. There is no inconsistency in accepting that and still appealing to our knowledge of such laws, understood moreover in a Humean manner, to derive empirical probabilities. Certain degrees of partial belief in a *B*-event attending an *A*-event are made reasonable by statistical laws, just as total belief in the attending *B*-event would be made reasonable by the truth of a deterministic law. None of this commits us to any non-Humean view either of what the laws themselves assert or of what makes it reasonable to believe them.

Let us now apply this account of what makes a CBQ reasonable to Laplace's biased coin. I described this (chapter 7, pp. 130–1) as a case of an event apparently having two chances; we can now clear the matter up. Two partial beliefs seem to be reasonable on the first toss of a biased coin: the CBQ $\frac{1}{2}$ displaying a propensity of the labelling set-up, and some other CBQ displaying the unknown bias of the coin. Which is really the more reasonable depends, on the above account, on what counts as repeating the bet. If further biasings of labelled coins, or labellings of biased coins, are what the gambler must break even on, his degree of partial belief should be $\frac{1}{2}$; if further tosses of the same biased coin, it should be something other than $\frac{1}{2}$.

There is no doubt in normal use that tossing the biased coin again is what counts as repeating the bet. The chance that displays the bias thus gives the more reasonable partial belief. Nobody who knew which way the coin was biased on its first toss would adopt the partial belief of degree $\frac{1}{2}$. That is because he knows the result of the labelling trial and does not envisage any repetition of it. We do not normally relabel or rebias coins by chance processes whose outcomes we bet on. But it is important to realise that we could do so, and that $\frac{1}{2}$ could be the more reasonable degree of partial belief. Imagine a machine that mints biased coins which it tosses once and then discards. Statistical tests on the discarded coins convince us that the machine's propensity is displayed in equal chances of the likely and unlikely sides of each coin being labelled 'heads'. We are to bet on the outcome heads of a toss on this machine. This is of course in each case the first toss of a biased coin the direction of whose bias is unknown. In this situation the CBQ $\frac{1}{2}$ is plainly more reasonable than any other. It is the only CBQ at which the gambler can know he will break even after enough repeated tosses of the machine. The chance of heads in this case really is $\frac{1}{2}$, and the propensity displayed in each trial is that of the machine, not that of any of the biased coins it produces.

What determines the more reasonable of the two partial beliefs is thus the propensity of the chance set-up on which the trial is conducted. Two trials satisfying the description 'toss of coin a with bias q_a' can display different propensities. Hence they can have different chance distributions over the results heads and tails. That no more makes chance relational than do the cases of chapter 4 (pp. 74–6) in which an unbiased coin is tossed by a biased machine. Most trials falling under this description clearly display one or other propensity and so have the one chance of heads or have the other. No one such trial need be supposed to have both distributions, and none of the heads resulting from them need be credited with two chances. Certainly conventions help to settle which propensity a given trial displays, but that does not make the matter any less settled or less objective. A man who adopts a CBQ $\frac{1}{2}$ on its first toss stands to lose no less money on repeated tosses of the same biased coin because it is a convention which makes that the appropriate repetition of his bet. And the same goes for the man who adopts any other CBQ on the first trial of our eccentric mint.

No doubt some cases could be unsettled. It could be unclear what counts as repeating the bet: another toss of the coin, or a first toss of another coin. It would then be unclear which propensity is displayed and hence not clear which partial belief is the more reasonable. It would then tempt and mislead equally to say either that there is no chance, or that there is one chance of which we are ignorant, or that there are two chances. Two degrees of partial belief are equal candidates for rationality in that there are propensities they could display. Either could be more reasonable than any third degree. There are just two partial beliefs, that is, which are not certainly objectively unreasonable. It is tempting to express this fact by saying that there are two chances. On the other hand no one partial belief is picked out as uniquely reasonable, and it is tempting to express this by saying that there is no chance. Or one could say that there must be a right way of repeating the bet even if no convention has so far settled it. In that case one of the two degrees of partial belief is the single chance, although we do not know which. The best thing is to describe the situation in terms of the propensities involved and not to talk of chance at all.

There is no need to regard the two CBQs involved in Laplace's biased coin case as picked out of a larger class of relational probabilities. We have seen in chapter 7 (pp. 146–50) that if we do so the partial belief of degree $\frac{1}{2}$ becomes a reasonable "prior" probability for Bayesian progress towards the chance revealed in repeated tosses of the biased coin. In particular its derivation from the propensity of the labelling device exhibits its empirical basis better than does the fiducial argument. We have equally seen no reason for propensity theory to commit itself to Bayesian progressions (chapter 2, pp. 45–9; chapter 7). We do not need to suppose objective Bayesian probabilities relative to evidence of the results of 0, 1, 2, 3, ... tosses of the biased coin.

It is contentious whether there are relative degrees of support measured by probabilities. They could not support unconditional betting quotients, precisely because they would be relative to evidence. Unconditional CBQs can therefore not provide a general measure of degrees of support. They could conceivably be measured by conditional betting quotients. But we have seen in chapter 2 (p. 49) that conditional quotients neither measure partial belief nor can be constrained by the Dutch book argument. It has not been shown either that there are logical relations of support or that they have a probabilistic measure (although the arguments mentioned on p. 28 may show that *if* support has a measure it is probabilistic).

Propensity theory need no more justify chances as privileged values of relational probabilities than as privileged values of relative frequencies. The demand for justification in either case presupposes an account of objective probability that propensity theory has no need to accept. Propensity theory need not deny that there are relative frequencies which are mathematical probabilities, and that these sometimes provide measures of chance. It need similarly not deny that there may be relational probabilities. If there are they are clearly connected to chance in a way statable by some formulation of Hacking's "frequency principle" (see p. 67 above). But deriving a relational probability from it does not make clearer how a chance can measure reasonable expectation. On the contrary, making the probability relative to evidence simply raises the question why just *this* amount of evidence should be appealed to.

The question, if raised, may be answered as follows. We wish to know if a possible future event will occur. As we proceed from a state of complete ignorance about it our rational expectation of the event may change with the changing evidence. We suppose, roughly speaking, that expectation based on more evidence is more rational than expectation based on less. Is there any non-arbitrary stopping point (short of conclusive evidence that will either entail the event occurring or it not occurring)? If not, then assuming a probabilistic measure of expectation, there are no objective probabilities in this field other than 1 or 0. What the propensity theory asserts in these terms is that the world can set a non-arbitrary limit to the relevant evidence we can get. It splits the relevant evidence into two sorts: evidence about a propensity of some persisting thing (the chance set-up) and evidence of the occurrence of another event (the trial). The chance is the probability relative to the evidence of the set-up's propensity and that the trial occurs. The latter is taken to be known independently, although we have had occasion to notice cases where it is itself an outcome of a chance trial. The former is a standing property of a thing. Knowledge of it is generally independent of knowledge of particular events in the thing's biography. Since it is widely connected with other standing properties and so detectable in diverse ways, a propensity is merely confirmed by accumulating evidence beyond a certain point. Once the evidence fixes the determinate values of the connected determinables further evidence is irrelevant. In terms of relational probability, a propensity signifies that all but a small amount of accessible evidence about the set-up is irrelevant – it leaves the relational probability (given always that the trial occurs) of the various outcomes unchanged.

Once the trial occurs one can conceive further evidence becoming available. As the tossed coin moves through the air evidence of its progress could conceivably support even weightier expectations of the outcome heads. We imagine ourselves proceeding through these expectations to the final state of knowing whether the coin lands heads. This is the picture of chance in relational terms, and it must be stressed that it is only a picture. There is no evidence that these further rational expectations exist or have any numerical measure. Nor would they be accessible before the toss, even if they existed. Inference from events before the toss, to details of the coin's trajectory affecting the rational expectation of heads, would require deterministic relations between them which *ex hypothesi* do not hold (see pp. 151–3 above).

Propensities are characteristics of things warranting conditional expectations of the future. They mark non-arbitrary positions between complete ignorance of the future and complete knowledge of it. In this respect propensities are like other dispositional properties. They too give knowledge of the future only on the unasserted condition of events occurring that occasion their displays. Its fragility tells us what will happen to a glass only if it is dropped. Again, dispositional knowledge of the future is subject to the unasserted condition that things continue to possess their present dispositions. We know what will happen when a fragile glass is dropped only if it stays fragile. Propensities differ from other dispositions only in yielding, subject to these conditions, not knowledge of what will happen in the future but mere reasonable expectation.

Temporally persisting things play an important rôle in our ontology by providing this sort of conditional knowledge of the future. If they can give reasonable full belief on these terms, they can surely give reasonable partial belief. If a thing can have dispositions at all, it can surely have propensities. It is foolish to swallow a coin's mass and strain at its bias. I can hardly doubt that we have conditional knowledge and reasonable expectations of future events; and what could conceivably provide them but presently detectable properties of things whose future biographies contain the events? So I credit things with persisting dispositions in general, and in particular with the relatively uninformative dispositions I call 'propensities'.

Perhaps Humeans cannot accept real dispositions. If so, they must reject propensities, though not for reasons peculiar to or enlightening about chance. I have argued above that objective chance is compatible with a Humean account of statistical law. I argue now for a Humean view of laws relating dispositions, to accommodate propensities as a special case. In so doing I assume that laws can relate properties of things as well as of events. Occasionally laws are restricted to events by definition (e.g. Swinburne, 1968, p. 177) but that is a mistake. We notoriously lack independent criteria for identity and diversity of events. Our ontology of events is derivative on our ontology of things (e.g. Prior, 1968, chapter 1). We have a usable ontology of identifiable and distinguishable things with persisting but changeable properties and relations. In terms of it events can be derivatively identified and distinguished, whereas the converse is not true. It is consequently most implausible to suppose that all deterministic laws are reducible to universal statements of causal relations between events. Suppose it is a law that all ravens are black. I can imagine this applied to a causal explanation of my turning black as an effect of being turned into a raven. But how about an existing raven? Must it staying black from moment to moment really be construed as a sequence of events which the law relates causally to members of the similar sequence generated by the bird staying a raven from moment to moment?

It seems quite clear that such laws are not applied to events at all but to persisting things. *Pace* Swinburne (1968, p. 180), they assert the invariable co-presence in such things of two logically independent properties or relations. That at least I take to be a Humean view of such laws. A non-Humean would no doubt take them also to assert some non-logical connection of necessity between the two properties by which their invariable co-presence is to be explained.

What sort of properties can laws of co-presence apply to? Presumably those which can meaningfully be attributed to things from moment to moment and in which things can change from moment to moment. A thing's having or lacking the property at one time entails nothing about its having or lacking the property at other times. Most physical properties are like this, e.g. colours. An object may be green now: if we discover that it is blue tomorrow, or destroy it, that in no way impugns our present knowledge of its colour.

In contrast we may set such supposed properties as that of being mortal. I take it that to be mortal is just to die at some (unspecified) time. Then a man who does die was *always* mortal and a man who doesn't *never* was. It makes no sense to say e.g. of Adam that he lost his immortality. It may be true that had Adam not eaten the apple he would have been immortal (i.e. still alive now as always). It is not true that before he ate it he had the property of immortality and that when he ate it an event occurred properly describable as his exchanging this property for that of mortality. I propose to say that there is in fact no such property as mortality, so understood. The predicate 'is mortal' is not correctly applied to a man by virtue of any instantaneously possessed, persisting and changeable property. It is applied simply by virtue of a single *event*, namely of an irreversible *change* in some persisting and instantaneously possessed properties of his body.

What now of dispositional predicates – do they denote properties in this sense? If they were given a Rylean sense perhaps they would not (Ryle, 1949, p. 119). Suppose dispositions differed from mortality only in being conditional. To say a glass is fragile would not be to say it will break unconditionally but to say it will break if dropped. Now suppose I take a fragile glass, heat-treat it so it ceases to be fragile, then drop it and (of course) it doesn't break. If 'is fragile' just meant 'will break when dropped' that would show the glass never was fragile, just as with 'is mortal'. In fact, of course, fragility *is* a property possessed by a glass from moment to moment. 'Is fragile' means 'would break if dropped *now*'. That this present tense subjunctive conditional is true of the glass plainly expresses a changeable property of the glass in the sense we require. The truth value of such a conditional statement can obviously change continually without the condition ever being realised. A glass may change continually in fragility without ever being dropped. And similarly of course for such other dispositional predicates as 'is soluble' and 'has a mass of 1 kilo'. These points have all been made before, and it counts neither against nor for them that the logic of subjunctive conditionals is not fully understood (*pace* Geach, 1957, pp. 6–7; and the patient who, when told his doctors could not understand how he was still alive, respectfully died).

Laws of co-presence can connect dispositions, and many do so. Gas laws connect the co-present volume, temperature and pressure of a gas sample. All these instantaneously possessed and changeable quantities are dispositions. Should anything in all this distress a Humean? Provided he will admit the existence of things with properties at all, I do not see why it should. I have credited him already with letting laws support counterfactuals, so he need hardly jib at singular dispositional ascriptions doing so. He can still maintain that their cash value in the world market of events is just the constant conjunction of (e.g.) whatever dropping-of-fragile-glass-events there happen to be with breaking-of-fragile-glass-events. But whether or not there are any such events, the truth or falsity of the present tense attribution of dispositional fragility constitutes a further fact about a glass. And a further Humean law can assert that whenever such true attributions can be made so can a true attribution of some other dispositional (e.g. chemical) property.

How about the special case of propensities? Consider first the relation between statistical laws and laws of co-presence connecting dispositions in general. Statistical laws quantify over trials, "disposition laws" over things. A statistical law could say that every toss of a certain kind L of an unbiased coin had a chance $\frac{1}{2}$ of resulting in heads. A disposition law could say that every glass of a certain independent kind K is fragile. The propensity theory shows these laws to be more alike than they seem. On the one hand the disposition law also entails a law about trials, namely that every standard dropping of a glass of kind K results in it breaking. The singular disposition of an individual glass that instantiates the law in turn supports a subjunctive conditional.

It is not indeed a peculiarity of statements which one takes as expressing laws of nature that they entail subjunctive conditionals: for the same will be true of any statement that contains a dispositional predicate. To say, for example, that this rubber hand is elastic is to say not merely that it will resume its normal size when stretched, but that it would do so if ever it were stretched. (Ayer, 1963, p. 229.)

No one indeed would accept such a generalisation who would deny it of a sufficiently similar individual. A sufficiently similar individual is one that has the same determinate values of every connected determinable property. The principle of connectivity appealed to here has been discussed and applied in earlier chapters. Here it ensures that every singular disposition does instantiate a law. If any glass is fragile, every glass of some (possibly unknown) independent kind K is fragile.

In particular a singular propensity is "universalisable" over all chance set-ups of some suitably similar kind. If a coin is unbiased, so are all coins which are like it in every connected property; if an atom has a half life T, so have all atoms of the same nuclear structure. Hence the entailed chance distributions of standard trials on one set-up are also universalisable over standard trials on all sufficiently similar set-ups. These universalised chance propositions are statistical laws as usually stated (see pp. 151–4 above). A singular propensity thus implies a statistical law, although *what* law will only be known if the connected properties of the set-up are known. If any coin a is unbiased, heads has a chance $\frac{1}{2}$ on every trial of a (possibly unknown) kind L, namely every standard toss of any coin sufficiently like a.

Whenever chances display propensities, the kind of event covered by the statistical law can be specified in terms of the kind of thing that has the propensity. I have suggested (pp. 169–70) that classifying events generally depends on classifying things. This may be why most if not all chances display propensities. In such cases at any rate the process of Humean generalisation over the events into the statistical law may be split into two stages, just as it may with deterministic laws connecting events. The first stage is a generalisation over all trials of a given individual with the propensity. The second is a generalisation in the form of a disposition law over all things of the kind that have that propensity. Thus it is a statistical law that every standard toss of every (suitably specified) coin has a chance $\frac{1}{2}$ of landing heads. It follows from this law that every standard toss of a coin a that meets the specification has a chance $\frac{1}{2}$ of landing heads. The ability of the overall statistical law to support subjunctive conditionals entails the same ability in the proposition that coin a is unbiased, which is derived from the law simply by instantiating the specification of the kind of coin. One could derive the proposition that a given glass is fragile in exactly the same way by instantiating the deterministic law that all standard droppings of a certain kind of glass result in breakage.

We thus have a statement to the effect that the coin a, while it remains of the specified kind, is such that it would be a fact about any standard toss of it that the most reasonable degree of partial belief in it landing heads would be $\frac{1}{2}$. This present tense subjunctive conditional statement may be true of a at one time, while it is unbiased, and false of it at others (after being bent, for example). We have, that is, a statement about the coin of precisely the form of other subjunctive conditionals we have already supposed (p. 171 above) Humeans able to admit as ascribing real dispositional properties. Why then should they deny that this statement does so? It ascribes to coin a the changeable, persisting, dispositional property of being unbiased, which is an instance of a propensity. The coin a is said to be now in such a state that if it were tossed the chance of heads would be $\frac{1}{2}$.

The property of the coin may of course enter into Humean laws of co-presence with other properties. It should be evident indeed from the above discussion, with its appeal to the principle of connectivity, that propensities must enter into lawlike relations. There must be some kind of coin of which it is non-trivially true that all coins of that kind are unbiased. So two things can no more differ in propensity than they can differ in any other dispositional property without at the same time differing also in some further explanatory respect. The question is whether this assertion and the principle of connectivity which backs it are acceptable to a Humean.

Connectivity is a regulative principle. Our scientific characterisation of things would not be allowed to be adequate if connectivity were not satisfied. It can certainly be violated in any fixed scientific vocabulary. Nothing in nature compels an explanatory difference to be statable in any terms science has so far used. But if it is not so statable, that is taken to show the need to extend the vocabulary. It shows there are properties of things not yet discovered. One could put all this by saying that it is necessary for two coins that differ in bias to differ in some other respect. But it does not follow, and a Humean will suppose it untrue, that there is any other respect in which it is necessary that they differ. Neither an acceptance of connectivity generally nor its application to propensities in particular entails accepting non-Humean necessary connections between any pairs of properties.

Humean scepticism finds its proper expression very simply in terms of propensities. While a coin remains unbiased it is most reasonable to adopt a partial belief of degree $\frac{1}{2}$ in heads resulting from a standard toss of it. But there need be no reasonable probabilistic measure of our expectation that this changeable disposition (of being unbiased) will continue to be possessed in the future. Connectivity may require that some other property changes if the bias does, but the Humean point applies equally to the other property. We have noted already (pp. 168–9) that all dispositional knowledge of future events is conditional and there is no uniquely rational degree of expectation that the conditions of it will be met. Propensities contribute no more than any other dispositions to solving the problem of induction; by the same token it provides no argument against their existence. Yet their scientific ascription may serve to explicate all the partial and conditional expectations of future events that we feel to be justified.

The test of a philosophical theory of chance is how much sense it makes of what usage shows everyone to suppose true of chance. I claim that the propensity theory makes sense of more than its rivals. It makes sense of chances being objective, empirical and not relational, and applying to the single case. No other theory I know of does as much. But it may be said, I am biased.

APOLOGY

A person of true refinement would have expressed much of that very differently, but nothing will ever make up for the lack of a classical education.

Ernest Bramah, *Kai Lung Unrolls His Mat*

References

The year given after an author's name in an entry is that in which the version of his work I refer to was first published. Another date later in the entry signifies that I have referred to this work in a republished or translated form, and it is to this form that page numbers cited in the text refer. If the later date comes after a book title it indicates that the book of that title would be available under the author's name. If it comes after the name of an editor, that indicates that the book would be available under the editor's name. In such cases I have added a separate entry to the list under the editor's name. Where a paper first appeared in an edited collection I have not, however, repeated the publication date after the editor's name in the author's entry.

ACHINSTEIN, P. (1964) On the meaning of scientific terms. *J. Phil.* **61**, 497–509.
AITCHISON, J. (1964) Bayesian tolerance regions. *J. Roy. Statist. Soc. Ser. B* **26**, 161–75.
ARMSTRONG, G. T. (1962) Vapour pressure. *Encyclopaedic Dictionary of Physics.* Edited by J. Thewlis. Volume 7, pp. 587–8.
ASTBURY, N. F. (1962) Bridge methods of electrical measurement. *Encyclopaedic Dictionary of Physics.* Edited by J. Thewlis. Volume 1, pp. 502–7.
AYER, A. J. (1936) *Language, Truth and Logic.* London: Gollancz.
  (1956) *The Problem of Knowledge.* London: Penguin Books.
  (1957) The conception of probability as a logical relation. *Observation and Interpretation.* Edited by S. Körner. pp. 12–17.
  (1963) *The Concept of a Person.* London: Macmillan.
AYERS, M. R. (1968) *The Refutation of Determinism.* London: Methuen.
BAILEY, N. T. J. (1957) *The Mathematical Theory of Epidemics.* London: Charles Griffin.
BAR-HILLEL, Y., Ed. (1966) *Proceedings of the 1964 International Congress for Logic, Methodology and Philosophy of Science.* Amsterdam: North Holland.
BAUMRIN, B., Ed. (1963) *Philosophy of Science: the Delaware Seminar Volume 2.* New York: Wiley.
BENNETT, J. (1956) Some aspects of probability and induction. *Brit. J. Phil. Sci.* **7**, 220–30, 316–22.
  (1963) The status of determinism. *Brit. J. Phil. Sci.* **14**, 106–19.
BERGMANN, G. (1943) Outline of an empiricist philosophy of physics. *Readings in the Philosophy of Science.* Edited by H. Feigl and M. Brodbeck (1953). pp. 262–87.
BLACK, M. (1967) Probability. *The Encyclopedia of Philosophy.* Edited by P. Edwards. Volume 6, pp. 464–79.
BOREL, E. (1924) Apropos of a treatise on probability. *Studies in Subjective Probability.* Edited by H. E. Kyburg Jr., and H. E. Smokler (1964). pp. 47–60.

BRAITHWAITE, R. B. (1932–3) The nature of believing. *Proc. Arist. Soc.* **33**, 129–46.

(1953) *Scientific Explanation.* Cambridge University Press.

(1957) On unknown probabilities. *Observation and Interpretation.* Edited by S. Körner. pp. 3–11.

(1963) The rôle of values in scientific inference. *Induction: Some Current Issues.* Edited by H. E. Kyburg Jr. and E. Nagel. pp. 180–95.

(1966) Why is it reasonable to base a betting rate upon an estimate of chance? *Proceedings of the 1964 International Congress for Logic, Methodology and Philosophy of Science.* Edited by Y. Bar-Hillel. pp. 263–73.

BRIDGMAN, P. W. (1927) *The Logic of Modern Physics.* New York: Macmillan.

(1938) Operational analysis. *Phil. Sci.* **5**, 114–31.

BRODBECK, M. (1962) Explanation, prediction and 'imperfect' knowledge. *Minnesota Studies in the Philosophy of Science Volume 3.* Edited by H. Feigl and G. Maxwell. pp. 231–72.

BROWN, B. (1962) Radioactivity. *Encyclopaedic Dictionary of Physics.* Edited by J. Thewlis. Volume 6, pp. 59–61.

(1962a) Radioactivity, artificial. *Encyclopaedic Dictionary of Physics.* Edited by J. Thewlis. Volume 6, p. 62.

BROWN, G. S. (1957) *Probability and Scientific Inference.* London: Longmans.

BROWN, R. (1962) Ohm's law. *Encyclopaedic Dictionary of Physics.* Edited by J. Thewlis. Volume 5, pp. 196–8.

(1962a) Resistance, electrical. *Encyclopaedic Dictionary of Physics.* Edited by J. Thewlis. Volume 6, pp. 285–9.

BUB, J. and RADNER, M. (1968) Miller's paradox of information. *Brit. J. Phil. Sci.* **19**, 63–7.

BUTLER, J. (1736) *The Analogy of Religion.* London.

CAMPBELL, N. R. (1920) *Physics: the Elements.* Cambridge University Press. (Reprinted (1957) as *Foundations of Science.* New York: Dover.)

CARGILE, J. (1969) The Sorites paradox. *Brit. J. Phil. Sci.* **19**, 193–202.

CARNAP, R. (1936) Testability and meaning. *Phil. Sci.* **3**, 420–68.

(1947) On the application of inductive logic. *Phil. Phenom. Res.* **8**, 138–40.

(1955) Statistical and inductive probability. *The Structure of Scientific Thought.* Edited by E. H. Madden (1960). pp. 269–79.

(1956) The methodological character of theoretical concepts. *Minnesota Studies in the Philosophy of Science Volume 1.* Edited by H. Feigl and M. Scriven. pp. 38–76.

(1962) *Logical Foundations of Probability.* 2nd edition. University of Chicago Press.

(1963) Replies and systematic expositions. *The Philosophy of Rudolph Carnap.* Edited by P. A. Schilpp. pp. 859–1013.

CHISHOLM, R. M. (1946) The contrary-to-fact conditional. *Mind* **55**, 289–307.

CHURCHMAN, C. W. and RATOOSH, P., Eds. (1959) *Measurement: Definitions and Theories.* New York: Wiley.

CHWISTEK, L. (1948) *The Limits of Science.* London: Kegan Paul.

CLEAVE, J. P. (1970) The notion of validity in logical systems with inexact predicates. *Brit. J. Phil. Sci.* **21**, 269–74.

COHEN, L. J. (1966) A logic for evidential support. *Brit. J. Phil. Sci.* **17**, 21–43, 105–26.

COLLINSON, A. J. L. (1962) Radioactive disintegration-rate measurement. *Encyclopaedic Dictionary of Physics*. Edited by J. Thewlis. Volume 6, pp. 44–5.

COLODNY, R. G., Ed. (1965) *Beyond the Edge of Certainty*. Englewood Cliffs, New Jersey: Prentice-Hall.

(1966) *Mind and Cosmos*. University of Pittsburgh Press.

COOPER, N. (1965) The concept of probability. *Brit. J. Phil. Sci.* **16**, 226–38.

CRAMÉR, H. (1945) *Mathematical Methods of Statistics* (1946). Princeton University Press.

DAVIDSON, D. *et al.* (1957) *Decision Making: an Experimental Approach*. Stanford University Press.

DE FINETTI, B. (1937) Foresight: its logical laws, its subjective sources. *Studies in Subjective Probability*. Edited by H. E. Kyburg Jr. and H. E. Smokler (1964). pp. 97–158.

(1951) Recent suggestions for the reconciliation of theories of probability. *Proceedings of the Second Berkeley Symposium on Mathematical Statistics and Probability*. Edited by J. Neyman. pp. 217–26.

(1969) Initial probabilities: a prerequisite for any valid induction. *Synthese* **20**, 2–16.

DELANEY, P. C. (1962) Radioactive disintegration theory. *Encyclopaedic Dictionary of Physics*. Edited by J. Thewlis. Volume 6, pp. 45–8.

DINGLE, H. (1950) A theory of measurement. *Brit. J. Phil. Sci.* **1**, 5–26.

(1970) Causality and statistics in modern physics. *Brit. J. Phil. Sci.* **21**, 223–46.

DUHEM, P. (1914) *The Aim and Structure of Physical Theory* (1954). Translated by P. P. Wiener. Princeton University Press.

EDWARDS, P., Ed. (1967) *The Encyclopedia of Philosophy*. New York: Macmillan.

ELLIS, B. (1966) *Basic Concepts of Measurement*. Cambridge University Press.

EWING, A. C. (1951) *The Fundamental Questions of Philosophy*. London: Routledge and Kegan Paul.

FEIGL, H. (1945) Operationism and scientific method. *Readings in Philosophical Analysis*. Edited by H. Feigl and W. Sellars (1949). pp. 498–509.

FEIGL, H. and BRODBECK, M., Eds. (1953) *Readings in the Philosophy of Science*. New York: Appleton-Century-Crofts.

FEIGL, H. and MAXWELL, G., Eds. (1961) *Current Issues in the Philosophy of Science*. New York: Holt, Rinehart and Wilson.

(1962) *Minnesota Studies in the Philosophy of Science Volume 3*. University of Minnesota Press.

FEIGL, H. and SCRIVEN, M., Eds. (1956) *Minnesota Studies in the Philosophy of Science Volume 1*. University of Minnesota Press.

FEIGL, H. and SELLARS, W., Eds. (1949) *Readings in Philosophical Analysis*. New York: Appleton-Century-Crofts.

FELLER, W. (1957) *An Introduction to Probability Theory and its Applications*. 2nd edition. Volume 1. New York: Wiley.

FEYERABEND, P. K. (1962) Explanation, reduction and empiricism. *Minnesota Studies in the Philosophy of Science Volume 3*. Edited by H. Feigl and G. Maxwell. pp. 28–98.

(1963) How to be a good empiricist. *Philosophy of Science: the Delaware Seminar Volume 2*. Edited by B. Baumrin. pp. 3–39.

(1965) Problems of empiricism. *Beyond the Edge of Certainty*. Edited by R. G. Colodny. pp. 145–260.

(1965a) On the 'meaning' of scientific terms. *J. Phil.* **62**, 266–74.

(1966) The structure of science. *Brit. J. Phil. Sci.* **17**, 237–49.

FEYERABEND, P. K. and MAXWELL, G., Eds. (1966) *Mind, Matter, and Method*. University of Minnesota Press.

FEYNMAN, R. P. (1951) The concept of probability in quantum mechanics. *Proceedings of the Second Berkeley Symposium on Mathematical Statistics and Probability*. Edited by J. Neyman. pp. 533–41.

FINE, A. (1967) Consistency, derivability and scientific change. *J. Phil.* **64**, 231–44.

(1968) Logic, probability, and quantum theory. *Phil. Sci.* **35**, 101–11.

FISHER, R. A. (1959) *Statistical Methods and Scientific Inference*. 2nd edition. London: Oliver and Boyd.

FISK, M. (1967) A defence of the principle of event causality. *Brit. J. Phil. Sci.* **18**, 89–108.

FLEW, A., Ed. (1960) *Essays in Conceptual Analysis*. London: Macmillan.

FLEW, A. (1966) *God and Philosophy*. London: Hutchinson.

GALL, D. C. (1962) Potentiometer. *Encyclopaedic Dictionary of Physics*. Edited by J. Thewlis. Volume 5, pp. 613–14.

GEACH, P. (1957) *Mental Acts*. London: Routledge and Kegan Paul.

GIEDYMIN, J. (1970) The paradox of meaning variance. *Brit. J. Phil. Sci.* **21**, 257–68.

GIERE, R. N. (1969) Bayesian statistics and biased procedures. *Synthese* **20**, 371–87.

GOGUEN, J. A. (1969) The logic of inexact concepts. *Synthese* **19**, 325–73.

GOMPERTZ, B. (1825) On the nature of the function expressive of the law of human mortality, and on a new mode of determining the value of life contingencies. *Phil. Trans. Roy. Soc. Ser. A.* **115**, 513–85.

GOOD, I. J. (1950) *Probability and the Weighing of Evidence*. New York: Charles Griffin.

GOODMAN, N. (1947) The problem of counterfactual conditionals. *J. Phil.* **44**, 113–28.

(1965) *Fact, Fiction and Forecast*. 2nd edition. New York: Bobbs-Merrill.

GREGORY, R. (1966) *Eye and Brain*. London: Weidenfeld and Nicolson.

GRICE, H. P. and STRAWSON, P. F. (1956) In defence of a dogma. *Phil. Rev.* **65**, 141–58.

GRÜNBAUM, A. (1962) The falsifiability of theories: total or partial? *Synthese* **14**, 17–34.

(1966) The falsifiability of a component of a theoretical system. *Mind, Matter, and Method*. Edited by P. K. Feyerabend and G. Maxwell. pp. 273–305.

HACKING, I. (1964) On the foundations of statistics. *Brit. J. Phil. Sci.* **15**, 1–26.

(1965) *Logic of Statistical Inference*. Cambridge University Press.

HACKING, I. (*cont.*)

(1967) Slightly more realistic personal probability. *Phil. Sci.* **34**, 311–25.

(1968). One problem about induction. *The Problem of Inductive Logic.* Edited by I. Lakatos. pp. 44–59.

HARE, R. M. (1963) *Freedom and Reason.* Oxford: Clarendon Press.

HARPER, W. L. and KYBURG JR., H. E. (1968) The Jones case. *Brit. J. Phil. Sci.* **19**, 247–51.

HARRÉ, R. (1961) *Theories and Things.* London: Sheed and Ward.

HEMPEL, C. G. (1962) Deductive-nomological *vs.* statistical explanation. *Minnesota Studies in the Philosophy of Science Volume 3.* Edited by H. Feigl and G. Maxwell. pp. 98–169.

(1965) *Aspects of Scientific Explanation.* New York: Free Press.

(1968) Maximal specificity and lawlikeness in probabilistic explanation. *Phil. Sci.* **35**, 116–33.

HESSE, M. B. (1963) A new look at scientific explanation. *Rev. Metaphys.* **17**, 98–108.

(1968) A self-correcting observation language. *Logic, Methodology and Philosophy of Science 3.* Edited by B. van Rootselaar and J. F. Staal. pp. 297–309.

HINTIKKA, J. (1969) Statistics, induction, and lawlikeness: comments on Dr Vetter's paper. *Synthese* **20**, 72–83.

HINTIKKA, J. and SUPPES, P., Eds. (1966) *Aspects of Inductive Logic.* Amsterdam: North-Holland.

HUME, D. (1739) *A Treatise of Human Nature* (1888). Edited by L. A. Selby-Bigge. Oxford: Clarendon Press.

(1777) An enquiry concerning human understanding. *Enquiries concerning the Human Understanding and Concerning the Principles of Morals* (1902). Edited by L. A. Selby-Bigge. 2nd edition. Oxford: Clarendon Press. pp. 5–165.

JEFFREY, R. C. (1965) *The Logic of Decision.* New York: McGraw-Hill.

(1968) Probable knowledge. *The Problem of Inductive Logic.* Edited by I. Lakatos. pp. 166–80.

JEFFREYS, H. (1957) *Scientific Inference.* 2nd edition. Cambridge University Press.

(1961) *Theory of Probability.* 3rd edition. Oxford: Clarendon Press.

JOHNSON, W. E. (1921) *Logic, Part I.* Cambridge University Press.

JONES, H. B. (1961) Mechanism of aging suggested from study of altered death rates. *Proceedings of the Fourth Berkeley Symposium on Mathematical Statistics and Probability.* Edited by J. Neyman. Volume 4. pp. 267–92.

KEMENY, J. G. (1963) Carnap's theory of probability and induction. *The Philosophy of Rudolph Carnap.* Edited by P. A. Schilpp. pp. 719–24.

KENDALL, M. G. (1949) On the reconciliation of theories of probability. *Biometrika* **36**, 101–6.

KEYNES, J. M. (1921) *A Treatise on Probability.* London: Macmillan.

KIRK, R. E. and OTHMER, D. F., Eds. (1947–56) *Encyclopedia of Chemical Technology.* New York: Interscience.

KNEALE, W. (1949) *Probability and Induction.* Oxford: Clarendon Press.

(1957) What can we see? *Observation and Interpretation.* Edited by S. Körner. pp. 151–9.

KOLMOGOROV, A. N. (1933) *Foundations of the Theory of Probability* (1956). 2nd. English edition. Translated and edited by N. Morrison. New York: Chelsea.

KOOPMAN, B. O. (1940) The bases of probability. *Studies in Subjective Probability.* Edited by H. E. Kyburg Jr. and H. E. Smokler (1964). pp. 161–72.

KÖRNER, S., Ed. (1957) *Observation and Interpretation.* London: Butterworths.
(1964) Deductive unification and idealisation. *Brit. J. Phil. Sci.* 14, 274–84.
(1966) *Experience and Theory.* London: Routledge and Kegan Paul.

KUHN, T. (1962) *The Structure of Scientific Revolutions.* University of Chicago Press.

KUMAR, D. (1967) Logic and inexact predicates. *Brit. J. Phil. Sci.* 18, 211–22.

KYBURG JR., H. E. (1958) R. B. Braithwaite on probability and induction. *Brit. J. Phil. Sci.* 9, 203–20.
(1961) *Probability and the Logic of Rational Belief.* Wesleyan University Press.
(1963) The role of values in scientific inference: comments on Braithwaite's paper. *Induction: Some Current Issues.* Edited by H. E. Kyburg Jr. and E. Nagel. pp. 196–9.
(1970) *Probability and Inductive Logic.* New York: Macmillan.
(1970a) More on maximal specificity. *Phil. Sci.* 37, 295–300.

KYBURG JR., H. E. and NAGEL, E., Eds. (1963) *Induction: Some Current Issues.* Wesleyan University Press.

KYBURG JR., H. E. and SMOKLER, H. E., Eds. (1964) *Studies in Subjective Probability.* New York: Wiley.

LAKATOS, I. (1963) Proofs and refutations. *Brit. J. Phil. Sci.* 14, 1–25, 120–39, 221–45, 296–342.

LAKATOS, I., Ed. (1968) *The Problem of Inductive Logic.* Amsterdam: North-Holland.

LAPLACE, P. S., Marquis de, (1819) *A Philosophical Essay on Probabilities* (1951). Translated by F. W. Truscott and F. L. Emory. New York: Dover.

LEBLANC, H. (1962) *Statistical and Inductive Probabilities.* Englewood Cliffs, New Jersey: Prentice-Hall.

LEPLIN, J. (1969) Meaning variance and the comparability of theories. *Brit. J. Phil. Sci.* 20, 69–75.

LEVI, I. (1966) Recent work in probability and induction. *Synthese.* 16, 234–44.
(1967) *Gambling with Truth.* New York: Knopf.
(1967a) Probability kinematics. *Br. J. Phil. Sci.* 18, 197–209.
(1969) Are statistical hypotheses covering laws? *Synthese* 20, 297–307.

LINDSAY, R. B. (1937) A critique of operationalism in physics. *Phil. Sci.* 4, 456–70.

LINDSAY, R. B. and MARGENAU, H. (1957) *Foundations of Physics.* 2nd edition. New York: Dover.

LOÉVE, M. (1955) *Probability Theory.* New York: Van Nostrand.

LUCAS, J. R. (1970) *The Concept of Probability.* Oxford: Clarendon Press.

MACKIE, J. L. (1963) The paradox of confirmation. *Brit. J. Phil. Sci.* 13, 265–77.
(1966) Miller's so-called paradox of information. *Brit. J. Phil. Sci.* 17, 144–7.
(1969) The relevance criterion of confirmation. *Brit. J. Phil. Sci.* 20, 27–40.

MADDEN, E. H., Ed. (1960) *The Structure of Scientific Thought.* Boston: Houghton Mifflin.

MARGENAU, H. (1950) *The Nature of Physical Reality*. New York: McGraw-Hill.

MAXWELL, G. (1962) The ontological status of theoretical entities. *Minnesota Studies in the Philosophy of Science Volume 3*. Edited by H. Feigl and G. Maxwell. pp. 3–27.

MELLOR, D. H. (1965) Experimental error and deducibility. *Phil. Sci.* **32**, 105–22.

(1965a) Connectivity, chance and ignorance. *Brit. J. Phil. Sci.* **16**, 209–25.

(1966) Inexactness and explanation. *Phil. Sci.* **33**, 345–59.

(1967) Imprecision and explanation. *Phil. Sci.* **34**, 1–9.

(1967a) Basic concepts of measurement [review]. *Brit. J. Phil. Sci.* **17**, 323–6.

(1967b) Connectivity, chance and ignorance. *Brit. J. Phil. Sci.* **18**, 235–8.

(1968) Models and analogies in science: Campbell *versus* Duhem? *Isis* **59**, 282–90.

(1969) Chance. *Arist. Soc. Suppl. Vol.* **43**, 11–36.

(1969a) God and probability. *Rel. Stud.* **5**, 223–34.

MILLER, D. (1966) A paradox of information. *Brit. J. Phil. Sci.* **17**, 59–61.

(1966a) On a so-called so-called paradox. *Brit. J. Phil. Sci.* **17**, 147–9.

(1968) The straight and narrow rule of induction. *Brit. J. Phil. Sci.* **19**, 145–52.

MONRO, D. H. (1967) *Empiricism and Ethics*. Cambridge University Press.

MYERSCOUGH, L. C. (1962) Radium. *Encyclopaedic Dictionary of Physics*. Edited by J. Thewlis. Volume 6, pp. 168–9.

NAGEL, E. (1938) Principles of the theory of probability. *International Encyclopedia of Unified Science*. Edited by O. Neurath *et al.* Volume 1, Number 6.

(1961) *The Structure of Science*. New York: Harcourt, Brace and World.

NEURATH, O. *et al.*, Eds. (1938) *International Encyclopedia of Unified Science*. University of Chicago Press.

NEYMAN, J. (1950) *First Course in Probability and Statistics*. New York: Henry Holt.

NEYMAN, J., Ed. (1951) *Proceedings of the Second Berkeley Symposium on Mathematical Statistics and Probability*. University of California Press.

NEYMAN, J. (1952) *Lectures and Conferences on Mathematical Statistics and Probability*. 2nd edition. Washington: Graduate School U.S. Department of Agriculture.

NEYMAN, J., Ed. (1961) *Proceedings of the Fourth Berkeley Symposium on Mathematical Statistics and Probability*. University of California Press.

OTHMER, D. G. and GILMONT, R. (1955) Vapour-liquid equilibria. *Encyclopedia of Chemical Technology*. Edited by R. E. Kirk and D. F. Othmer. Volume 14, pp. 614–21.

PAP, A. (1959) Are physical magnitudes operationally definable? *Measurement: Definitions and Theories*. Edited by C. W. Churchman and P. Ratoosh. pp. 177–91.

(1963) *An Introduction to the Philosophy of Science*. London: Eyre and Spottiswoode.

PEIRCE, C. S. (1931) *Collected Papers*. Edited by C. Hartshorne and P. Weiss. Harvard University Press.

PITCHER, G., Ed. (1964) *Truth*. Englewood Cliffs, New Jersey: Prentice-Hall.

POINCARÉ, H. (1913) *The Foundations of Science.* Translated by G. B. Halsted. Lancaster, Pennsylvania: Science Press.

POPPER, K. R. (1950) Indeterminism in quantum physics and in classical physics. *Brit. J. Phil. Sci.* 1, 117–33, 173–95.

(1957) The propensity interpretation of the calculus of probability, and the quantum theory. *Observation and Interpretation.* Edited by S. Körner. pp. 65–70.

(1957a) The aim of science. *Ratio* 1, 24–35.

(1959) *The Logic of Scientific Discovery.* London: Hutchinson.

(1959a) The propensity interpretation of probability. *Brit. J. Phil. Sci.* 10, 25–42.

(1963) *Conjectures and Refutations.* London: Routledge and Kegan Paul.

(1966) A comment on Miller's new paradox of information. *Brit. J. Phil. Sci.* 17, 61–9.

(1966a) A paradox of zero information. *Brit. J. Phil. Sci,* 17, 141–3.

PRICE, H. H. (1969) *Belief.* London: Allen and Unwin.

PRIOR, A. N. (1968) *Papers on Time and Tense.* Oxford: Clarendon Press.

PRZELECKI, M. (1969) *The Logic of Empirical Theories.* London: Routledge and Kegan Paul.

PUTNAM, H. (1962) The analytic and the synthetic. *Minnesota Studies in the Philosophy of Science Volume 3.* Edited by H. Feigl and G. Maxwell. pp. 358–97.

QUINE, W. V. O. (1936) Truth by convention. *Readings in Philosophical Analysis.* Edited by H. Feigl and W. Sellars (1949). pp. 250–73.

(1951) Two dogmas of empiricism. *Phil. Rev.* 60, 20–43.

(1960) *Word and Object.* New York: Wiley.

(1961) *From a Logical Point of View.* 2nd edition. Harvard University Press.

RAMSEY, F. P. (1926) Truth and probability. *The Foundations of Mathematics* (1931). Edited by R. B. Braithwaite. London: Kegan Paul. pp. 196–211.

REICHENBACH, H. (1949) *The Theory of Probability.* 2nd edition. University of California Press.

VAN ROOTSELAAR, B. and STAAL, J. F., Eds. (1968) *Logic, Methodology and Philosophy of Science 3.* Amsterdam: North-Holland.

ROZEBOOM, W. W. (1969) New mysteries for old; the transfiguration of Miller's paradox. *Brit. J. Phil. Sci.* 19, 345–53.

ROYAL INSTITUTE OF CHEMISTRY (1961) *A Chemists' Introduction to Statistics, Theory of Error and Design of Experiment.* By D. A. Pantony. Lecture Series 1961, number 2.

RUSSELL, B. (1905) On denoting. *Logic and Knowledge* (1956). Edited by R. C. Marsh. London: Allen and Unwin. pp. 41–56.

(1919) *Introduction to Mathematical Philosophy.* London: Allen and Unwin.

(1921) *The Analysis of Mind.* London: Allen and Unwin.

(1948) *Human Knowledge: Its Scope and Limits.* London: Allen and Unwin.

RUSSELL, L. J. (1928) The logic of modern physics [review]. *Mind* 37, 355–61.

RYLE, G. (1949) *The Concept of Mind.* London: Hutchinson.

SALMON, W. C. (1967) *The Foundations of Scientific Inference.* 2nd Edition. University of Pittsburgh Press.

SAVAGE, L. J. (1954) *The Foundations of Statistics.* New York: Wiley.

184   *References*

SAVAGE, L. J. (*cont.*)

    (1961) The foundations of statistics reconsidered. *Proceedings of the Fourth Berkeley Symposium on Mathematical Statistics and Probability.* Edited by J. Neyman. Volume 1, pp. 575–86.

SCHILPP, P. A., Ed. (1963) *The Philosophy of Rudolph Carnap.* La Salle, Illinois: Open Court.

SCHLEGEL, R. (1970) Statistical explanation in physics: the Copenhagen interpretation. *Synthese* **21**, 65–82.

SCHLESINGER, G. (1963) *Method in the Physical Sciences.* London: Routledge and Kegan Paul.

    (1967) Operationalism. *The Encyclopedia of Philosophy.* Edited by P. Edwards. Volume 5, pp. 543–7.

SELLARS, W. (1961) The language of theories. *Current Issues in the Philosophy of Science.* Edited by H. Feigl and G. Maxwell. pp. 57–77.

SHAPERE, D. (1966) Meaning and scientific change. *Mind and Cosmos.* Edited by R. G. Colodny. pp. 41–85.

SHIMONY, A. (1955) Coherence and the axioms of confirmation. *J. Symb. Logic* **20**, 1–28.

SKLAR, L. (1970) Is probability a dispositional property? *J. Phil.* **67**, 355–66.

SNEED, J. D. (1970) Quantum mechanics and classical probability theory. *Synthese* **21**, 34–64.

SPECTOR, M. (1966) Theory and observation. *Brit. J. Phil. Sci.* **17**, 1–20, 89–104.

STALNAKER, R. C. (1970) Probability and conditionals. *Phil. Sci.* **37**, 64–80.

STEVENS, S. S. (1959) Measurement, psychophysics and utility. *Measurement: Definitions and Theories.* Edited by C. W. Churchman and P. Ratoosh. pp. 18–63.

STRAWSON, P. F. (1950) On referring. *Mind* **59**, 320–44.

    (1952) *Introduction to Logical Theory.* London: Methuen.

    (1963) Carnap's views on constructed systems versus natural language in analytic philosophy. *The Philosophy of Rudolf Carnap.* Edited by P. A. Schilpp. pp. 503–18.

    (1964) A problem about truth – a reply to Mr Warnock. *Truth.* Edited by G. Pitcher. pp. 68–87.

SUPPES, (1957) *Introduction to Logic.* New York: Van Nostrand.

    (1966) Probabilistic inference and the concept of total evidence. *Aspects of Inductive Logic.* Edited by J. Hintikka and P. Suppes. pp. 49–65.

SWINBURNE, R. G. (1968) *Space and Time.* London: Macmillan.

    (1969) Vagueness, inexactness, and imprecision. *Brit. J. Phil. Sci.* **19**, 281–99.

TARSKI, A. (1944) The semantic conception of truth. *Readings in Philosophical Analysis.* Edited by H. Feigl and W. Sellars (1949). pp. 52–84.

TAYLOR, W. F. (1961) On the methodology of studying aging in humans. *Proceedings of the Fourth Berkeley Symposium on Mathematical Statistics and Probability.* Edited by J. Neyman. Volume 4, pp. 347–68.

THATCHER, A. R. (1964) Relationships between Bayesian and confidence limits for predictions. *J. Roy. Statist. Soc. Ser. B* **26**, 176–92.

THEWLIS, J., Ed. (1962) *Encyclopaedic Dictionary of Physics.* Oxford: Pergamon Press.

TOULMIN, S. (1950) Probability. *Essays in Conceptual Analysis.* Edited by A. Flew (1960). pp. 157–91.

TURNER, J. (1955) Maxwell on the method of physical analogy. *Brit. J. Phil. Sci.* **6**, 226–38.

VENN, J. (1888) *The Logic of Chance.* 3rd edition. London: Macmillan.

VETTER, H. (1969) Logical probability, mathematical statistics, and the problem of induction. *Synthese* **20**, 56–71.

VON MISES, R. (1957) *Probability, Statistics and Truth.* 2nd English edition. London: Allen and Unwin.

VON WRIGHT, G. H. (1957) *The Logical Problem of Induction.* 2nd edition. New York: Macmillan.

WARNOCK, G. J. (1960) The logic of scientific discovery [review]. *Mind* **69**, 99–101.

WATLING, J. (1969) Chance, *Arist. Soc. Suppl. Vol.* **43**, 37–48.

WILL, F. L. (1954) Kneale's theories of probability and induction. *Phil. Rev.* **63**, 19–42.

WITTGENSTEIN, L. (1958) *Philosophical Investigations.* 2nd edition. Oxford: Blackwell.

WORLD HEALTH ORGANISATION (1958) *Annual Epidemiological and Vital Statistics, 1955.* Geneva: World Health Organisation.

Index

References with italicised page numbers are to chapter sections so titled.